Citizenship Today

REFERENCE

**Frontispiece**   T. H. Marshall.

# Citizenship today

## The contemporary relevance
## of T. H. Marshall

*Edited by*

Martin Bulmer
*University of Surrey*

Anthony M. Rees
*University of Southampton*

LONDON AND NEW YORK

© Martin Bulmer, Anthony M. Rees and contributors 1996, except
Chapter 6 © London School of Economics 1991
Chapter 7 © British Sociological Association 1987
Chapter 8 © Cambridge University Press 1984
Chapter 9 © Basil Blackwell 1987

First published in 1996 by UCL Press


Reprinted by Routledge
11 New Fetter Lane
London EC4 P4EE


*Routledge is an imprint of the Taylor & Francis Group*


Transferred to Digital Printing 2003


**British Library Cataloguing in Publication Data**
A catalogue record for this book is available from the British Library.


**Library of Congress Cataloging-in-Publication Data are available.**


ISBNs
1-85728-471-2 HB
1-85728-472-0 PB


Typeset in Bembo.
Printed and bound by
Antony Rowe Ltd., Eastbourne, East Sussex.

*For Nadine Marshall*

# Contents

CONTENTS

# Foreword

## J. H. Smith

*Professor Emeritus of Sociology in the University of Southampton*

The first T. H. Marshall Memorial Lecture was given at the University of Southampton in November 1983, two years after Marshall's death in his 88th year. The lecture series was immediately established as a major event, attracting speakers who were united by their distinction in the social sciences and their readiness to pay homage to one of Britain's greatest sociologists. Bringing the first 12 lectures together in the present volume recognizes the substantial contribution that the Marshall Lectures have already made to current debates on a wide range of academic and policy issues. It also gives the reader an opportunity to appreciate the many ways in which Marshall's work in sociology and social policy continues to influence and challenge us.

This dual purpose of celebrating Marshall's memory and the force of his ideas as an example was the principal objective of the Department of Sociology and Social Policy in founding the series. Tom Marshall's formal link with Southampton dated from 1969, when the university awarded him the honorary degree of DSc (Social Sciences). It was in fact the first academic honour of this type he had received, although others soon followed.

On the face of it, this belated recognition may seem surprising. Marshall, by then in his mid-seventies, had enjoyed a long, distinguished and highly distinctive career and was continuing to publish papers of lasting value. He had held the premier professorship of sociology in the country – the Martin White Chair at the London School of Economics – which he vacated in 1956 to spend four years as Director of Social Sciences at UNESCO. From 1944 to 1949 he was head of the Department of Social Science at LSE, immediately prior to Richard Titmuss's appointment to the first chair of social administration in the country. Marshall had moved freely and easily between academic life and public service. In the Second World War he had worked in the Foreign Office Research Department (for which he was awarded the CMG) and he later served as Educational Adviser to the British High Commissioner in Germany from 1949 to 1950.

His knowledge of German society and culture had its roots in his enforced stay as a prisoner in the German civilian internment camp outside Berlin, Ruhleben, during the First World War, that he himself described as "the most powerful formative influence of my early years". The period in captivity also brought a significant change of direction in terms both of his career and of Marshall's sociological awareness. Had it not been for this experience, his life-pattern would almost certainly have set firm in the typical upper-middle-class mould of Edwardian England. His father was a successful London architect, with a house in Bloomsbury and country retreats. By the time he was 19, Marshall's education had followed the familiar path from preparatory to boarding school (Rugby) to Cambridge, with a Foreign Service career as the predictable destination. Instead, after a spell back in Cambridge as an economic historian, he moved to the LSE in the mid-1920s, initially as a tutor in social work. Subsequently in 1930 he joined the Department of Sociology to teach comparative social institutions. His background in economic history fused with the evolutionary sociology of Hobhouse and Ginsberg to equip him – in his own words – with "some skills in the analysis of social systems and the interpretation of social change".

For over 25 years, until his retirement from LSE in 1956, Marshall displayed these skills to great effect in his teaching on comparative social institutions. Those of us who heard those lectures retain a vivid sense of Marshall's style and substance. He combined an impressive platform presence with an intellectual assurance made all the more acceptable by a singular blend of irony and diffidence. He clearly enjoyed performing – he was also an accomplished violinist and by all accounts a talented amateur actor – and there was no doubt that he found teaching a particularly important and rewarding form. At conferences, his courtesy and clarity made him an outstanding rapporteur.

In the immediate post-war years at the LSE, Marshall provided one of three equally distinguished but very different role models for the aspirant sociologist. The others were Morris Ginsberg and David Glass. Ginsberg, the senior of the three, was lucid, philosophical and sorrowful. His great learning was shot through with a sense of unease; mostly because although he remained in no doubt of his late mentor Hobhouse's importance for sociology, he was forever trapped in that inheritance. In the sharpest contrast, David Glass, the youngest and most recently appointed to a chair, combined a sense of high aspirations for sociology as a profession with a formidable and radical vitality that was a driving force for the post-war generation.

Ginsberg and Glass could be taken as fully representative of the twin roots of the discipline in social philosophy and in sociological research. Their respective strengths left no doubt as to the importance, or the difficulties, of the possibilities inherent in sociology. Marshall's appeal was more ambiguous. His charm and modesty, together with his civilized detachment from what others might see as urgent priorities for the sociological enterprise, led some to underrate him. But for those students who wondered, then as now, whether sociology really was an acceptable thing to be studying, the Marshall persona could be greatly reassuring. Here after all, was a gentleman in the authentic sense, who had expressed a clear preference for sociology and the LSE and had, moreover, forsaken the safer haven of Oxbridge history.

It is possible that these impressions lingered and delayed a proper appreciation of Marshall's place in British sociology. But the publication in 1950 of his *Citizenship and social class* added high-level inspiration to the comfort that Marshall had already brought to his discipline. The lectures reprinted in this volume are a living testimony to that particular work, but David Lockwood's assessment, written to celebrate Marshall's 80th birthday, cannot be bettered. He said of Marshall:

> There is a finely balanced tension of opposites: on the one hand a gentle scepticism about the achievements of sociology and on the other a quiet enthusiasm for its potentialities; a subtle appreciation and mastery of work that combines conceptual discrimination with a stringent regard for evidence; and an understanding that although Sociology has a life of its own that it must cherish, it is also liable to academic anaemia if it is not continuously in contact with and refreshed by the

practical concerns of the society that harbours it. These qualities pervade all his writings but are nowhere more evident than in the pages of the only work of post-war British Sociology that in the boldness of its perspective and conceptualization bears comparison with, and stands in a direct line of succession to those classical texts that mark the origins of modern sociology. I refer, of course, to *Citizenship and social class*.

Happily, this was not simply the culmination of Marshall's career. In a long and fruitful retirement, he continued to write and to advise, producing what remains a standard text on social policy, as well as a volume of papers edited by Robert Pinker that appeared only a few months before Marshall's death. These reflect – as do all his publications – the delicate and telling balance he achieved between his concerns with mainstream sociological analysis and the issues facing contemporary society. Maintaining that balance over more than half-a-century was itself a remarkable personal achievement that, as the lectures demonstrate, has become a landmark in the social sciences. As A. H. Halsey has said, "It is hard to think of anyone more valuable than T. H. Marshall."

The publication of this volume also provides an opportunity to thank, in addition to the Marshall lecturers, Mrs Nadine Marshall and members of her family and the many friends who gave their enthusiastic support. Particular mention must be made of those who shared warm memories of Marshall as a friend and colleague and who came to Southampton to chair individual lectures. They included Sir Ralf Dahrendorf, Mrs Jean Floud, Professor Ernest Gellner, Professor Donald Macrae, Sir Claus Moser and Professor Robert Pinker.

## A note on publications

T. H. Marshall's seminal lecture on citizenship, which is the starting point of this collection, was first published in *Citizenship and social class and other essays*, published by Cambridge University Press in 1950. T. H. Marshall's collected works, including this essay, are to be found in *Sociology at the crossroads*, first published by Heinemann in 1963 (American edition with a foreword by S. M. Lipset 1964) and *The right to welfare and other essays*, London: Heinemann, 1981. His text *Social policy* was first published by Hutchinson's in 1965; the fifth edition, *T. H. Marshall's social policy in the twentieth century* by Anthony M. Rees appeared posthumously in 1985.

Marshall wrote one brief personal memoir "A British sociological career" (*International Social Science Journal* **25**(1/2), 1973). Personal recollections and assessments of Marshall include A. H. Halsey, "T. H. Marshall: past and present, 1893–1981", *Sociology* **18**(1), 1984; D. Lockwood, "For T. H. Marshall", *Sociology* **8**(3), 1974; D. G. MacRae, "Tom Marshall 1893–1981: a personal memoir", *British Journal of Sociology* **33**(3), 1982; eightieth birthday tributes in the *British Journal of Sociology* **24**(4), 1973 by R. Dahrendorf and S. M. Lipset; and R. Pinker's introduction to Marshall, *The right to welfare and other essays* (1981). The prison camp society of Marshall's youth is recaptured in J. Davidson Ketchum, *Ruhleben: a prison camp society* (Toronto: University of Toronto Press, 1965), reviewed by Marshall himself in *Sociology* **1**(1), 90–93, January 1967.

# Preface

The 12 T. H. Marshall Memorial Lectures published here were given between 1983 and 1995 at the University of Southampton under the auspices of the Department of Sociology and Social Policy. The first 12 lectures of what is a continuing series have an unusual unity around the theme of citizenship. The series was the brainchild of Professor John Smith, Professor of Sociology and holder of the first chair in the subject at the university. As he notes in the Foreword, T. H. (Tom) Marshall (1893–1981) was one of the most influential scholars in interwar and immediate post-war sociology and social policy, making particularly important contributions to the study of social stratification and to social policy. The authors contributing to this volume concentrate upon his seminal conceptualization of *Citizenship and social class and other essays* in the (Alfred) Marshall lectures of 1949 given at the University of Cambridge (published in Marshall 1950), which opened up a series of themes in both sociology and social policy that have been pursued ever since, and that have returned to prominence, particularly in sociology, in recent years.

The subject of citizenship encompasses and links a number of central themes in the analysis of contemporary society. What are the boundaries of a society? Which groups belong and which do not? What criteria for full citizenship are invoked? What entitlements to social benefits and services do different members of the society enjoy? What is the relationship between the actual distribution of rights and their ideal distribution? The concept thus connects the empirical studies of sociology and social policy to the more abstract concerns of social and political theory and philosophy. The concept of "social" citizenship in particular addresses central questions of obligation and entitlement in contemporary society.

Marshall's contribution to the study of citizenship needs to be put in the context of his overall contribution to sociology and social policy as fields for academic study. His life and career are briefly touched on above by John Smith in the Foreword, in more detail by A. H. Halsey in Chapter 5 and in the further reading given at the end of the Foreword.

That the University of Southampton department should have sponsored the lectures was particularly appropriate, since it is a joint department of Sociology and Social Policy, a combination comparatively rare on the British academic scene today, but one that closely mirrors T. H. Marshall's own interests. The lectures are delivered annually at a public lecture attended by Mrs Nadine Marshall and other members and friends of the Marshall family. Each lecture is chaired by a distinguished social scientist well known in their own right. Indeed the Marshall lecturers and chairs listed below represent many of the leading figures of two generations of British sociology. Of the twelve lecturers, ten at the time of writing are resident in the United Kingdom; nine of these are listed in the 1995 edition of *Who's who*, and all ten appear in the 1996 edition, the tenth having become a vice chancellor.

The chronological sequence of the lectures published in this book, with the chair, was as follows:

| Marshall Memorial Lecturer | Chair taken by |
|---|---|
| 1983–4 James Meade | Donald G. Macrae |
| 1985 Ronald P. Dore | J. H. Smith |
| 1986 Michael Mann | Ernest Gellner |
| 1987 A. H. Halsey | J. H. Smith |
| 1988 Ralf Dahrendorf | Jean Floud |
| 1989 J. H. Goldthorpe | J. H. Smith |
| 1990 William Julius Wilson | Ralf Dahrendorf |
| 1991 Howard Newby | Sir Claus Moser |
| 1992 Janet Finch | Robert Pinker |
| 1993 Anthony Giddens | Christopher Bryant |
| 1994 W. G. Runciman | Howard Newby |
| 1995 Patricia Hewitt | Raymond Plant |

Lectures are usually given in the spring, however, the first lecture was given in November 1983, two years after T. H. Marshall's death.

The sequence of chapters adopted for the book is not purely chronological, but has a strong thematic element. They move from the more theoretical and philosophical at the beginning, by Ralf Dahrendorf, A. H. Halsey, Anthony Giddens and Michael Mann, to those with a more substantive emphasis, by James Meade, Ronald Dore, Janet Finch and William Julius Wilson. Some are not as easily classified. W. G. Runciman addresses theoretical issues via an argument about war as a caesura in twentieth-century British history. John Goldthorpe addresses issues in the methodology of "grand historical sociology" that have aroused strong responses and a subsequent symposium in 1994 in the *British Journal of Sociology* (see p. 119) where his chapter first appeared. Howard Newby opens up a new field for the analysis of citizenship, that of the environment, while Patricia Hewitt, starting from some basic concerns in social policy, extends the discussion to the global dimension. In Chapter 1, Anthony Rees, who has a special interest in Marshall's work and is the author of the fifth, post-humous, edition of Marshall's text on *Social policy*, reflects on some of the historical themes in the study of citizenship as an introduction to the collection. The concluding chapter by the editors points to some of the salient likely future concerns of debate in the area.

Of the 14 chapters in the book, only five have previously appeared, and we are indebted to the publishers and the authors for permission to reprint them here. They are:

Chapter 2 by Ralf Dahrendorf, © 1988 Ralf Dahrendorf reproduced by permission of the author and the publishers, Weidenfeld & Nicolson, from Ralf Dahrendorf, *The modern social conflict* (London: Weidenfeld & Nicolson 1988, pp. 24–47).

Chapter 6 by John H. Goldthorpe, © 1991 London School of Economics reproduced by permission of the author and the publishers, Routledge, from the *British Journal of Sociology* 42(2), 211–30, 1991.

Chapter 7 by Michael Mann, © 1987 British Sociological Association reproduced by permission of the author and the British Sociological Association from *Sociology: the Journal of the British Sociological Association* 21(3), 339–54, 1987.

Chapter 8 by James Meade, © 1984 Cambridge University Press, reproduced by permission of the author and the publishers,

Cambridge University Press, from the *Journal of Social Policy* **13**(2), 129–46, 1984, James Meade, "Full employment, new technologies and the distribution of income".

Chapter 9 by Ronald Dore, © 1987 Basil Blackwell, reproduced by permission of the author and the publishers, Basil Blackwell, from the *British Journal of Industrial Relations* **25**(2), 201–25, 1987.

It remains to thank those who made this collection possible. Our main debt is to the 12 Marshall Memorial Lecturers appearing here, who readily agreed to the publication or republication of their work and made appropriate changes to the text originally delivered as a lecture.

Some of the contributions have been revised more then others. Generally those that have already appeared in print are reproduced in the form in which they then came out; there may, of course, have been considerable changes from the original lecture. The authors of those which are published for the first time, however, have sometimes taken the opportunity to update them.

Justin Vaughan at UCL Press has been a supportive and encouraging editor. In the Department of Sociology and Social Policy, Roger Lawson, Doreen Davies, Glynis Evans and Gwen Gordon have provided help at key points. Our greatest debt, however, is to T. H. Marshall's widow Nadine, whose support for the lectures since their inception in 1983 has been unstinting, and whose encouragement and interest has been an example to us all. We are delighted to dedicate this book to her.

Martin Bulmer & Anthony M. Rees
Guildford and Southampton

# Notes on contributors

*Martin Bulmer* is Professor of Sociology at the University of Surrey and was previously Professor of Sociology at the University of Southampton from 1993 to 1995.

*Ralf Dahrendorf* (Lord Dahrendorf of Clare Market) is Warden of St Antony's College, Oxford and was previously Director of the London School of Economics and Political Science, 1974–84.

*Ronald Dore* is Senior Research Fellow in the Centre for Economic Performance, London School of Economics and Political Science.

*Janet Finch* is Vice-Chancellor, University of Keele.

*Anthony Giddens* is Fellow of King's College and Professor of Sociology, University of Cambridge.

*John H. Goldthorpe* is Official Fellow in Sociology, Nuffield College, Oxford.

*A. H. Halsey* is Professorial Fellow Emeritus of Nuffield College and Emeritus Professor of Social and Administrative Studies, University of Oxford.

*Patricia Hewitt* is Head of Research at Andersen Consulting and was previously Deputy Director of the Institute of Public Policy Research from 1989 to 1994.

*Michael Mann* is Professor of Sociology at the University of California, Los Angeles.

*James Meade* was Professor of Political Economy, University of Cambridge and Nobel Laureate in Economics, 1977.

*Howard Newby* is Vice-Chancellor of the University of Southampton, and was previously chairman of the Economic and Social Research Council from 1988 to 1994.

*Anthony M. Rees* is Senior Lecturer in Social Policy, University of Southampton

*W. G. Runciman* is Senior Research Fellow, Trinity College, Cambridge

*J. H. Smith* is Professor Emeritus of Sociology in the University of Southampton, where he was foundation Professor of Sociology from 1964 to 1991.

*William Julius Wilson* is Lucy Flower University Professor of Sociology and Public Policy and Director of the Center for the Study of Urban Inequality, University of Chicago.

# CHAPTER 1

# T. H. Marshall and the progress of citizenship

## Anthony M. Rees

A social thinker and critic who dies at the age of 87 might reasonably have expected that he would have outlived the vagaries of fashion, and, in particular, the years of indifference that frequently seem to follow the brief excitement attendant upon the publication of an apparently new, relevant and challenging set of propositions. In T. H. Marshall's case this did not happen, perhaps partly because his most seminal ideas were either not crystallized and written down, or did not command wide attention, until after he retired, at the age of 62 in 1956, from his professorship at the London School of Economics. What is always regarded as his most important work, *Citizenship and social class*, was given as the (Alfred) Marshall Lectures in Cambridge in 1949, and was published by the Cambridge University Press in the following year, but did not achieve its full impact until 1963, when Heinemann made it the centrepiece of *Sociology at the crossroads*, a collection of essays and lectures produced or delivered over the previous 30 years (Marshall 1963).

Shortly before Marshall's death in 1981, Robert Pinker edited a second collection of essays brought together under the title of *The right to welfare* (Marshall 1981), together with a thoughtful introduction from his own pen and a series of "afterthoughts" to the principal articles contributed by Marshall himself. It is, however, an indication that the quickening of interest in Marshall's work at the time was only modest that the book failed to appear in paperback. The obituaries themselves were warm and appreciative (Halsey 1984) but, as is the way with obituaries, they seemed to be closing a chapter rather than opening one. The tone of commentators was respectful and indeed overt hostility to Marshall has been very rare, although in a review of Martin Bulmer's *Essays on the history of British sociological research,* Stanislav Andreski (1986) referred to Halsey's chapter on the LSE Sociology Department, and declared:

> He glosses over some nasty intrigues which went on there and is overgenerous in attributing intellectual merit, especially to T. H. Marshall whose contribution to knowledge was nil.

This summary verdict may be eccentric, but others have regretted that Marshall was so sparing in the deployment of the statistical and research skills acquired in his first academic career as a historical demographer during his later career as a sociologist and social policy specialist. He explained himself that when he accepted Ginsberg's offer to join the LSE Department of Sociology as a lecturer in 1930:

> I realized that broad comparative studies in the Hobhouse tradition must be built on secondary sources, and the thought that I might leave the basic task of fact collecting to others appealed enormously to my lively and impatient mind. (Marshall 1973)

It is interesting to place this slightly ingenuous admission in the context of Goldthorpe's strictures in Chapter 6 on the recent school of "grand historical sociologists". Would Goldthorpe apply them to Marshall, one wonders? Anyway, Marshall became a "sophisticated consumer" of other people's data (Halsey 1984), and this, together with the fact that detachment does not breed many disciples, may help to account for the non-emergence of "a Marshallian 'school' of social administrators of the kind that Titmuss gathered together during his lifetime" (Pinker 1981). Marshall came to be seen as a synthesizer; and the fate of the synthesizing "man of wisdom", it was insinuated, is that lapidary observations and incisive insights do not often have a very long shelf-life. Yet even this more measured conclusion fails to account for the very considerable influence that Marshall exerted over many of his most distinguished successors in the next two generations, those who came to intellectual maturity in the 20 years after the

Second World War. Michael Mann (p. 126) lists Reinhard Bendix, Ralf Dahrendorf, Ronald Dore, A. H. Halsey, S. M. Lipset, David Lockwood and Peter Townsend, and that is clearly naming only a few. And since the mid-1980s – when the Marshall Memorial Lecture series that forms the basis for this book started – there has been an explosion of interest in Marshall's ideas among a newer generation of scholars. Whole books have been written commenting on – and in the view of their authors, improving on – Marshall's conception of citizenship (Turner 1986, Barbalet 1988). Most of the contributions to the numerous edited collections on citizenship contain at least one reference to *Citizenship and social class* – sometimes these are mere tokens, sometimes extended commentaries on his seminal formulation (Andrews 1991, Vogel & Moran 1991, Coote 1992, van Steenbergen 1994).

It could be argued that what has been rediscovered in the later 1980s and the 1990s is less Marshall himself than the central importance of citizenship, interest in which in Britain has been much subject to intellectual fashion. In three periods it has come to the fore. What might be called the "first wave" occurred in the 30 years or so before the First World War: it was associated with the brief dominance of Idealist thought in British intellectual life under the influence of T. H. Green, but was carried forward by later thinkers like Hobhouse who were very critical of Idealist assumptions. The "second wave" lasted from the Second World War to the 1960s: it might be roughly demarcated by the publishing history of *Citizenship and social class* (see above). During this period Marshall almost single-handedly revived the notion of citizenship, and disseminated a particular view of it so successfully that it came to be seen (at least in England) as the only possible account. The fact that the writers of the "third wave" – which is, of course, with us today – so very often use Marshall as their starting point is therefore a justifiable act of homage.

There is no space here for more than a little speculation about why the concept of citizenship has moved in and out of favour. One clue may be afforded by the fact that the two most obviously "dead" periods – the 1930s and the 1970s – were marked by a brief fleuraison of Marxist thought. However, this has always been rather a thin story in Britain. A more important factor must be that the "three waves" coincided with vigorous and anxious debates about appropriate welfare systems, centring respectively on the social legislation of the

New Liberalism, the implementation of the post-war social democratic welfare state and the Thatcher/Major recasting of the late 1980s and early 1990s. This emphasis on "social citizenship" was, of course, very much in line with Marshall's own central preoccupation.

For in *Citizenship and social class* Marshall had a tale to tell. It is one of the gradual evolution of citizenship so that it culminates in the coming of age of the British welfare state after mid-century. In Marshall's later writings a darker element intrudes – he became less convinced of the strength and reality of social rights, and of citizenship as a unifying concept (Rees 1995). However, it is from Marshall's classic formulation of his case in *Citizenship and social class* that modern commentators have drawn inspiration, and it is with this evolutionary account that this chapter is concerned. The aim is to consider how, why and with what justification it has been adopted, adapted, criticized and utilized. To this end, I shall begin by setting out Marshall's schematic presentation of the historical development of citizenship in more detail. Then, in three longish sections I shall consider three questions, each of which has attracted a considerable volume of literature. First, does Marshall give a correctly ordered account of what transpired in Britain, full enough for his (and our) purposes? Secondly, is this account universalizable, applicable to other societies and polities that have undergone similar transformations in the past two centuries? Thirdly, does Marshall describe too consensual, too bland an evolution, one that lacks an emphasis on the crucial factor of struggle?

## Marshall's account of the progression of citizenship

In this section, I shall use Marshall's own words where possible, although a health warning is in order: *Citizenship and social class* contains a number of complex reworkings and modifications of statements that appear more baldly and quotably near the start of the text, so things are not always quite as they seem (Rees 1995). How Marshall describes the three elements in citizenship is set out below (all quotes from Marshall 1963: 74). It should be noted that not only does he ascribe the development of civil, political and social rights to the eighteenth, nineteenth and twentieth centuries respectively, but he also argues that each was accompanied by the rise of a set of characteristic institutions.

1. The civil element is composed of the rights necessary for individual freedom – liberty of the person, freedom of speech, thought and faith, the right to own property and to conclude valid contracts, and the right to justice.

The institutions most associated with the establishment of these rights are the civil and criminal courts of justice:

2. By the political element I mean the right to participate in an exercise of political power, as a member of a body invested with political authority or as an elector of such a body.

In this case the corresponding institutions are Parliament and local elective bodies. We may note here that Marshall's equation of political citizenship with the extension of the franchise and related opportunities for political participation is not followed by all contributors to this volume. Dahrendorf, for example, includes significant elements of civil citizenship – freedom of association, freedom of speech – under the political rubric.

3. By the social element I mean the whole range from the right to a modicum of economic welfare and security to the right to share to the full in the social heritage and to live the life of a civilized being according to the standards prevailing in the society. The institutions most closely connected with it are the educational system and the social services.

Here Marshall names the educational system and the social services, although responsibility for these has always been divided between central government administration and local councils. There is not therefore any very clear distinction between political and social rights in this respect.

In the Middle Ages, according to Marshall, "these three strands were wound into a single thread ... because the institutions were amalgamated" (Marshall 1963: 74). He goes on:

In feudal society status was the hall-mark of class and the measure of inequality. There was no uniform collection of

5

rights and duties with which all men – noble and common, free and serf – were endowed by the membership of the society. There was, in this sense, no principle of the equality of citizens to set against the inequality of classes. (Marshall 1963: 75)

The process that Marshall traces in later centuries is one both of fission and of fusion – the former because the three elements in citizenship rights were separated out and followed different paths, the latter in the sense that rights and duties no longer conferred a status that was specifically local or municipal but had, so to speak, been nationalized. Marshall actually devoted little space to the emergence of a specifically national sense of citizenship, and what he did have to say mainly occurs in passages about the eighteenth century (Marshall 1963: 96). As a sociologist whose teaching career spanned the three decades of the 1930s, the 1940s and the 1950s he was more concerned to define the relationship between social class and citizenship. Today, when social class is commonly seen as a waning force both as an integrator and a divider, and citizenship is often sanitized of overt class connotations, this perhaps needs stressing:

> If I am right in my contention that citizenship has been a developing institution in England at least since the latter part of the seventeenth century, then it is clear that its growth coincides with the rise of capitalism, which is a system, not of quality, but of inequality. Here is something that needs explaining, How is it that these two opposing principles could grow and flourish side by side in the same soil? What made it possible for them to be reconciled with one another and to become, for a time at least, allies instead of antagonists? The question is a pertinent one, for it is clear that, in the twentieth century, citizenship and the capitalistic class system have been at war. (Marshall 1963: 87)

The words "in the twentieth century" indicate that Marshall is thinking here especially of social rights, and is putting forward one of the most frequently claimed ways in which they may be said to be "different". To the conundrum he has set himself in this passage he gives an answer a few pages further on:

Nevertheless it is true that citizenship, even in its early forms, was a principle of equality, and that during this period (ie the eighteenth and early nineteenth centuries) it was a developing institution. Starting at the point where all men were free and, in theory, capable of enjoying rights, it grew by enriching the body of rights which they were capable of enjoying. But these rights did not conflict with the inequalities of capitalist society: they were, on the contrary, necessary to the maintenance of that particular form of inequality. The explanation lies in the fact that the core of citizenship at this stage was composed of civil rights. And civil rights were indispensable to a competitive market economy. They gave to each man, as part of his individual status, the power to engage as an independent unit in the economic struggle, and made it possible to deny to him social protection on the ground that he was equipped with the means to protect himself. (Marshall 1963: 90)

## Criticisms of Marshall's periodization

I now want to consider some recent objections and emendations to Marshall's account of the rise of citizenship. I will start with some observations of Gertrude Himmelfarb (1984), which might be read as a commentary on the passage quoted at the end of the last section. She sets out Marshall's theory of historical development, and continues:

It is this sequence that gives rise to the familiar idea that political rights are less advanced, less progressive than social rights, that they are "merely formal", insubstantial, illusory, until fleshed out with a full complement of social rights. (Himmelfarb 1984: 268)

Himmelfarb then refers to the "moral economy" of the eighteenth century that so pervades the thought of Adam Smith and many of his contemporaries, and suggests that to a nineteenth-century radical – "an 'Old Corruption' radical or a Tory radical" – the location of rights might have appeared very differently. Social citizenship already existed in the form of a tissue of rights and obligations that tied together a

7

single society – not "two nations" – based on rank. This paternalistic order was threatened in the early nineteenth century by soulless Utilitarians and greedy industrialists, but it was nevertheless *there*, precisely because it was a natural order, enshrined by tradition, and in the hearts of men and women. Himmelfarb says that according to this view political rights might be seen as "a later stage in the advance of civilization".

One difficulty in Marshall's theory is that if in the Middle Ages civil, political and social rights were already present – in however "fused" a condition – they had at some point to go underground, in order to re-emerge in the shape and sequence that Marshall postulated. So far as social rights are concerned, it would seem quite plausible to argue that the institutions of the moral economy continued throughout the eighteenth century, although eroded by such developments as the decline in wage regulation, until they were given a legislative quietus in the first 40 years of the nineteenth century, and particularly with the coming of the New Poor Law in 1834. The story therefore becomes one of fracture, even if the line was broken only for a comparatively brief spell. It might be argued that the establishment of capitalism required a temporary suspension of ground rules.

Next, it might be instructive to set out a far from recent alternative account to Marshall's, supplied by Leonard Hobhouse, a leading figure of the "first wave" and an acknowledged proximate influence on Marshall – he held the Chair of Sociology at the LSE that Marshall was later to occupy when the latter arrived there to teach in 1929. At the peak point of Edwardian social reform, Hobhouse brought out his little Home University Library book on *Liberalism* (Hobhouse 1911). In one of the chapters in which he gears himself up to his main themes (Ch. 2), Hobhouse contributes what he terms "a sketch of the historical progress of the liberalising movement". The chapter is entitled "Elements of Liberalism", and consists of a categorization of various kinds of liberty, which Hobhouse arranges in the chronological order of their realization. Although Hobhouse talks primarily of liberty, he uses the word "rights" freely.

Hobhouse starts with "Civil Liberty", which means the reign of law, due process, the establishment of impartial legal institutions, and so on. He goes on to "Fiscal Liberty" – principally freedom from arbitrary taxation. The third section is called "Personal Liberty", and this includes freedom of thought and speech, and of religious observance.

Hobhouse then proceeds to "Social Liberty", by which he intends not social rights in Marshall's sense but freedom to choose an occupation and the abolition of posts reserved to particular status groups. These four add up to what Marshall would call the civil element in citizenship, although there are differences in what the two authors mention and stress.

Hobhouse continues, however, not with the "political element" in citizenship, but with what he terms "Economic Liberty". This category includes rights attendant on factory legislation as well as freedom of contract and association – Hobhouse has, of course, particularly trade union rights in mind here. In this way he bridges the gap between Marshall's civil and social elements. Next, he introduces a category of "Domestic Liberty", in which he includes both the Married Women's Property Act and early protection of children, which are not matters specifically considered by Marshall. It will be noted that, although Hobhouse is not precise on dates, he has by this stage travelled a long way through the nineteenth century.

We have, however, still not reached political rights. The next section is concerned with "Local, Racial and National Liberty", meaning essentially the self-determination of communities and peoples. Here, as elsewhere, Hobhouse seems more concerned with collectivities than Marshall. There then follows an understandably brief section on "International Liberty". And, at last and lastly, we come to "Political Liberty and Popular Sovereignty". This seems to have been left to so late a point in the chapter because of the importance Hobhouse attached to the extension of the franchise in 1884, although he also wants to ruminate on whether "popular sovereignty" can be considered a form of liberty at all. Furthermore, full adult male suffrage was not attained until 1918, and full adult female suffrage not until 1928 – and if Hobhouse was in no position to appreciate the significance of this, Marshall certainly was.

*Liberalism* was published too early for an appreciation of the full import of such measures as the Old Age Pensions Act of 1908 or the National Insurance Act of 1911. As a result, Hobhouse's treatment of the "social element" is truncated, but in his publications of the 1920s this omission was rectified (Hobhouse 1924): Barbalet indeed credits him with "the germ of the idea that citizenship comprises three parts" (Barbalet 1988: 7). His sketch of the historical progression is considerably more complex than Marshall's: it is also much messier, but then so surely was the reality. Hobhouse's general tendency is to throw social rights and Marshall's social element in citizenship back in time, and political rights and the political element in citizenship forward. His formulations also draw attention to some lacunae in Marshall's historical scheme of things, particularly in the sections on "Economic Liberty" and "Domestic Liberty".

Let us take the latter first. As Bottomore points out, Marshall, like most of the social scientists who were his contemporaries, paid scant attention to the particular situation of women (Bottomore 1992: 67). Unlike Hobhouse, he was writing at a time when the claims of feminism were not insistent. Yet this scarcely seems an excuse, and one recent historian, Susan Pedersen, takes Marshall to task most severely in an interesting comparison with Beveridge:

> ... Beveridge ordered the sexes hierarchically, treating men as representatives of "the family" as a whole and women as autonomous citizens primarily in the absence of men. Yet Beveridge was convinced enough of the desirability of a family form based on male "breadwinning" and female dependence to leave this unequal treatment naked for all to see, covered only by the rhetorical fig leaf of his claim to be treating such couples as a "team". Marshall, by contrast, developed a theory of "social citizenship" that claimed to be universal but was constructed in such a way as to be applicable only to men. Women were not defined by Marshall as "dependent" – they disappeared from the picture entirely – and with their going the manifold ways in which the welfare state addressed family and dependency relations vanished as well. (Pedersen 1993: 6)

If the experience of citizenship of more than half the adult population is taken fully into account, perhaps becoming a touchstone for its attainment, a very different picture from Marshall's emerges – much foreshortened, occurring considerably later in time. Civil and political rights were achieved by women in Britain in the approximately 50 years from the Married Women's Property Act to the attainment of the franchise on an equal basis with men in 1928. Even then there were many gaps, particularly in respect of the right of entry to certain occupations, or, once admitted to them, to remain after marriage or childbirth. And it is only since 1990 that women have been taxed separately from their husbands as a matter of course.

As for social rights, most feminists would maintain that they are not fully with us yet. British social security still marches falteringly to the beat of a Beveridgean social order resting on the lifetime earnings of a male breadwinner, and treating many women as appendages to men. Social insurance has not found it possible to provide adequately in old age for women with broken employment records, and has excluded major and growing groups like non-working single parents. On a wider front, there has been great reluctance (on the part of both public authorities and employers) to provide services of importance to women, such as suitable child care facilities. Furthermore, any conception of "domestic citizenship" poses a sharp question about the continuance of gender-ascribed roles in the provision of goods and services for and within the household. One recent feminist writer notes that this would make "radical and problematic demands on the reorientation of political theory" since "it expands the centre of citizen commitments to a domain the exclusion of which has traditionally been assumed in the distinctive meaning of citizenship" (Vogel & Moran 1991: 79).

Hobhouse's "Economic Liberty" broadly parallels Marshall's subcategory of "industrial citizenship", which has often been thought anomalous. Before going on to this, however, we need to note that Hobhouse includes restrictions on hours of work, control of working conditions, safety requirements and the other elements of early workplace regulation. Marshall deals with these measures by arguing that like the Poor Law, they were developments separate from the expansion of citizenship, since the protection they gave was initially accorded only to women and children, manifestly non-citizens by the standards of the mid-nineteenth century. However, the early factory legislation still represents a problem for Marshall, as it did for Marx. This is because the protection was quite soon extended to adult working men, so we have an example of social rights before the time allotted to them in Marshall's scheme.

The timing problem with trade union rights is in the opposite direction. Since they enable the pursuit of gains for workers through direct contractual bargaining with employers, rather than via the political system, Marshall treats them as an outgrowth of civil rights. However, they were clearly secured much later than most other such

11

rights. Marshall suggests that trade unionism has "created a secondary system of industrial citizenship parallel with and supplementary to the system of political citizenship" (Marshall 1963: 98) This is not merely "secondary", it is also unsatisfactory, not least because democratization has in almost all respects stopped well short of the gates of the workplace. The cause of "industrial citizenship" in any meaningful sense currently has rather few advocates, but is kept just about alive by Robert Dahl and a small group of "market socialists" (Dahl 1985, Miller 1989).

In the second volume of his mammoth trilogy *The sources of social power* Michael Mann turns to Marshall's account, deciding that two of his types of citizenship are, on inspection, heterogeneous (Mann 1993: 19). He thus creates a five-category rather than a three-category scheme. One of the categories he splits into two is civil rights, distinguishing individual and collective sub-types and noting that the latter were not granted, in any of the countries he has studied, until the late nineteenth century or, in some cases, well into the twentieth. This revised classification presents some problems. Mann makes it clear that he means by collective civil rights primarily organizing rights for workers, yet many other civil rights are in some sense collective, such as rights of assembly, association and freedom of worship. Furthermore, limited liability and related institutional forms, essential for the success of the Second and Third Industrial Revolutions, were corporate statuses bestowed on collectivities. An irony pointed out by Marshall is that British trade unionism, in the nineteenth century and later, doughtily resisted incorporation, and thereby embraced curiously individualistic styles of collective action.

Mann's second candidate for splitting into two is social rights:

> I also subdivide social citizenship (Marshall's "sharing in the social heritage") into ideological and economic sub-types – rights to an education, allowing cultural participation and occupational attainment, and rights to direct economic subsistence. Through the long nineteenth century, ideological-social citizenship was attained by all middle-classes, but economic-social citizenship remained minimal (as Marshall noted). (Mann 1993: 19)

12

The trouble with this is that it makes too jagged a tear in the unity of social citizenship. "Allowing occupational attainment", included under "ideological-social citizenship", sounds quite economic, and it is not clear where one could fit into this classification the "health-care citizenship" discussed by Michael Moran in a recent chapter (Moran 1991). There might be some sense in distinguishing between "cultural citizenship" and (other forms of) social citizenship: such a distinction would draw a line through the middle of education. It might recall a very transatlantic argument advanced by Milton Friedman in *Capitalism and freedom* in which he separates out both basic skills, such as numeracy and literacy, and the introduction to the general cultural heritage (including the inculcation of Americanism) from the more vocational aspects of education (Friedman 1962). (He thinks that the costs of the latter, but not the former, should be recouped from the beneficiaries.) Otherwise, if social citizenship is heterogeneous, it is because it involves access to a very mixed assortment of services and benefits, in respect of each of which different allocation rules may be appropriate.

Since Marshall wrote, things have moved on, and many recent commentators are not satisfied with a view of citizenship revolving so much around occupational social class, the ownership and control of industry, and the distribution and redistribution of income and wealth – the issues that have fitted so easily with a political spectrum running from left to right. I have already indicated that some feminists see social class as a series of spaces occupied principally by men, but this rejection runs wider than that. Introducing an edited volume of articles, Bart van Steenbergen notes that "it will become evident in this book [that] the notion of social citizenship as the *final* stage is not accepted". He lists a host of "new types of citizenship" set out by his contributors "in the light of new developments and problems with which we are confronted today" (van Steenbergen 1994: 3, emphasis in original). In addition to "cultural citizenship" (put forward by Turner (1993b) in his collection), these are "neo-republican citizenship", "active citizenship", "race-neutral citizenship", "gender-neutral citizenship", "global citizenship", "European citizenship" and "ecological citizenship". Some of these themes are echoed in various of the Marshall lectures, and with this fragmentation comes the danger that the concept will disintegrate into a cacophony of unrelated tunes, cross-cutting and obscuring each other.

13

## The Englishness of Marshall's account

One persistent criticism of Marshall is that he is far too Britocentric (or perhaps more accurately Anglocentric) in his approach to citizenship. His sequence of civil, political and social rights fits Britain well, it is suggested, but is misleading when applied to other countries. In particular, the notion that social citizenship is the inevitable capstone of the edifice has been questioned. It is remarkable how often the British experience has been taken as paradigmatic of welfare state development: this must be one of the few British post-war coups in the history of ideas, and Marshall, along with others such as Titmuss, must receive much of the credit for it (or alternatively bear the blame).

In Chapter 7, originally given as a Marshall lecture in 1986 some years before volume II of *The sources of social power*, Michael Mann grapples with the English-centredness of Marshall's account. Basing his analysis on the nature of regimes and the calculations made by leading members of the ruling class, he demonstrates that the particular ordered sequence found in Britain was not necessarily replicated elsewhere. He identifies five "strategies" pursued by advanced industrial countries, terming them liberal, reformist, authoritarian monarchist, Fascist and authoritarian socialist. Interestingly, he finds Britain to be an impure case, mixed liberal/reformist. It has deviated in a reformist direction from the liberal strategy of the United States, with its denuded and unprestigious conception of social citizenship: however, according to Mann, the reformist possibility is better exemplified by the Scandinavian countries, where social rights have been more securely lodged in a more corporatist framework of assumptions and institutions.

The relevant contrast is with "authoritarian-monarchist" Wilhelmine Germany. There, limited social rights, in the form of Bismarckian social insurance, were granted as a deliberate, and rather cynical, substitute for full political citizenship. Thus in Germany in a real sense social rights preceded rather than succeeded political rights, an order corresponding to that recommended by Himmelfarb. Mann concludes in Chapter 7 that, had it not been for certain unpleasant geopolitical events starting in 1914, the "authoritarian monarchical" strategy "could probably have survived into advanced, post-industrial society, providing a distinctive, corporately organized, arbitrary combination of partial civil, political and social citizenship". "This was not", he adds, "envisaged by Marshall, or indeed by any modern sociologist" (Mann, pp. 139–40).

Mann shares Marshall's concern with the institutionalization of class conflict and in particular with the incorporation of the working classes and their organizations into society and polity. However, his emphasis on the strategies followed by national elites seems to owe more to Barrington Moore (1966) than to Marshall. As we have seen, his classifications revolve more around such strategies than around the order in which the elements in citizenship made their appearance. This may be why Mann under-theorizes France, which appears to be placed in the reformist column, but as a "contested regime" (alongside Spain and Italy) in which reactionaries and secular liberals spent the nineteenth century, and a good slice of the twentieth too, in squabbling over citizenship.

Yet the French experience would seem to repay attention for more than one reason. First, the modern version of republican citizenship was virtually invented in late eighteenth-century France, and the traditions thereby created have left a deep imprint. The republican virtues – as seen in the emphasis upon military service – have always been severely masculine (van Gunsteren 1994): this may help to explain why the franchise was not extended to women in France until after the Second World War.

Secondly, and apparently paradoxically in view of the above, the French developed certain aspects of social citizenship early, and on less deeply gendered lines than in Britain. France is often taken as a latecomer among welfare states, chiefly because a comprehensive, "modern" social insurance system was not in place until after 1945, yet it was a pioneer in family policy. "It would be an over-simplification", writes John Baker, "to say that in France childrearing is regarded as a service to society that entitles those performing it to adequate reward and assistance, but no more so than to say that in Britain having children is regarded as a private indulgence of parents that should concern the community no more than their buying a house or car" (Baker 1986: 422). It is not difficult to see in this cautious formulation the germ of a distinctively French approach to citizenship, in which the state's duty to advance the welfare of children – future French citizens – is seen as more important than a one-sided emphasis on the rights and obligations of the male breadwinner.

Thirdly, the French conception of citizenship has been strongly assimilationist. This is a feature common to France and the United States, even though the former has never been in the same sense as the latter a country of immigration. However, according to the French republican tradition, immigrants will be regarded as French, provided that they espouse French cultural values, and behave (and especially speak) like a French person.

In line with the law of *jus soli* most of those born to immigrant parents in France have been ascribed French citizenship on attaining the age of majority (although it should be noted that French nationality law has recently been altered under the Balladur Government). In Germany the situation has been very different. There, *jus sanguinis* rules: citizenship is essentially a matter of blood and descent. Brubaker, who has added much to our knowledge of citizenship in both countries, sums up the distinctive German understanding of the concept as "restrictive toward non-Germans, yet expansive toward German immigrants"(Brubaker 1992: 15). For other immigrants the processes of naturalization are difficult and very low proportions either seek it or obtain it, even after a generation of residence (Layton-Henry 1991). Social rights have not been the stumbling block to the incorporation of German guest-workers, since a virtually complete array of them has been made available, along with civil rights (Brubaker 1989). Thus, to employ Brubaker's terms, substantive citizenship has been partly uncoupled from formal citizenship. However, political rights have been confined to those with formal membership of the national community, except in two Länder that were for long periods under Social Democratic control, where rights of voting in local elections have been conceded.

British approaches to citizenship have been different again. Citizenship is acknowledged to be a status based upon membership, yet there has been surprisingly little interest, especially in the academic debate, about to whom this status should be offered, and on what conditions. It is true that there have been bitter controversies over immigration and that British governments have adopted an increasingly restrictive stance. Britain admits to its territory for humanitarian reasons far fewer migrants than does the Federal Republic of Germany. However, there has been a strange tendency to wall off the question of initial entry, and the processes of gradual admission to membership that may follow through the granting of residential status, naturalization, et cetera (see Layton-Henry 1991), from the core conception of citizenship as reported in these pages. Abundant concern about exclusion has been expressed in Britain, but it has been directed more at internal than external exclusion. That is to say, it has been less about the policed boundaries of the nation-state (which have simply been presumed) than about whether particular groups, whose full citizenship status is mostly not in dispute, are being denied access to lifestyles that are customary in British society. Hence the anxiety about "underclasses". These emphases cross the Atlantic: Brubaker notes the relative neglect of formal citizenship among both British and American sociologists and political scientists (Brubaker 1992: 22).

Marshall clearly played quite some role in fixing this preoccupation with the substantive rights of citizenship, and in particular with the social rights supposedly guaranteed by the welfare state. However, some contextual considerations need to be taken into account. Marshall's lectures were given in 1949 when the question of state membership was not of active political concern. Large-scale immigration from the New Commonwealth had not yet taken place, so that its effects could not have made themselves felt. The relaxed atmosphere at the time is well illustrated by the Ireland Act of 1949, according to which the Labour Government continued to grant full citizenship rights to settlers from a country that had voluntarily left the Commonwealth and had not offered reciprocal arrangements to Britons moving to its own territory.

By the time Marshall composed his later writings this situation had clearly changed, and the questions raised by immigration had forced themselves closer to the centre of the political stage. Marshall's emphases, however, remained of a piece with his earlier works. In the early editions of *Social policy* (Marshall 1965, 1970) the only references to immigrants occur in a section about the strains placed upon housing provision in particular localities by newcomers – who, of course, might be of any origin. For the fourth edition, however, he wrote a new page in which he suggests that "the problem of race relations, *and of immigrants in general,* is basically one of participation and community development" (Marshall 1975: 210, my italics). He then discusses the Community Relations Commission and the Race Relations Board, the statutory bodies set up some years previously to promote harmonious relations and to prevent racial discrimination. Such a commitment to the ending of internal exclusion – however limited the results in practice – is not generally found elsewhere in the European Union, although similar legislation exists in the Netherlands.

## T. H. Marshall and the role of conflict

Another respect in which Marshall has attracted some shellfire, notably from Anthony Giddens, is because of his perceived failure "to emphasize that citizen rights have been achieved in substantial degree only through *struggle*" (Giddens 1982: 171, emphasis in original). Giddens maintains that "each of the three sets of citizenship rights . . . had to be fought for, over a long span of historical time" (*ibid.*). Albert O. Hirschman in a typically sparkling contribution, agrees: taking Marshall's, or the English, order as the "normal" order, and applying it to the whole Western world, he argues that each assertion of citizenship rights by the advocates of progress was met by a bitter response from the forces of reaction (Hirschman 1991). And Barbalet considers that "Marshall's conflict is more contradiction than struggle" (Barbalet 1988: 30), meaning that the opposition is between principles, of citizenship on the one hand and class or capitalist society on the other, rather than a matter of long-running battles between warring groups of actors.

However, many commentators have argued to the contrary, sometimes through taking too literally Marshall's statement that in the twentieth century citizenship and the capitalist class system have been at war (Halsey 1984) (Later in *Citizenship and social class*, Marshall (1963:115) grants that this phrase may have been "rather too strong", and replaces it with the more cautious formulation that citizenship has "imposed modifications" on the capitalist class system.) Marshall makes scattered references to struggle in Giddens's sense, but there seems little doubt that his stress is on the development of institutionalized forms of conflict with most of the teeth drawn.

Probably the best way to defend Marshall against the charge of underplaying struggle is to argue that he accurately portrays what actually happened in Britain. One relevant consideration is that throughout the nineteenth century the working classes and their representative institutions were very wary of a central state whose most positive activity was selling postage stamps (Pelling 1968). Otherwise, it taxed the working man's beer and baccy, recruited the working-class young into the armed forces, ran courts, prisons and other corrective establishments, policed strikes and assemblies, raised rents through housing regulations, and took away valuable household income by insisting on school attendance. Not all these activities were unpopular, especially among the respectable and often skilled working class, but they too preferred independence from the state, through the development of a network of self-helping mutual benefit associations. The coming of national insurance did not, at least initially, redress the balance, since compulsory deductions from the wage packet were an innovation unwelcome to many working-class people. Pressure from below before 1914, especially for social rights, can easily be exaggerated.

Of greater importance was the British ruling class's customary practice of doling out reforms (or "concessions") in small parcels. "The political rights of citizenship", says Marshall, "unlike the civil rights, were full of potential danger to the capitalist system, although those who were cautiously extending them down the social scale probably did not realize quite how great the danger was" (Marshall 1963: 96). There are many reasons why this danger was averted, but the process of piecemeal incorporation itself surely played a considerable part. Referring to extensions of the franchise, Mann notes that "at any particular point in time emerging dissidents – petty bourgeois radicals, artisan and skilled factory worker socialists, feminists – have been partially inside, partially outside the state" (Mann, p. 131). This must have helped to turn conflict into constitutional and reformist channels.

Marshall's lack of emphasis on struggle and violence may not only have been in the interests of good description. One would guess that it also reflected a normative preference, and this needs exploration, which I will attempt via a closer look at *The rhetoric of reaction* (Hirschman 1991). Hirschman builds an elegant argument on the foundations laid in Marshall's categories of civil, political and social rights – a tribute paid by the author of *Exit, voice and loyalty* to one of his few rivals in the production of fruitful triads. He starts with the "difficulty and opposition" that the "socioeconomic dimension of citizenship" has run into 35 years after Marshall "painted [his] magnificent and confident canvas of staged progress" (Hirschman 1991: 2). He continues, however:

> Is it not true that not just the last but each and every one of Marshall's three progressive thrusts has been followed by

ideological counterthrusts of extraordinary force? And have not these counterthrusts been at the origin of convulsive social and political struggles often leading to setbacks for the intended progressive programs as well as to much human suffering and misery? The backlash so far experienced by the Welfare State may in fact be rather mild in comparison with the earlier onslaughts and conflicts that followed upon the assertion of individual freedoms in the eighteenth century or upon the broadening of political participation in the nineteenth. (Hirschman 1991:3)

Hirschman goes on to suggest that "reactionary" arguments – he insists that he uses the adjective in as neutral a sense as possible – have been remarkably constant in the forms they have taken, and have come in very few varieties. Indeed, he creates yet another threesome:

According to the perversity thesis, any purposive action to improve some feature of the political, social, or economic order only serves to exacerbate the condition one wishes to remedy. The futility thesis holds that attempts at social transformation will be unavailing, that they will simply fail to "make a dent". Finally, the jeopardy thesis argues that the cost of the proposed change or reform is too high as it endangers some previous, precious accomplishment. (Hirschman 1991: 7)

Hirschman stresses that these arguments are not the exclusive property of the Right, a point especially pertinent in the 1980s and 1990s when the defenders of large-scale state welfare provision on the political left and centre have been pushed into the conservative position. However, he also goes further, in that he finds arguments in "progressive" rhetoric that form counterparts to each of his "reactionary" theses. Thus the jeopardy thesis can be metamorphosed into a "mutual support" thesis – progressive reforms reinforce rather than threaten valued gains – or an "imminent danger" thesis – not to act promptly on lines recommended by the forces of progress will produce disorder or disaster. Paralleling the futility thesis are views that earmark for the progressive cause the laws underlying the development of human societies: history is on the side of change, so it is futile to resist it. The perversity thesis is a little more difficult, so central has it been in conservative strategies, but Hirschman suggests that a Burkean insistence on the wisdom encapsulated in existing institutions has, on occasion, been effectively countered by the argument that so desperate is the situation "that the old order must be smashed and a new one rebuilt from scratch *regardless* of any counterproductive consequences that might ensue" (Hirschman 1991: 162). He concludes his excursion into progressive rhetoric with the observation that, "(L)ike its reactionary counterpart, it turns out to be richer in maneuvers, largely of exaggeration and obfuscation, than it is ordinarily given credit for" (Hirschman 1991: 163).

Hirschman clearly believes that out of rhetoric is brought forth daggers. He therefore conceives it as his moral duty to puncture its pretensions, and his paired triplets of reactionary and progressive arguments certainly cut them down to size (Hirschman 1991: 167). This all seems rather unlike anything in Marshall but otherwise the two men have much in common. The stance of both is humanitarian, mildly ironic, favouring the liberal consensus and the middle way.

On his very first page, Hirschman talks of Marshall proceeding "to explain, very much in the spirit of the Whig interpretation of history, how the more enlightened human societies had successfully tackled [the civil, political and social] dimensions [of citizenship] one . . . after the other" (Hirschman 1991: 1). Was Marshall a Whig? It is not too difficult to find excerpts from *Citizenship and social class* that seem to express a *de haut en bas* perspective. For example: "(T)he familiar instruments of modern democracy were fashioned by the upper classes and then handed down, step by step to the lower" (Marshall 1963: 96). However, the imputation of Whiggery rather wrenches these words out of context: they occur in a passage in which Marshall is talking about a very early stage in the story of citizenship, and in any case he was arguably only reporting how things developed. Marshall was not charting an inevitable progression to the sunny uplands of the 1950s and a then contemporary version of the end of history. On the contrary: the last pages of *Citizenship and social class* record Marshall's recognition of the precariousness of the post-1945 welfare reforms, and show that he expected there to be further phases in the development of democratic citizenship (which is perhaps optimistic rather than Whiggish) (Marshall 1963: 127).

Nevertheless, Halsey's remark that "Marshall was in one sense the outstanding sociological interpreter of British Butskellism" (p. 81) is suggestive. Some recent historians have found Butskellism to be a highly contestable phenomenon (Rollings 1994) and the extent of the agreement among leading politicians about the essentials of policy can indeed be questioned, although it does seem that for a time they marked out rather a large number of areas as not being in dispute between them. And if any intellectual figure of the period can be said to embody the spirit of the "post-war settlement" it is Marshall. This can be seen, first, in his eagerness to spread the credit for the attainment of the social element in citizenship. In a well known passage in *Social policy* he wrote:

> The three pillars of the British Welfare State were the Education Act, the National Insurance Act, and the National Health Service Act. They are associated with the names of Butler, Beveridge, and Bevan – a Conservative, a Liberal and a Socialist. When one remembers the mixed origins of social policy at the beginning of the century it is not surprising to find that the Welfare State, when it eventually saw the light, was of mixed parentage. (Marshall 1965: 86)

Secondly, a careful reading of his treatment of "class abatement" suggests that his statement that twentieth-century capitalism and citizenship were "at war" was profoundly misleading rather than just in need of modification:

> . . . mass production for the home market and a growing interest on the part of industry in the needs and tastes of the common people enabled the less well-to-do to enjoy a material civilization that differed less markedly in quality from that of the rich than it had ever done before. All this profoundly altered the setting in which the progress of citizenship took place. Social integration spread from the sphere of sentiment and patriotism into that of material enjoyment. (Marshall 1963: 100)

Thus the spread and success of consumer capitalism seem to have become preconditions for citizenship, a line of thought later developed in his essay on the "hyphenated society" of welfare-capitalism (Marshall 1981).

I will conclude with a look at a *tour-de-force* article that, *inter alia,* sets Marshall within a philosophical context. Geraint Parry outlines four models of citizenship, each associated with one or more recent political thinkers (Parry 1991). The first of these has Michael Oakeshott as its principal advocate: a "minimal" conception of citizenship based on no more than the "watery fidelity" necessary for "persons who are related to each other merely by virtue of their recognition of certain rules which regulate their conduct within the jurisdiction in which they find themselves" (Parry 1991: 168). The second theory discussed is a "human rights" one, most fully developed by Alan Gewirth (1982): people have rights because of what they share in common as human beings, namely the capacity for agency. Such a view downplays the significance of national boundaries and of national and local loyalties. It is sharply distinct from the third model, put forward by communitarian thinkers like Sandel (1982), Macintyre (1981) and Walzer (1983). Human identities are deeply embedded in, and therefore cannot be abstracted from, the history of particular societies and the experience of living in them. Citizenship depends on community and, at the same time, the sense of a common life feeds concern for the welfare of all those defined as fellow citizens, so the relationship is seen in terms of mutual reinforcement. Parry's fourth conception, which he terms the mutual society model, is in some senses intermediate between the other three. Citizens have agency, rights, common understandings, some shared purposes, and obligations to one another, as in a mutual society that is freely joined.

The question is: where are Marshall's views fitted into this scheme? Parry's answer is somewhat mixed, as he recognizes that Marshall blends in a modicum of gentle communitarianism. However, he is essentially seen as standing with Oakeshott. Indeed, Parry uses Marshall to fill out the "minimalist" conception historically, saying that "the successive stages of Marshall's evolution of citizen rights may, with some adjustments, be regarded as a pursuit of the intimations of the notion of free and equal subscription to the rules of civil association" (Parry 1991: 171). The yoking together of these two professors at the London School of Economics, one avowedly conservative, the other social democratic, seems at first sight inappropriate. But perhaps they were fellow liberals under the skin, of a sceptical, patrician kind.

# CHAPTER 2

# Citizenship and social class

## Ralf Dahrendorf

### Origins of inequality

Life chances are never distributed equally. We do not know of a society in which all men, women and children have the same entitlements and enjoy the same provisions. We do not even know of one in which all men have the same status. Probably there cannot be such a condition. "Similars do not constitute a state", said Aristotle. If all were alike, or even nearly alike, there might be human sand-dunes or other molecular formations brought about by the elements, but there would be no structure, no meaning, no progress. Society is necessary because different people have to create common institutions to survive and advance their lot. Their differences matter at least in so far as their various interests encroach on each other, if not because some are able to impose their will on others whether by force or the evil eye.

To reflect upon these matters has become popular again in the late twentieth century. All of a sudden, the social contract has been unearthed by philosophers, economists and political theorists. For the most part, the reason for this interest differs today from what it was two, three and four centuries ago.[1] Then, authors from Hobbes to Locke and on to Hume and Rousseau were arguing that some elements of a deliberate social order are necessary. In the midst of civil upheavals, they tried to establish the rule of law and civil government. Today, the sense is widespread that government and the law are everywhere. The dominant "contractarian" question is how little government would suffice to guarantee law and order. Even those who do not exactly advocate a minimal state insist that reasons must be given for social institutions such as property or democracy. The rediscovery of the social contract arises from the search for fundamental structures in a jungle of superstructures of many kinds.

This is as it should be as long as one point is well understood. The social contract is not an unchanging skeleton of the body politic. It is not there once and for all, but itself subject to change. Even the American constitution – the nearest to a deliberate social contract in modern history, and of course in part a result of the eighteenth-century debate on the subject – had to be adapted by amendments, court rulings and practice to stay alive. The social contract is not the basis of society but the subject of history. It is written and rewritten by each generation. Its lasting elements are at best a grammar of society; everything else is variable, capable of improvement but liable also to take a turn for the worse. The question is not whether we should return to the everlasting articles of the social contract, but how we can write such articles anew to advance liberty under changed conditions.

Still, a little grammar helps one understand the language. We need not pursue the question of natural inequalities of humans here, save to say that people's motives and interests differ, and that all societies have found ways of organizing these differences in ways that involve both co-ordination and subordination. The division of labour co-ordinates different tasks to common effect; social stratification subordinates some to others by applying a scale of values on which some rank lower than others. Both, but notably subordination, require a group and an agency that set the tone. Some speak of hegemony, others simply of power. In the grammar that is used here, the old distinction between a "contract of association" and a "contract of domination" is at best of analytical usefulness. In practice it is difficult to think of human association without an element of domination. Where there is society there is power.

Certain authors like to use a less orthodox grammar and separate the two contracts. They dream of an association freed of all elements of domination.[2] Theirs is the language that appeals in revolutionary moments of elation. It has little use at other times, except to prepare people for unusual days that cannot last. Like all absolute perspectives it detracts from the tasks before real people in real conditions. These have to do with the domestication, not the abolition, of power. Of course, power is never benevolent. Society is not nice, but it is necessary. The question is therefore how power and the inequalities generated by it can be turned to advantage in terms of liberty.

Modern societies have gone some way towards this objective. Aristotle's statement about similars who do not constitute a state was not as bland as its isolated citation sounds. The early chapters of his *Politics* (1988) abound with statements that we would regard as entirely unacceptable. For Aristotle, slaves are not a part of the state, because they are "by nature" slaves. Women differ somewhat from slaves, but again they are "by nature" inferior to men. Children, the sons of free men at any rate, grow up to be citizens, but are not citizens yet. There is obviously an issue of inclusion here that has accompanied the history of mankind through the centuries, and of which many would say that it is still unresolved. It is clear, however, that modern societies have a more generous concept of who belongs and who does not than Aristotle did.

How did this come about? Even the benevolent reader of this chapter and its subject will not fail to notice a melancholy weakness of social analysis. There is a theory of how change comes about, and there is history. The theory is not bad, in that it directs our attention to certain actors and motives, and even helps us anticipate the eventual outcome. But the ways of human progress are not so simple. Things happen for reasons not foreseen in the theory and at times at which they should not have happened at all.

The unequal distribution of life chances is a result of structures of power. Some are in a position to lay down the law by which the standing of others is measured. For many centuries, it looked as if very few were able to do this; the rule of kings remained virtually unchallenged by the people. Even then, there were good rulers and bad ones (and great rulers somewhere in between). Gradually, more people came to be involved in making the law, though it was still administered by a minority. The difference is not only one of times, but also one of places. A degree of democracy was characteristic above all of certain islands of association in the oceans of domination. They were often co-extensive with cities, from the Greek *polis* to the medieval burgh. The rise of modernity can be described also as the gradual spread of such experiences. As the power of a few was brought under the control of more and ultimately of the many, inequalities lost their fateful, ascribed character and social positions became at least in principle attainable as well as shedable. The route from status to contract was also one from status to class.

It is as well that society is not nice. If it was, men and women would, as Immanuel Kant put it, "live an Arcadian, pastoral existence of perfect concord, self-sufficiency and mutual love. But all human talents would remain hidden forever in a dormant state, and men, as good-natured as the sheep they tended, would scarcely render their existence more valuable than that of their animals." Man's "unsociable sociability" is the sting that produces the antagonisms from which progress flows, including more life chances within an improved social contract. Power generates not just inequality but by the same token conflict. It creates interests in change as well as interests in the status quo. But such interests find different expressions in a world of hierarchy than they do in a world of contract. It would be instructive to speculate in another context about the pre-modern social conflict. Was it merely a battle of elites? How important was the formula of bread and circuses for maintaining power? When did elements of class begin to enter the scene? In the eighteenth century they certainly did. With the revolutions of modernity the quality of conflict has changed. As a result, large numbers of people are involved, and visible conflicts become the motive force of change. Class conflict enters the scene.

One little noticed internal contradiction in Marx's theory of class mars the stringency of the theory but testifies to the honesty of the author. In the *Communist manifesto*, Marx and Engels talk briefly about different epochs. As the bourgeoisie had to turn feudal relations of production upside down, they say, in order to help new forces of production break through, so the proletariat will have to put an end to bourgeois relations of production. Neither Marx nor his followers ever identified the forces of production that had the proletariat as their herald and bearer. But there is another point. The bourgeoisie can hardly be described as the oppressed class of feudal society and compared to the proletariat in bourgeois society. The Third Estate may have lacked political rights, but the recognized estates had long been economically dependent on its services when the revolutionary grumblings began. In fact, the proletariat has a unique place in Marx's schema of history, and the authors of the *Communist manifesto* knew it: "All previous historical movements were movements of minorities, or in the interest of minorities. The proletariat is the self-conscious, independent movement of the immense majority." Leaving hyperbole and the hang-up with epochs on one side, it is not unfair to translate this into the statement that class, in the sense of open political conflicts based on social position and involving large numbers of people, is a modern phenomenon.

The origin of the class conflict then is to be found in structures of power that no longer have the absolute quality of entrenched hierarchy. The subject of the class conflict is life chances. More precisely, it is the unequal distribution of life chances. Those at the disadvantaged end demand from those in positions of advantage more entitlements and provisions. The struggle, first latent and barely visible, then open and fully organized, leads to a wider spread of both. But it has above all one effect that describes the history of modern societies from the eighteenth century to the present: it transforms differences in entitlements into differences in provisions. From qualitative inequalities we move progressively to quantitative inequalities. Status barriers give way to degrees of status. This is the story that has to be told in greater detail before the next stage in the history of modern conflict can be described.

## Enter citizenship

One of the more important developments that accompanied the rise of modernity was the creation of the nation-state. The process was in most cases the deliberate work of monarchs and their first ministers, but it was in the evident interest of a social group that could not rely on traditional territorial powers. The nation-state was also a necessary vehicle for the establishment of the modern contract in the place of feudal bonds. It provided the framework for law and the institutions to uphold it. Not uncharacteristically, the first modern societies were also the first nation-states, and those who came later had as much trouble with problems of nationality as with those of citizenship.

No contemporary of the second Thirty Years War, or even of the wars between the new nations of the post-war period, would call the nation-state an unmixed blessing. Many would not call it a blessing at all. But they are wrong. Historically at least, the nation-state was as much a necessary condition of progress as it unfortunately turned out to be a source of regression and inhumanity. The alliance of nationalism and liberalism was a force for emancipation during the revolutionary decades from 1789 to 1848. To this day, no other guarantee of the rule of law has come to the fore than the nation-state, its constitution of checks and balances, due process and judicial review.[3] Not the least advantage of the nation-state was that it generalized the ancient idea of citizenship.

The citizen is the city-dweller, and in the first instance the (male, free) inhabitant of Athens in the fifth century BC. When the first dead were brought home from the Peloponnesian War, Pericles spelt out to the survivors the values for which their loved ones had fallen and described the constitution of the city.

Its administration favours the many instead of the few; this is why it is called a democracy. If we look to the laws, they afford equal justice to all in their private differences; if to social standing, advancement in public life falls to reputation for capacity, class considerations not being allowed to interfere with merit; nor again does poverty bar the way, if a man is able to serve the state, he is not hindered by the obscurity of his condition.

The translation of Thucydides' report on the speech is perhaps a little too modern,[4] but many of the characteristics of citizenship can be found in the famous funeral oration: equality of participation, equality before the law, equal opportunity and a common floor of social status. It was to take a long time, and harsh battles, before any modern nation was brought close to this ideal: but then one remembers that Athens was exceptional and fought a very different Sparta, that within Athens the majority even of grown-ups were by nature excluded from citizenship. and that the great experiment did not last. Its significance was that it established the possibility of a great idea, for there is no better way of doing that than by making things real in one place. Citizenship was not a Utopian idea; it was the development of an ancient experience.

The experience was never entirely lost. Contrary to some, I would not praise the Romans for "the wit to distinguish between civil rights – rights of equality before the law – and political rights – rights of membership in the sovereign body".[5] Once this distinction is made, civil rights tend to evaporate into distant skies of morality whereas rights of membership quickly turn into the duties of subjects. But there is a Roman history of citizenship; there are the Italian cities, the Hanseatic cities and others during the Middle Ages. The difference is that for many centuries the principle was dormant. It served to defend the few rather than to envelop all. The momentum of the principle of citizenship begins with the creation of political units within which civil rights and civic participation become necessary elements of the constitution. We are back to the nation-state.

Citizenship describes the rights and obligations associated with membership in a social unit, and notably with nationality. It is therefore common to all members, though the question of who can be a member and who cannot is a part of the turbulent history of citizenship. Its turbulence is still much in evidence. It has to do with the issue of lateral or national (as against vertical or social) exclusion and inclusion.[6] It affects people's identity because it defines where they belong. More often than not, it involves drawing boundaries that are visible on maps or by the colour of people's skin or in some other way. These are processes that quickly raise the temperature of human relations. Lateral exclusion has probably given rise to more violence than social exclusion. Disputes about definition are also among the more intractable human conflicts.

There is no shortage of examples. Multiracial societies are the exception rather than the rule even in the modern world. Civilization has not led to a noticeable decline in people's desire to be among their own. Few societies have managed to integrate as many ethnic groups as those of North America; but even there, the hyphen – Italian-American, Polish-American, etc. – has become as important as American citizenship, and the blacks mind that they alone do not seem to have one. After the Hapsburg Empire, the United Kingdom is an outstanding example of a country that includes several nations. This is acceptable in Wales, just bearable in Scotland and the source of civil strife in Ireland. The concept of national self-determination that emerged from the great carve-up of empires after the First World War has confirmed the strain towards homogeneity that seems still characteristic of human societies. It has also weakened the force of citizenship by detracting attention from its rights in favour of mere membership. I am a Latvian, Tyrolean, Basque, etc. and liberty must wait until that is recognized . . .

Perhaps it was wrong to imply that modern societies should find it easier to live with difference than earlier ones. Are the Quebecs and Irelands, the Lebanons and Belgiums not issues of fiercer conflicts today than 100, let alone 200 years ago? Versions of these issues are moreover evident everywhere. Has a Jewish convert from a reformed community a claim to Israeli citizenship? Can an Egyptian immigrant be trusted to run a Swedish business? Should asylum seekers be given even the most elementary rights of membership? Do they not belong in camps, like the boat people in Hong Kong. or the Cambodian refugees in Thailand? Some countries are more border-conscious than others; perhaps they have special identity problems. But everywhere it appears that as traditional bonds become weaker, boundaries of membership become more important.[7] The subject is complicated. Mobility plays a part in it, as the characteristic social role of the century increasingly seems to be that of the migrant for the more fortunate. and of the refugee for the unlucky. As one considers the result, it is hard to conclude that mankind has made great strides of civilization. A civilized society is one in which common citizenship rights combine easily with differences in race, religion or culture. It is also one that does not use its civic status as a weapon for exclusion, but regards itself as a mere step on the road to a world civil society. We shall not lose sight of the dream as we take stock of the real world.

Citizenship then is a set of rights and obligations for those who are included in the list of members. The phrase "rights and obligations" comes easily, but has its pitfalls. Clearly, I am not simply talking about a value, an ideal. Citizenship is a real social role. It provides entitlements. Entitlements are of course rights, such as the right to conclude a free contract, or the right to vote, or the right to an old age pension. But what is meant by obligations?

One obvious obligation of citizenship is to comply with the law. (I am leaving the question of civil disobedience on one side, though it does not alter the basic proposition.) But it has long been argued that this is not enough. One recent author has made the point forcefully that what is wrong with the welfare state is the neglect of obligations in favour of entitlements.[8] Obligations should include not just compliance, but also "civility", "activity and competence". The "common obligations of citizenship" encompass "both political and social duties", and among the social obligations the most important is work. Indeed, apart from "law-abidingness", "learning enough to be employable", "fluency and literacy in English", "contributing . . . to the support of one's family" and "work in available jobs for heads of families . . . and for other adult families that are needy" are all part of the "operational definition of citizenship in its social dimension".

I believe this view is fundamentally mistaken and destroys an important concept if not, by its application, the rights of people. The objections could be argued in terms of the history of work but they can be made in general terms too. Citizenship is a social contract, generally valid for all members; work is a private contract. In societies in which the private contract of labour does not exist there is no citizenship either. This is true for feudal relations of dependence and for some versions of really existing socialism. It is no accident. For when the general rights of citizenship are made dependent on people entering into private relations of employment, these lose their private and fundamentally voluntary character. In an indirect but compelling manner, labour becomes forced labour. It is imperative that the obligations of citizenship are themselves general and public as it were.

This is not to say that they are necessarily confined to compliance with the law. Paying taxes has become an obligation associated with membership, although (income) taxes are levied only on those who can afford them. (The argument put forward here is by implication an argument for civic rather than work taxes.) It may well make sense to ask all citizens to give some time of their lives to the community. Conscription is the obvious example, though some form of community service could be one method of dealing with issues that the market does not resolve by itself. Such service, whether military or civilian, is of course also "forced labour". But it is strictly circumscribed and in all respects a part of the public domain in which citizens exist.

Thus both the rights and the obligations of citizenship can vary over time. However, they are under all conditions not only public but in principle universal. Moreover, it is an important issue of liberty to what extent they may include calls on what people actually do rather than on what they have the right to do. Probably, such demands should be minimized rather than maximized. Compulsory voting is a dubious interpretation of citizenship rights. In principle the rights of citizenship are not conditional, but categorical. What citizenship offers does not depend on the readiness of people to pay a price in the private domain. Citizenship cannot be marketed.

These caveats are important when it comes to understanding the related concept of civil society. The term has a long and distinguished history. From Aristotle to the eighteenth century, it was used interchangeably with the political community, the body politic, the commonwealth or even the state.[9] Then people – liberal people – began to distinguish between society and the state. One of the productive forces of the bourgeoisie was society as against the state, or more precisely a new society against an old regime. It was but a small step from this confrontation to an understanding of civil society that associated the notion with market exchanges and capitalist economic relations generally. The ambiguity of the German term, *burgerliche Gesellschaft*, helped such misunderstandings; to some, the *citoyen* and the *bourgeois* appeared as two sides of the same coin. In fact, they are not. The two coins may have been minted at about the same time, but they are two coins, and it is conceivable that one will lose its currency long before the other.

There is no reason, in other words, why civil society should cease to be desirable, or real, once the bourgeoisie has left the social and political stage. This means in turn that the eighteenth-century distinctions may have served their purpose, but need not be maintained. The separation of civil society from the state is, like that of the contract of association from the contract of domination, analytically useful but misleading in practice. Civil society is not a private game of intelligent discourse apart from the institutions of government, let alone against them. It is rather the inclusive concept for social units in which citizenship is the guiding principle. All members possess certain equal entitlements that have the quality of social norms. They are enforced by sanctions and protected by institutions. This is effective only if there are structures of power to back them up. The search for a civil society, and ultimately a world civil society, is one for equal rights in a constitutional framework that domesticates power so that all can enjoy citizenship as a foundation of their life chances.

## T. H. Marshall's case

As we turn from the outer or lateral boundaries of citizenship to the inner or social ones, we encounter another issue of membership. It is Aristotle's issue, or rather the one that he left unresolved when he suspended slaves and women and children from his polity. One of the themes of the modern social conflict has been the extension of citizenship to more members of society. One way of describing this process is to tell the story of suffrage. First, property qualifications or tax classes were abolished for men and the right to vote extended to all adult males. The process took more than a century even in countries that started it early. Then the fight for women's suffrage began in countries that had limited voting to men. While the suffragettes may seem a quaint memory today, they represent a stage in a difficult battle that in most countries was not won before 1919, and in some, like Switzerland, considerably later. Eventually, adulthood was redefined, and the voting age lowered to 21 and further to 18 years.

This is only a part of a difficult story. Many civil rights issues in the developed world have been issues of inclusion. The right to vote meant little to segregated blacks in the American South, and perhaps to American blacks generally. Action was needed to bring them in, by literacy programmes and by forcing employers to give blacks a chance. The process has remained incomplete to the present day, and some see a reversal of trends. Women's rights too are not confined to suffrage. They touch on deeper cultural obstacles to equal participation and require both a change in attitudes and one in prevailing norms. The road from the assertion of equal rights to the acceptance of comparable worth is long. Then there is the vexing issue of the place of children in the scheme of citizenship. The simultaneous attempt to give them more rights and to grant them exemptions has not worked very well. Contemporary societies are loath to deal with the incompatible facts that most crimes of violence are committed by people who are not held fully responsible as citizens for reasons of age or incompetence.

If I turn to class at this stage, this is not to detract from the importance of these issues of citizenship, much less to claim that minority and women's rights are essentially questions of class. The reason is rather a sense that the crucial momentum of change in the last two centuries has been the extension of citizenship to new dimensions of social position. Advocates of minority rights or women's rights will object, and they may have a case, but I would argue that their fight makes sense only if citizenship has become a full and rich status. The class conflict for the extension of the entitlements of citizenship is the precondition for extending the range of those eligible for them.

The English sociologist T. H. Marshall has told this story in a series of lectures given in 1950 that provide one of the gems of social analysis. I have borrowed the title of his lectures for this chapter, *Citizenship and social class*.[10] The lectures were given in Cambridge in honour of T. H. Marshall's (unrelated) namesake, the economist Alfred Marshall, which fact led the lecturer to begin with a question raised by the author of *The future of the working classes* in 1873: "The question is not whether all men will ultimately be equal – that they will certainly not – but whether progress will not go on steadily, if slowly, till, by occupation at least, every man is a gentleman." The question sounds a little dated, not only to women who would have an equal claim to be ladies (or gentlewomen). Since we are here concerned with entitlements one must wonder also whether they actually progress "steadily, if slowly", or in bursts and stages. But T. H. Marshall merely uses the quotation for his own formulation of the problem that is close to ours in concept and language. He distinguishes between what he calls "quantitative or economic inequality" and "qualitative inequality". The former may not disappear, but the latter can, and if it does the former will lose its sting. The way to bring about this result is to include more people as members of society with more rights. This has in fact happened. "The basic human equality of membership . . . has been enriched with new substance and invested with a formidable array of rights . . . It has been clearly identified with the status of citizenship."

This then is Marshall's thesis. Modern social change has transformed patterns of inequality and the conflicts resulting from them. What used to be qualitative political differences between men have become quantitative economic ones. This has happened in two stages, by the revolution of modernity itself, and by the transformations of the modern world (to use our words rather than Marshall's).

Marshall begins by discussing feudal hierarchy with its legally defined privileges and exclusions. This is the world of status which when invaded by modern contract fell apart. In the old world, entitlements formed an apparently immutable pattern of inequality: "The impact of citizenship on such a system was bound to be profoundly disturbing, and even destructive." It meant the end of legally defined entitlement barriers, no less. But no more either. It did not mean the end of inequality. Marshall says somewhat apologetically, "it is true that class still functions" once the principle of citizenship has been established. There is no need to apologize. In some ways, class only begins to function on the basis of common citizenship for all. It is the driving force of the modern social conflict.

It may help to avoid confusion if I add at this point that the modern class conflict too has to do with entitlements. Many remnants of an earlier age are left over, including titled families and local landlords who enjoy privileges long after these have lost their legal sanction. New entitlement barriers emerge that may not have the binding force of the law but are nonetheless solid obstacles to full citizenship rights for all. They include real incomes as well as social discrimination, barriers to mobility as well as to participation. The modern social conflict is no longer about removing differences that (in Marshall's words) "have the essential binding character of the law". The principle of citizenship has destroyed such differences. (At least, it has done so "in principle".) The only legally binding status left is in fact that of citizenship. The modern social conflict is about attacking inequalities that restrict full civic participation by social, economic or political means, and establishing the entitlements that make up a rich and full status of citizenship.

T. H. Marshall distinguished three stages of this process, which he called civil rights, political rights and social rights, and being lucky enough to be English he could make the otherwise suspiciously tidy claim that it is possible "to assign the formative period in the life of each to a different century – civil rights to the eighteenth, political to the nineteenth and social to the twentieth". Perhaps there was more overlap between the three even in Britain, but the distinction remains useful.

Civil rights are the key to the modern world. They include the basic elements of the rule of law, equality before the law and due process. The end of hierarchy means the beginning of civil rights. No-one is above the law, all are subject to it. The law constrains power and those who hold it while giving those in a temporary or permanent minority position a haven of integrity. The discussion about whether the rule of law can be defined in purely formal terms or requires certain substantive elements will never end. Due process in the United States is a formal concept that has nevertheless served to protect human rights; many other countries have found it preferable to take up the ancient notion of natural rights and embody these in the preamble to their constitutions. "We hold these truths to be self-evident . . .". Certainly, a purely formal notion of the rule of law can be abused. Hitler started his regime with an Enabling Law to abolish the rule of law. Despite such twentieth-century ambiguities, the notion that all members of society are citizens, all citizens are subject to laws. and all are equal before the law was the first definition of citizenship.

It was also a necessary condition of Western versions of capitalism. Free wage labour presupposed the modern contract. Markets work only to the extent to which people have access to them as equal participants. This is not to say that everyone has to have access: for many decades capitalism meant increasing provisions for a minority. It is not to say that civil rights are a sufficient condition for growth either. Neither the Protestant ethic nor entrepreneurial initiative or technical inventiveness follows from civil rights. But if the eighteenth century bourgeoisie had any one subject that tackled both entitlements and provisions, it was civil rights. Civil rights were and are one of the strategic changes of the modern world. They are therefore the first necessity for all countries embarking late on the course of modern development.

The most obvious weakness of civil rights is that the laws in which they are embodied may themselves be biased. They are intended to be rules of the game, but some rules of the game benefit one side more than the other. The labour contract is an obvious example. What does "free and equal" mean if one party needs labour to survive whereas the other can pick and choose, hire and fire? Unless all citizens have an opportunity to feed their interests into the law, the rule of law leaves serious inequalities of entitlement. This is why political rights were a necessary supplement to civil rights. They include not only suffrage, but also freedom of association, freedom of speech, and the whole panoply of rights discussed by John Stuart Mill in his treatise *On liberty* (1989). The political public corresponds to the economic market; its structures are similarly complicated and similarly imperfect; but in the first instance it has to be open to all. Political rights are the entry tickets to the public.

Liberal reformers fought for both civil and political rights. Not all were prepared to "attach political rights directly and independently to citizenship as such"; some thought that civil rights were sufficient and politics was the task of the chosen few. But, on the whole, reformers recognized that the rule of law and universal suffrage were conditions of liberty. However, most did not want to go any further. The largest free country – and civil society - never fully accepted that the story of citizenship does not end here. In the United States, a notion of opportunity prevailed that interpreted equal starting chances restrictively and subsequent choices extensively. Civil rights, political rights and the open frontier summed up the American concept of liberty. To some extent they still do. The poor deserve help if they help themselves; otherwise their condition is their affair. In Europe, the twentieth century is marked by a different development. Whether the logic of citizenship and the class struggle or the tradition of an all-embracing state inspired the process, members of society were deemed to need more than civil and political rights. Social rights were added so that the status of citizenship came to include, as Marshall put it, "a universal right to a real income which is not proportionate to the market value of the claimant". It is an entitlement.

The underlying argument is clear enough. Civil rights are not only curtailed by the exorbitant power of some, but also by the economic weakness of many of those who have them. It makes a difference whether one can afford to defend one's interest, or one's honour, in a court of law or not. Political rights mean little if people lack the education to make use of them. They can also have a social and economic cost that prohibits their use. Unless everybody can live a life free of elementary fears, constitutional rights can be empty promises and worse, a cynical pretence of liberties that in fact stabilize privilege. The conclusions to be drawn from the argument are not so clear. Whereas civil and political rights can be established as such and embodied in laws or even constitutions, it is less easy to see how social rights can be entrenched. Some have tried, but neither a minimum wage nor the right to work nor other social "rights" have proved very durable.

In this connection it is telling that the case for social advances has often been made in terms of provisions. When Keynes pleaded for a more conscious management of demand, he did not argue for higher real wages as such, but for purchasing power as an engine of growth. The debate about educational expansion in Europe in the 1960s began not as one about education as a civil right, but as one about educational opportunity and economic growth. In widely publicized OECD papers, it was argued that there was a correlation between GDP growth and the proportion of graduates. It is worth mentioning also that the notion of social rights, or of transfer payments as an element of citizenship, blurred the line between equality of opportunity and equality of results. T. H. Marshall anticipated Fred Hirsch's questions when he wondered whether social citizenship rights had not gone beyond the original intention of "raising the floor-level in the basement of the social edifice" and "'begun to remodel the whole building" so that they "might even end by converting the skyscraper into a bungalow ".

Why not, one might ask? The quick answer is that inequality is a medium of liberty if it is inequality of provisions rather than entitlements. It fills the supermarket, which is highly desirable especially once everybody has access to it. But our initial concern here is with what the extension of citizenship rights has done to class. We assume for the moment that the process itself is a result of class conflict. The have-nots of the rudimentary civil society have organized to push their demands for political and eventually social rights; the haves have reluctantly given way. As a result, the progress of citizenship from the civil through the political to the social sphere is also a process of "class-abatement". Indeed, at the end of the day, what is there left for classes to struggle about? T. H. Marshall is cautious in his conclusions. Still, he leaves no doubt that citizenship has brought many changes affecting class. "They have undoubtedly been profound, and it may be that the inequalities permitted, and even moulded, by citizenship do no longer constitute class distinctions in the sense in which that term is used for past societies." They are economic inequalities that are subject to market conditions, not social inequalities that require political action. The classless society at last?

## A perfect world?

T. H. Marshall gave his lectures in 1950. Like many sociologists, he anticipated social trends as much as he observed them. During the 1950s, several authors would claim that modern societies had reached the end of the class war, and perhaps of class. The striking thesis hinges in part on definitions. But if one associates class with modern entitlements, it might indeed have seemed for a while that the battle was almost over. In the early centuries of the modern age, modernity itself was at stake. Legally entrenched differences in entitlements – privileges – had to be broken and the principle of citizenship established. Then the struggle for giving this principle civil, political and social substance began. From the point of view of the 1950s, it was quite successful.

The gist of this struggle was to eliminate inequalities of entitlement. This was done by bringing about two related changes. One of these had to do with raising the floor on which everyone stands. The other concerned the ceiling for those in an exceptional position of wealth or prestige. The point in both cases was to decouple civic status from economic position. Put differently, constitutional rules had to be introduced to prevent the translation of wealth into the power to deny the citizenship rights of others. Other measures were designed to empower all citizens to participate in the economic, social and political process. The combination may be described as the domestication of power. Numerous particular developments of the last two centuries find their place in this story. Apart from those already mentioned they include tax and antitrust laws, the separation of Church and state, parliamentary committees of enquiry and administrative law as well as the traditional foundations of democratic constitutions.

The basic idea throughout is that inequalities of provisions are acceptable if and when they cannot be translated into inequalities of entitlements. There is a degree of functioning wealth that gives those who have it illegitimate power, and there is a degree of poverty that deprives those who suffer it of civic participation, but between the two, distinctions of rank and of income do not give rise to the same kind of conflict. Little has been said about provisions in this chapter. Yet more than one question could and should be asked. For example, why did T. H. Marshall not relate the progress of citizenship to the advances of economic performance? Would one have been possible without the other? Is not the key factor the rising level of general prosperity? Does not class detract from the individual opportunities for increasing life chances? Is not the American example the model for the rest? (In the words of Werner Sombart's book of 1906: *Why is there no socialism in the United States?*) And if one looks at things the other way round, are not citizenship rights an optical illusion in view of continuing inequalities? Should one not focus on the fact that inequalities of income distribution, of educational opportunity, of the incidence of social mobility appear to have changed little in the last decades?

This is quite a mouthful of partly contradictory questions. Yet they can probably be reduced to two. One is analytical. How do increases in provisions affect entitlements, and vice versa? The other is normative. Why should the unequal distribution of provisions be acceptable as long as it cannot be translated into unequal entitlements? The normative question goes to the heart of liberal theory. So far, I have merely asserted that qualitative inequalities are incompatible with free societies, whereas quantitative inequalities may even be a stimulus to growing life chances. The analytical question goes to the heart of the issue.

Adam Smith believed that there would be a "natural progress of opulence".[11] He thought that the market entailed the force for its own extension, so that in the end inequalities are swept away "and a general plenty diffuses itself through all the different ranks of the society". One notes the paradox: there is a "general plenty" but there are also "different ranks of society". *Prima facie,* this could be the opposite of the picture drawn here with the help of T. H. Marshall; it could mean equal provisions in a structure of unequal entitlements. On reflection, however, this makes little sense. After all, what are entitlements for, if not for provisions? Perhaps what we really see here is an early version of a curious weakness of much economic analysis. Almost by definition, it concentrates on the provisions side of change. Economics is the science of provisions. Great claims are made for increases in provisions, in incomes, standard of living and welfare. Who would deny that the long economic miracle since the Industrial Revolution has changed the social scene? But underlying social structures are almost anxiously held constant, as if the whole approach of economics would collapse if they changed.

Moreover, this is true independent of the political persuasion of economists. Friedrich von Hayek praises the pathbreakers, but assumes that others will lag behind. For him this is bearable because "even the poorest today owe their relative wellbeing to the results of past inequality". At the other end of the spectrum, Robert Heilbroner is concerned about those who are capable of "denying to others access to the goods which constitute wealth", but regards the fact as a kind of law of nature, because wealth for him "is a social category inseparable from power". The decoupling effect of citizenship does not occur. In between Hayek and Heilbroner, Fred Hirsch bemoaned the failure of an extension of "material goods" when it comes to the lasting scarcities of "positional goods". Again, the assumption is that inequalities of entitlement are inevitable.[12]

In fact, they are not. One must not confuse the shortcomings of economic analysis with those of reality. Capitalism – the growth of provisions – does not solve all problems, nor does it create them. Adam Smith was wrong in expecting too much from the "natural progress of opulence", and Karl Marx was wrong in expecting the contradictions of capitalism to lead to the dramatic dissolution of the Gordian knot of provisions and entitlements. As a rule, the two revolutions of modernity do not merge into one event, nor is there one theory to explain them both. The theory of class conflict and that of the incompatibility of new forces and old relations of production are after all two theories. Markets fail to achieve entitlement changes, and governments fail to achieve increases in provisions, but it would be wrong to hold them responsible for what they cannot do. True, the separation is not total. Civil rights provide access to markets and thereby help their extension: rising incomes are a necessary condition of an entitlement to a decent standard of living. Time and again, we shall seek the points at which the twain meet, because they are the levers of strategic change. But "the twain" they remain. Different processes advance provisions and entitlements. For example, active minorities – pathbreakers, entrepreneurs, innovators – play a much more important role in the progress of opulence than that of classes. The story of citizenship does not invalidate economic analysis (unless it makes exorbitant claims for encompassing everything); it must be added to it. The same is true the other way round. The creation of a common floor of entitlements and the domestication of power do not make the separate study of economic growth superfluous; they merely supplement it. Political economy is perhaps too facile a concept for what we need; politics and economics are as close and as far apart as entitlements and provisions. Social analysis, however, falls short if it simply holds either constant; it is in some ways always about their interrelations.

Whatever citizenship does to social class, it does not eliminate either inequality or conflict. It changes their quality. Several authors have compared the result to a marching column. People have their place at very different points in the column; but since the whole column is moving, the last will eventually reach the point at which the first were before them. Some state this with delight, others with irony, again others with frustrated anger.[13] When the last reach the point that the first passed some time ago, will it still be the same? The marching column is too orderly a simile. In fact, it is an economist's metaphor since it holds the relative position of everyone constant. It would be more apposite to think of one of those shambolic urban marathons that paralyse large cities once a year. The chaos is not total: some start in front and try to win the race, some have just joined to have fun, many want to prove that they can do it. There are surprises and disappointments. The important point is to be a part of the race.

Is not such a state of affairs the best of all possible worlds? The question was bound to arise in the reader's mind as I went along taking more and more citizens into the modern marathon. It is fundamental to this argument. While the answer that will be given must disappoint those who expect a straight yea, yea or nay, nay, it is nevertheless clear. Moreover, the line of argument that responds to the expectations or suspicions of perfection can now be sketched. It will be extended, embellished, illuminated, but its direction is clear.

In one sense, the world of citizens is a perfect world. It is hard and costly to achieve. The process involves many pains and aches, of which some are literally unbearable. Even the scourge of totalitarianism has something to do with the halting progress of modernity. There is also the price in ligatures that Marx and Tocqueville described so vividly. But the establishment of civil, political and social citizenship rights for all marks true progress. If it is coupled with significant growth in the quantity and diversity of provisions it creates a highly desirable state of civilization, and of liberty. Even the best of all possible worlds is however not perfect.

In the first instance, the process is far from complete. Three major issues remain on the agenda of citizenship and entitlement struggles. The first arises from the fact that much remains to be done to assure all members of even the OECD societies of their citizenship rights. The old class struggle is by no means fully played out. Boundaries of membership give rise to violent struggles. The rights of women and of minorities remain under-recognized. Such conflicts may involve playing out old themes rather than adding new ones, but they concern millions of human beings and need to be fought and won.

The second issue may on the contrary be a sign of things to come. The modern society of citizens has created new social problems. While it may have seemed to some as if everyone was on board, or a part of the race, it suddenly emerged that not only had some been left behind, but new groups were pushed to the margin and beyond. Persistent poverty and long-term unemployment are new issues of citizenship, and the old instruments of the social state do not seem able to cope. It is not easy (yet?) to tell what form the conflicts arising from a new exclusion will take. They are not likely to be traditional class conflicts because those at the margin are scattered, disorganized and weak. But they represent a living doubt in the contract of society that cannot fail to affect the rest. Perhaps law and order is the subject that tells the story.

In the meantime, those who are included are discovering new kinds of entitlement issues. They enjoy full citizenship rights but are also affected by threats to their natural environment, by the deterioration of their habitat, perhaps by the absence of certain services as a result of the cartel of special interests. Such deprivations do not constitute classes, because they affect everyone. The few who can escape them by moving to the South Seas are hardly relevant, and may even be in for surprises there. But everyone is affected only with a part of his or her social existence. A disparity of social position has been replaced by "disparities of realms of life".[14] The resulting conflicts mobilize everyone to some extent, though there are always activists for a cause. The resulting social movements or, more modestly, civic initiatives add an element to modern conflicts for which class-based institutions are ill prepared.

The third issue is the biggest of all. Perhaps socialism in one country is possible, even if it is not viable; but a civil society in one country is strictly not possible. Let there be no misunderstanding. Of course, one can and must start at home building a civilized society of citizens. But as long as this is confined to the boundaries of nations it is also coupled with attitudes. policies and rules of exclusion that violate the very principles of civil society. The historic task of creating civil society will be complete only once there are citizenship rights for all human beings. We need a world civil society.

This is the second or third time that I have mentioned the notion that some will regard as hopelessly Utopian. Whatever it is, Utopia it is not. As Pericles' Athens turned citizenship from a dream to a reality on which to build modern societies, so the civil societies of Europe and North America and some other places on the globe prefigure what is evidently possible everywhere. The process will take time and strategic action, but it is worth embarking on. We have to embark on it if we do not want to see the achievements of citizenship jeopardized. It is unfortunate that even our instruments of analysis are geared to the national boundaries of progress. When one says "society", this is usually a euphemism for the territorial boundaries of nations. Social analysis is to all intents and purposes national analysis. (It is only honest for Germans to call economics *Nationalökonomie*.) As we try to tackle wider interrelations, we flounder. The study of international relations (note the expression!) has yet to become a serious subject, and there are only rudiments of genuine international law. Some instructive studies of war have been written, though fewer of peace, and numerous stilted vacuities about strategy in the nuclear, or any other age. The application of economic approaches to the global scene has suffered from an overdose of ideologies of the Establishment, of the International Monetary Fund, or the equally established Left, of dependency and decoupling theories. These are overstatements of course, but I believe they overstate a valid case. It would be wonderful and important to know more about the conditions and processes of extending civil society. This would include an understanding of conflicts that involve geographically dispersed groups, of entitlement struggles and the growth of provisions worldwide. Knowledge does not necessarily lead to action, but it might help. In any case, there is a vast field for theory as well as practice in an issue that figured prominently even in Immanuel Kant's project for a "general history with cosmopolitan intent" 200 years ago; it is to create a general civil society under the rule of law.

It is clear then that citizenship has changed the quality of the modern social conflict. Remnants of class in the old sense continue to be with us and may even provide the underlying pattern of social and political antagonisms for some time to come. But increasingly they are overlaid with other, less familiar contests. It is certainly possible to use the term "class" for them also. After all, inequality and power continue to be forceful factors making for divergent interests and strife. Often, a farewell to class is coupled with an overly idyllic picture of things to come. But if one retains the concept of class after citizenship, one has to qualify it and spell out the difference. For purposes of analysis, it is sufficient to note that the days of entitlement conflicts are not over. Though most differences of income and status may have become gradual, and some of the old barriers are still there, new ones have been erected. In the world at large, such barriers of privilege remain the key issue. Citizens have not arrived, they have merely gained a new vantage point in the struggle for more life chances.

## Notes

1. Some of the important recent protagonists of this debate are of course John Rawls (1971), Robert Nozick (1974), James Buchanan (1975). For the history of the concept of social contract I happily rely on J. W. Gough (1957).
2. One recurrent theme of this book is the debate with Jürgen Habermas, notably (though by no means only) with his *Theorie des kommunikativen Handelns* (1985). The debate is complicated in that I share certain basic values with

Habermas, including an appreciation of the rule of law and the need for a "constitutional patriotism". When it comes to German questions, we are clearly on one side. I do not share either the Hegelian roots or the Rousseauean hopes with Habermas, however. He too thinks in terms of systems and total change; and he dreams of the expansion of niches of "unconstrained communication" to the whole of society. The reference here is therefore to Habermas, but the debate remains open.

3. Raymond Aron wrote a remarkable paper on the subject, "Is multinational citizenship possible?" (1974). He asks: "How could a citizen possibly belong to several political entities at once?" His answer is that he cannot. Human rights are real only within the confines of nation-states. "The Jews of my generation cannot forget how fragile these human rights become when they no longer correspond with citizenship rights." The European Community does not alter this fact, for "there are no such animals as 'European citizens'"; it may even "weaken people's sense of their citizenship". This may sound surprising from one of the few Frenchmen of his generation who remained unimpressed by de Gaulle. It has a hard analytical core, however, in that citizenship and the law are inseparable, and the only law we know is national.

4. I have used the translation of Thucydides' *History of the Peloponnesian War* by Richard Crawley, revised by R. Feetham and published by the Encyclopaedia Britannica in its series of Great Books in 1952.

5. MacIver (1926), 97.

6. The distinction is mine. Harry Eckstein (1984) uses "civic inclusion" for "the processes by which segments of society previously excluded from membership [in Charles Tilly's sense] in political and socio-economic institutions are incorporated into these institutions as 'citizens'". See also Tilly (1978).

7. In a letter to me, Giovanna Zincone has pointed out that modern citizenship is not transportable. Unlike medieval citizenship people do not carry it with them, but it is linked to the territory to which they belong (with limited international guarantees).

8. Mead (1986).

9. To my knowledge, the best account of the history of the concept is Manfred Riedel's dictionary article "Gesellschaft, burgerliche", in *Geschichtliche Grundbegriffe*, Otto Brunner, Werner Conze, Reinhart Koselleck (eds) (Stuttgart: Klett, 1975). The extensive piece has, however, a distinctly German bias and is less satisfactory on the English term "civil society".

10. Published under this title in 1950, and later included in the volume *Class, citizenship and social development* (1964). The three lectures are short, so that I have not identified all page references.

11. The title of Chapter I in Book Three of the *Inquiry into the nature and causes of the wealth of nations*, from which the quotation is also taken.

12. von Hayek (1960), 46; Heilbroner (1985), 45; Hirsch (1977), passim.

13. Friedrich von Hayek is delighted, Fred Hirsch angry, and the irony is that by Michael Young & Peter Wilmott(1973), 167.

14. The notion of "disparities of realms of life" was first held against class theory by authors of the Frankfurt School. See Jochen Bergmann, Gerhard Brandt, Klaus Korber, Ernst Theodor Mohl, Claus Offe, "Herrschaft, Klassenverhaltnis, Schichtung", in *Spatkapitalismus oder Industriegesellschaft*, Proceedings of the 16th German Sociological Congress (Stuttgart: Enke, 1969). John Kenneth Galbraith's distinction between "private wealth" and "public squalor" (in *The affluent society*) is not dissimilar.

# CHAPTER 3

# Why social inequalities are generated by social rights

## W. G. Runciman

I did not know Tom Marshall well. But I knew him well enough to recognize in his person as well as in his writings those qualities of mind that, in the words that David Lockwood used in his 80th birthday tribute in 1974, provided "exemplary inspiration" to successive generations of pupils and colleagues (Lockwood 1974: 363). Like many others, I regretted both that his published output was not more abundant than it was and that Cambridge did not create a chair of sociology in time for him to be, as he would unquestionably have been, the first person offered it. And from the first of many readings, I shared the universal admiration for *Citizenship and social class*.

I am not sure just how many times I have in fact read *Citizenship and social class*. But when I last re-read it, I found that it was not only the classic exposition of the evolution from legal through political to social rights that I remembered but also a warning about the difficulty of reconciling equality of condition with equality of opportunity. That, perhaps, says as much about me as about Marshall. But it also says something about what has happened in the world in the decades since *Citizenship and social class* was written. At that time, the changes in social policy that followed the Second World War were fresh in everybody's minds. For the first time in British history, a nominally socialist government had held office with an impregnable majority in the House of Commons. A "welfare state" had been created that offered protection from the cradle to the grave. And there was a widespread sense that the social inequalities of the interwar period had been, if not abolished, at least significantly and lastingly reduced. Half a century later, things look very different – as no doubt they always do after such a length of time. The 1945–51 government no longer occupies the place it then seemed likely to do in the history of British society. For David Marquand, for example, writing in the aftermath of the general election of 1992, 1945 was no more than a "golden moment" when "the Labour ethos and the national mood ran so close that a Labour government seemed to embody a progressive conscience extending well beyond the frontiers of its own constituency" (Marquand 1992: x). We can now see, in a longer perspective, that Lloyd George's administration of 1918 to 1922 was more important for the evolution of Britain's social institutions than Attlee's of 1945 to 1951 (Runciman 1993); and my first theme, accordingly, is the revision that needs, with hindsight, to be made to Marshall's perception of the historical context within which *Citizenship and social class* was written.

But if history has not stood still, nor has sociology. My second theme, therefore, is the commentary that a present-day sociologist might be disposed to offer in a notional introduction to a new edition of *Citizenship and social class*. For this purpose, the text is ready to hand in Lockwood's tribute of 1974, which points firmly to the issue that struck me on my own re-reading. To quote Lockwood directly, "citizenship does possess an inner logic, and the conflicting group interests that shape its institutional form at any one particular stage are themselves in turn changed and have their social force redirected as a consequence of both the practical working out of these arrangements and the principles dormant in them; principles that are as yet unrealized in social relationships and which have the potential for exacerbating as well as diminishing the impact of class" (Lockwood 1974: 365).

To some extent, the two themes are interwoven, since the contrast between the aftermath of the First World War and the aftermath of the Second is often drawn in terms of the visible manifestations of class conflict in 1919–20 and the seeming lack of them in 1946–7. But this is one of several contrasts that is more apparent than real. Britain's working classes were no more authentically revolutionary after the First World War than its middle and upper classes were authentically acquiescent after the Second World War. The most obvious circumstantial difference between the two aftermaths was the maintenance of full employment after 1945 in contrast to the onset of persistent, large-scale unemployment in the "staple" industries that followed the collapse of the short-lived post-war boom in the summer of 1920. But there is no necessary correlation between the level of unemployment and the incidence of class conflict.

It is true that there was a vocal minority of far-Left working-class trade unionists after the First World War, just as there was a vocal minority of far-Left middle-class intellectuals after the Second World War. But both remained a minority. There was far more consensus after 1918 on parliamentary democracy and a free labour market, and far less consensus after 1945 on government control of the economy and the compulsory redistribution of income and wealth, than some commentators have supposed. It can still be claimed for Attlee's administration that its pledges of social reform were translated, unlike those of Lloyd George, into effective legislation. But this contrast too can be overdrawn. The policies initiated by Lloyd George's government in the fields of health, housing, education and unemployment relief were progressively, if sometimes haltingly, expanded by its successors. Those initiated by Attlee's government were progressively eroded by its successors – or, where not eroded deliberately, tacitly permitted to diminish in their effect.

The most important single innovation in the field of social policy in the aftermath of the First World War was the first provision of so-called "uncovenanted" unemployment benefit in March of 1921 – a measure that was intended as a short-term palliative for an unforeseen difficulty but which, in the event, enshrined both the principle and practice of what was subsequently nicknamed the "dole" (Mowat 1955: 127–8). But it was only one of a series of changes that, for all the rhetoric about a return to "normalcy", made the pre-1914 world of minimal income tax, Poor Law and Friendly Society safety-nets, private rented accommodation, charity- or market-driven health care, rudimentary working-class education, private legislation for local social initiatives, non-interference by both the Treasury and the Bank of England in economic policy, poverty wages for unskilled labour, fragmented trade unions, and Gladstonian principles of public finance increasingly remote.

By the outbreak of the Second World War, social service provision in Britain could be claimed to be the most advanced in the world (Addison 1975: 33) and "middle opinion", as it was called (Marwick 1964), was fully reconciled to the principles that underlay it. It still remained for a national health service and a comprehensive national insurance scheme to be implemented in one form or another. But the wish to see this done was not a simple function of wartime fellow-feeling. Richard Titmuss, whose official history of wartime social policy is very much a product of the same period and milieu as *Citizenship and social class,* may have been right about the psychological responses of the British population to Dunkirk and the Blitz (Titmuss 1950: 508). But he was wrong to suppose either that any lasting innovations of a collectivist kind can be attributed to them or that they did more than temporarily obscure the deep-seated differences of view both among and between the members of different classes about the kind of society they wanted to emerge from eventual victory (Harris 1986: 238).

A possible rejoinder at this point might be that a revision of Marshall's periodization does not undermine his central argument about the evolution from legal through political to social rights. Nor does it. There has indeed been such an evolution. What is more, Marshall rightly saw the importance to the explanation of it of both the trade union movement and universal adult suffrage. But seen from 1994, the outcome looks more like an expression of the ideals of 1918–22 than of 1945–51. To Marshall, "citizenship" implied a universal entitlement to free health care, free secondary education, legal aid (with, perhaps, a means test but no income limit), subsidized public housing, and, in the sphere of work, protection against untrammelled market forces by means of strong trade unions and a government policy of full employment. But in the 1920s, it had implied only the vote, scholarships for able working-class children, "dock briefs" in court, local authorities as residential landlords competing with the building societies, free hospital care in emergencies but fee-charging general practitioners, limited unemployment relief, and qualified old age pensions and national insurance. As implemented in the 1990s, therefore, social rights would appear to enshrine priorities and preoccupations more of Lloyd George's time than of Attlee's – to say nothing of the issues of ethnicity and gender that were hardly on the agenda when *Citizenship and social class* was being written, even though they had both been very much on the agenda in the form of the Irish Question and the Suffragettes when Lloyd George was Chancellor of the Exchequer in 1914.

I make no attempt here either to explain how this has come about or to evaluate how far it is a good thing or a bad thing that it has.

Instead, the question that I wish to pose is: what conditions would have had to obtain for it not to? One such condition would have been the prolongation into peacetime of the domestic policies of the wartime coalition: conscription, rationing, physical controls, incomes policy, and allocation of labour and materials in accordance with priorities dictated by government. But this would never have been accepted in peacetime, least of all by the trade unions (Brooke 1991), and was never intended by Attlee's government any more than it had been by Lloyd George's. The "bonfire of controls", sometimes mistakenly attributed to the incoming Conservative government of 1951, was in fact lit by Harold Wilson at the Board of Trade; rationing was retained, or reintroduced, not by choice but by necessity; and by 1951 trade union leaders were no longer either willing or able to deliver wage restraint. It is sometimes argued that if Labour had won the election of 1951, it might have been able, with the help of rising real incomes and favourable terms of trade, to stay in power for a generation; and that might have meant that British society would have evolved in the direction of a more egalitarian form of social democracy on the Swedish model. But the subsequent evolution of Swedish society is not, from that point of view, encouraging. Sweden's "historical compromise" of the 1930s had transformed a fragmented and confrontational system of industrial relations into a centralized and bureaucratic one in which the unions accepted constraints on free collective bargaining in return for influence on governmental decision-making and the employers accepted trade union influence in the management of their enterprises in return for freedom in the international market place. But even at its most apparently consensual that system was being attacked from the Right as stifling personal freedom and from the Left as perpetuating capitalist control of the means of production; and both Left and Right came to see that maintenance of the level of universal welfare benefits depended on increasing subsidization by the productive of the unproductive – including those workers whose unemployment was concealed in the official statistics by costly government- funded retraining schemes and large-scale absenteeism underwritten by notional sick pay. It is always hazardous to draw inferences from what has actually happened in one society to what might have happened but didn't in another. But if, by 1990, this form of social democracy was no longer sustainable even in Sweden, where for many reasons the institutional environment was more favourable to it, it is surely implausible to suppose that it would have been sustainable in Britain.

The context in which Marshall wrote, therefore, looks with hindsight less and less like the symptomatic expression of a progressive trend, and more and more like the product of short-term political pressures and a short-lived ideological mood. It is a sociological commonplace that the most egalitarian forms of social organization are likely to be found where the total resources available for distribution are least. Although Britain in the 1940s is hardly to be equated with the foraging bands of the Kalahari Desert, the years of and immediately after the Second World War were a time of relative austerity. It is, accordingly, at least arguable that the egalitarian sense of national unity that Titmuss saw fostered by the events of the war extended into the early years of peace. But as economic recovery got under way from 1952 onwards, so did the different aspirations of different classes increasingly diverge and conflict. The "welfare state" remained as popular among the middle as among the working classes, if only because they benefited from it as much if not more than the working classes did. But by the time that the Conservative Party was back in power, the world of queues, rationing, shortages, "spivs", the five-shilling restaurant meal and the foreign travel allowance was on its way to becoming a world of free competition for increasingly abundant resources in an expanding consumer-driven market.

In that world, the aspirations of manual workers and their families re-emerged looking much as they had after the First World War, when near-universal suffrage, an autonomous Labour Party, and trade unions strengthened by the government's dependence on their members for the war effort all combined to integrate the organized working class into the institutions of British society to an extent hardly dreamed of by progressive opinion before 1914. There had been nothing very egalitarian about those aspirations. But why should there be? Manual workers wanted to be better paid, to work shorter hours, to be more comfortably housed, and to be more fully protected against the poverty consequent on sickness, unemployment and old age. But they were as tenacious in defence of differentials in earnings, and as vehement in their disapproval of "scroungers", as non-manual workers were. They were hostile to bureaucracy, jealous of the right to strike, and resentful of being preached at from either the Right or the Left. And in their political opinions, a larger minority of them were

Conservatives than were socialists in any but a nominal sense.

None of this implies a repudiation of Marshall's conception of citizenship. How, indeed, could anyone dispute that legal and political rights do not add up between them to social rights, and that formal or "negative" freedom is of little value without the resources adequate to realize positive choices about how to make use of it? But as soon as those choices can be made, and are, there reappears the conflict between equality of opportunity and equality of condition. The dilemmas posed by this conflict for egalitarian reformers are thoroughly familiar. But my point is again to contrast how they look today with how they looked in 1950. Not long after *Citizenship and social class* was published, Tawney published an epilogue to his well known Halley Stewart Lectures of 1929 on *Equality*, of which the last pre-war edition had been published in 1938. In it, Tawney quotes approvingly from both Marshall and Titmuss on the changes brought about during the war and its aftermath. He still sees what he regards as indefensible disparities persisting in the educational system and the inheritance of wealth. But he is confident that if the electorate wants them tackled, Parliament and the civil service will do the job. He does not see social rights in Marshall's sense as inimical to liberty because, on the contrary, they enlarge the liberty of wage-earners unable to find employment, of consumers unable to protect themselves against extortionate prices, and of parents unable to afford to send their children to fee-paying schools. And he concludes with a characteristically eloquent burst of rhetoric that I quote in full:

> A society is free in so far, and only in so far, as, within the limits set by nature, knowledge, and resources, its institutions and policies are such as to enable all its members to grow to their full stature, to do their duty as they see it, and – since liberty should not be too austere – to have their fling when they feel like it. In so far as the opportunity to lead a life worthy of human beings is needlessly confined to a minority, not a few of the conditions applauded as freedom would more properly be denounced as privilege. Action which causes such opportunities to be more widely shared is, therefore, twice blessed. It not only subtracts from inequality, but adds to freedom. (Tawney 1952: 268)

To which the (or at least my) reply in 1994 has to be: well – yes, but what exactly are the consequences, in Lockwood's words, of "both the practical working out of these arrangements and the principles dormant in them"? All citizens – every wage-earner, every consumer, every schoolchild – have the right to be enabled to grow to their full stature and to have their fling when they feel like it. But what actually happens when they are all in a position to exercise that right?

One reason, I suspect, why Tawney hadn't fully thought through the answer to that question is that in 1950 the aspirations of the organized working class as formulated by its upper-middle-class sympathizers still seemed unproblematically straightforward. For all the complaints by, or on behalf of, the middle classes voiced under the Attlee government about narrowing differentials and high taxation, the continuing difference between the circumstances of the middle and of the working classes was there for all to see. Indeed, it still is. Now as then, middle-class people have careers, with all that the term implies. Working-class people have jobs, the going rate for which is a function not of individual effort but of collective organization on the one hand and supply and demand on the other. No doubt clerical, technical and sales employees are at risk of unemployment too, as the 1930s had shown (and the 1980s were to do again). No doubt, too, even the high-salaried managers, the comfortable *rentiers* and the well credentialled professionals are respectively at risk of their companies failing, their investments declining in value and their practices losing custom to their competitors. But by comparison with manual workers, including the most skilled, their more favourable opportunities in good times and more reliable protections in bad ones are an almost self-evident demonstration of the case for common citizenship to be translated into common social rights that, in the words of a later namesake and fellow sociologist, Gordon Marshall, and his co-authors, "determine the welfare of individuals independently of their market capacities, and in an egalitarian manner" (Marshall et al. 1987: 60).

What that leaves out, however, is among other things the extent of differentiation within the working class. Marshall, who unlike many of his academic contemporaries was never drawn into the ideological embrace of Marxism, did not need to be told that the British proletariat was not being driven inexorably downwards into a state of common immiseration. But he cannot be expected to have foreseen the gap that was to widen between working-class households with several earners and working-class households with none (Pahl 1984), or the return of unemployment on a scale fully comparable to the 1930s with the consequent exacerbation of the division between the "idle buggers and dole wallahs" – the words are those of striking miners in the Yorkshire pit village of South Elmsall in 1985 (Jenkins 1987: 231) – and those in work, or the spread of home ownership to the point that a significant number of working-class families would become possessors of appreciating capital assets, or the rise in gross full-time adult earnings to a level where the standard rate of income tax would be a serious consideration in the calculation of many manual workers' take-home pay.

Nor can he be expected to have foreseen what would happen in the sphere of education. The right to education is for Marshall an unequivocal right of citizenship, and free secondary education for all had been the avowed aim of progressive opinion since 1918. But what sort of education? And with what purpose in mind? Here again, there is a familiar dilemma. For working-class children to be given an education that is both shorter in duration and poorer in content than that given to middle-class children is in clear contradiction to the concept of citizenship as Marshall understands it. But what if it turns out that working-class children neither want nor can put to use a curriculum devised by and for the exponents of middle-class interests and tastes? Do middle-class reformers have any more business to thrust the values of science and scholarship down working-class throats than had their Victorian predecessors to thrust down their throats the values of thrift and "useful" hobbies? Don't children who are destined for working-class jobs both need and deserve a different kind of education from those who are destined for middle-class careers? If the consequence is a two-tier, or even three-tier, system either within comprehensive schools or between grammar, secondary modern, and perhaps also technical schools, does that infringe the social rights of those who are not and do not want to be taught the grammar-school curriculum? It may be that whatever the resources devoted to the secondary modern and technical schools, they will never enjoy "parity of esteem" with the grammar schools (or not, at any rate, in the eyes of those who go to the grammar schools and from these into middle-class careers). But does that matter? Need it mean any more than that, in Marshall's own words, "status differences can receive the stamp of legitimacy in terms of democratic citizenship provided they do not cut too deep" (1950: 75)?

Here, however, we come up against the further dilemma posed by the facts of social mobility. It was Marshall himself who first presented to the Social Research Division of the London School of Economics a memorandum calling for a long-term programme of research into social selection and differentiation in Britain (Glass 1954: v); and by the time that *Citizenship and social class* was published, Glass and his associates had carried out the interviews that formed the basis for the volume on *Social mobility in Britain* which they were to publish in 1954. Both the methods and the results of that study remain to some extent controversial. But it, like the subsequent study of men aged between 20 and 64 in 1972 by Goldthorpe and his collaborators (Goldthorpe 1980), confirmed two conclusions already familiar in outline to contemporary observers: first, that middle-class children are much likelier than working-class children to end up in middle-class roles; and second, that despite this, an increasing number of middle-class roles are occupied by working-class children.

The explanation of the first has not yet been precisely established: we simply do not know to what extent it may be due to a correlation with inherited ability combined with individual effort as opposed to institutional restrictions on the opportunities available to the children of working-class parents. But the explanation of the second is straightforwardly arithmetical. Even though relatively few middle-class children leave openings to be filled by working-class children by themselves moving into working-class roles, the expansion in the number of middle-class roles that are there to be filled is such that many of them are bound to be filled by children of working-class parents. Whatever the process of selection by which some but not other working-class children then become middle-class adults, the secondary schools must therefore – must they not? – provide working-class children with an equal opportunity to acquire the education that is designed to lead to a middle-class career. But this then implies after all that all children should be similarly educated irrespective of social origin. And will this not in practice exacerbate once again the conflict between equality of opportunity and equality of condition?

These, as I have said, are familiar dilemmas. But were Marshall's warnings then prophetic? Were Tawney's hopes naïve? Although equality of opportunity and equality of condition are very different objectives they are in conflict for reasons of sociology, not logic. Suppose the citizens of Britain all supported steeply progressive taxes on income and wealth, accorded parity of esteem to different educations, occupations, subcultures and lifestyles, and conformed to shared legal and customary norms of behaviour towards one another. In that event, could they not all enter the adult role of their choice without there being generated in the process any more significant or lasting inequalities in economic, ideological or political power than Marshall was willing to accept? That this isn't what happens is not because it is inconceivable, but because of the way in which, to go back to Lockwood's phrase, the principles inherent in the concept of citizenship are realized in practice. It depends, in other words, on what equal opportunity is equal opportunity *for*. A possible response at this point is simply to complain that almost everybody is too selfish, except in wartime, to subordinate their determination to get as much as they can of whatever they want to the joint pursuit of the common good. But to say this is not to say very much, even if the moralistic overtones of "selfish" and "common good" are suitably discounted. What sociologists, as opposed to moralists, want to know is whose opportunities get in the way of whose, and to what extent the resulting inequalities are inescapable.

There are, to begin with, certain constraints that are indeed inescapable. Not everybody can have an income above the median, or own a Georgian manor house, or send their children to the best school in the county, or claim entitlement to unlimited medical care. To suggest that any of these things should be rights to which all citizens are entitled would be absurd. But everybody can want, and try to obtain, more money, a more attractive home, a better education for their children, and more nearly complete protection against sickness and injury. Indeed, to prevent the citizens of Britain from trying to obtain these things would be to deny them what is as much a right of citizenship in what calls itself a free society as is the right to the accepted minimum of income, housing, education and health care in what calls itself a civilized one. But as more and more people make more and more determined attempts to "grow to their full stature", and "have their fling when they feel like it", there will inevitably result widening inequalities between those who are more and less successful in doing so. What is more, those who succeed are likely to feel that if they have done so fairly as a result of their own effort, they have no less right to the rewards of their success than to the initial opportunity to pursue it. And if the state denies them those rewards in order to redistribute goods and services in favour of the unsuccessful, this will be a very different matter from the progressive taxation of the luxuries of the rich to provide necessaries for the poor. As equality of opportunity becomes more and more of a reality for the previously underprivileged, the principles inherent in the concept of citizenship will increasingly find expression in conflict over resources and priorities between citizens who are fellow members of the same class.

This conflict is, in practice, mediated by the various agencies responsible for allocating the goods and services redistributed through taxation of one kind or another by the institutions of the welfare state. But the exercise by those agencies of the discretion placed in their hands is itself unavoidably invidious. I do not suppose that Marshall foresaw any more than Tawney or Titmuss did the degree of frustration that would be aroused among successive generations of claimants by their treatment at the hands of public service officials who were themselves strongly unionized and often in the employ of Labour-controlled councils elected in the very boroughs where claimants were likely to be concentrated (Donnison 1982: 127). Social-administrative stigmatization (Page 1984: Ch. 2) is in part a reflection of the long-standing and deep-seated distinction in the minds of officials, the public and claimants (or non-claimants) themselves between the deserving and the undeserving poor. But it is a reflection also of the roles of public officials as gate-keepers, arbitrators and monitors in a system open to conflicting interpretation of rules as well as to direct abuse. Of all the issues of welfare policy where these problems have been experienced since Marshall wrote, perhaps the most contentious has been the allocation of local authority housing of variable quality to tenants competing in accordance with criteria defined by others than themselves – an allocation made yet more contentious by its connection with the increasingly salient issue of ethnic discrimination (Henderson & Karn 1987).

Meanwhile, it has become increasingly evident also that the establishment of a universal minimum for income, housing, education and health care does not automatically prevent inequality not only above but below it – that, so to speak, the new safety-net cannot be sufficiently tightly meshed to prevent some people from falling through it. I do not mean to imply that Marshall was unaware of the problems of social policy posed by homelessness, vagrancy, single parenthood, truancy, illiteracy, petty crime, alcoholism (and drug dependence), and incapacitating mental and physical illness. But these were some of the very problems that the "welfare state" was supposed to address. How many of Marshall's original audience imagined that a generation later unemployment would rise to levels equal to the worst of the interwar depression, or that a so-called "underclass" would come to be discussed in the same tones as the so-called "residuum" had been in the period before the First World War? It is true that now, as then, there is no justification for equating the two. Although workers who experience unemployment once are more likely to do so again, their attitudes to work are, except for a minority consisting predominantly of older men and younger mothers, not significantly different from those of the employed (Gallie & Marsh 1994), and the long-term unemployed of the 1980s, as of the 1930s, are "not so much stable members of an underclass as unstable members of the working class" (Buck 1992: 19). But there unmistakably is an "underclass" in the value-neutral sense of a category of citizens who for a variety of reasons, whether you regard them as good or bad, are permanently dependent on income or services (or both) provided by the state; and within that category there are some who, again for a variety of reasons, either cannot be induced to take up their rights or, having done so, fail to take advantage of them.

These are notoriously complex issues – more so, as I fully realize, than can be adequately summarized here. But I hope that I have said enough to vindicate my chosen title. It may seem almost a contradiction in terms to suggest that social rights can *generate* social inequalities. Does not bringing those below the stipulated minimum up to it diminish the pre-existing degree of inequality by definition? But, for the reasons I have given, inequalities of a new and different kind do then arise as a direct, even if unintended, consequence. Raising more people to a higher minimum level will inevitably intensify competition for goods of a kind that cannot be distributed equally; it will inevitably bring into being a professional bureaucracy that in order to perform its functions will have to outrank its potential clients in both authority and expertise; and it will inevitably create a gap between those of the clients who do and those who do not need sustained and disproportionate attention if they are to be raised to, and kept at, the minimum level, which not all of them will or can be. It does not, to be sure, follow that these consequential inequalities are unjustifiable. Indeed, it can be argued that they are justifiable precisely to the extent that they are a necessary condition of the achievement of the desirable end of providing all citizens with the stipulated minimum. My point, however, is that the extent to which they are inevitable is much easier to see – or perhaps I should say, much harder to avoid seeing – in 1994 than it was in 1950.

Before I conclude, however, I must firmly disavow an impression that I might seem to be wanting to leave behind. I might fairly be asked whether I have been leading up to the conclusion that the pre-suppositions that underlie the text of *Citizenship and social class* are not merely out-of-date but inherently misconceived. But the answer is an emphatic no. This is not the place for me to start expounding my own political views. But the fact is that they are close to what I take to have been Marshall's own and I do not regard anything that I have said as conflicting with them. I agree that legal and political rights ought to be supplemented by social rights to a minimum level of income, education, housing and health care, and I believe that the minimum level should be progressively raised as the country as a whole becomes more prosperous: in the words of Adam Smith, "Under necessaries, therefore, I comprehend not only those things which nature, but those things which the established rules of decency have rendered necessary to the lowest rank of people" (1961, vol. II: 400).

That said, the sociological question to which I might now be expected to offer a parting answer is: what prospect is there of British society evolving in a direction that would bring it closer than it is at present to Marshall's implied ideal? But I have no more to say in response than to repeat that there is nothing that logically, as opposed to sociologically, rules the possibility out. Any guess I might make as to whether it will happen, and if so how or when, is of no more value than anybody else's. Here again, I think I am at one with Marshall, who as far as I know never held that sociology either was, or could be, a predictive science. But I would go further. Any sociologist who uses a lecture like this one to offer an *ex cathedra* prediction of the state of his or her society in another 50 years should be made to sit down and write out a hundred times the dictum initially enunciated by Frank H. Knight for the benefit of his American fellow economists: "Never try to forecast anything, least of all the future."

# Note

This lecture is reprinted more or less as delivered. I have, however, as well as adding references where appropriate, substantially altered the concluding section in response to comments from Professor David Lockwood for which I am very grateful. I am grateful to him also for letting me see an unpublished paper on "Civic stratification", of which an earlier version was published as "Schichtung in der Staatsburgergesellschaft", in *Theorien der Ungleichheit*, B. Giesen & H. Haferkamp (eds) (Giessen, 1987).

CHAPTER 4

# T. H. Marshall,
# the state and democracy

## Anthony Giddens

Tom Marshall is remembered above all for the brilliance of his work on citizenship. Modest in size, Marshall's classic work *Citizenship and social class* (1950) has enjoyed a continuing influence for some half a century. In that book Marshall described a balancing act between the divisive effects of class inequalities and the integrative implications of citizenship rights. Marshall did not use the term "democracy" all that often, but his analysis of the progressive development of citizenship certainly can be regarded as a theory of democratic evolution.

Marshall's views were strongly shaped by a critical reaction to Marx and Marxism. Marshall wanted to defend the claims of reformist socialism as contrasted to its bolder and violent cousin, revolutionary communism. He wanted to show also that class conflict was neither the main motor of social transformation nor a vehicle for political betterment. With Max Weber, Marshall accepted class inequality as an inherent element of a capitalistic industrial society. Class division, however, in Marshall's view is only one dimension of such a society. The other, integrative, dimension is that of universal involvement in the national community, given concrete form in the welfare state. The term "welfare state" was first coined during the Second World War, to contrast the idea of a cohesive and protective national community with the "warfare state" of Nazi Germany. The new welfare policies were designed to treat all citizens as part of a more inclusive national order and in so doing to recognize state responsibility for caring for those who were in some way prevented from active economic participation. Marshall recognized the influence of the war effort upon the shaping of welfare institutions, but placed them in a much longer evolutionary context. His theory of citizenship rights, nevertheless, was at the same time a theory of the welfare state as the realization of a programme of socialist reform.

Marshall's critical reaction to Marx's interpretation of class conflict is a clear and evident feature of his work. Less obvious, and less explicit, is his critique of Marx's account of democracy. Marx recognized that the universal qualities of democracy run counter to the class-divided nature of capitalist societies. He was able to preserve the primacy of class in his theory by treating democratic rights as narrow and partial. In democratic systems people only get to vote occasionally, every few years: there is little or no participatory democracy. Even more important, democratic rights are limited in two ways. In Marx's time only a small proportion of the British population, essentially male middle-class property owners, had the right to vote. Moreover, political rights made no impact upon the economic sphere. The worker, as sheer "labour power", sacrificed all control over his or her body when entering the workplace. Many have argued that Marx was undemocratic or even anti-democratic. A charitable reading of his texts, however, would suggest that he believed class revolution to be the means of widening and deepening of democratization. A genuine universalizing of democratic rights would be accompanied, in other words, by some form of economic democracy having the participatory traits noted by Marx in his discussion of the Paris Commune.

Whether consciously or not, Marshall provided an alternative interpretation of democratization to that offered by Marx. On the one hand, Marshall was more clearly aware than was Marx of the essential importance of civil or legal rights in a democratic society. Legal rights that guarantee effective freedoms protect individuals both from the overweening power of the state and from the organized use of violence or coercion.

In his discussion of economic rights, however, Marshall in effect picks up Marx's theme of the partial nature of democracy. Marshall was not a proponent of economic democracy, but his advocacy of welfare rights, in the context of his overall analysis of citizenship, can be understood as a theory of democratization. Welfare rights round out and deepen the "hollow" character of democracy that Marx diagnosed. When combined with the other two types of citizenship right, rights of welfare provide for a full and "complete" integration of the citizen into the wider social order. The citizen is no longer simply the "abstract voter" but instead appears as a flesh-and-blood individual with material needs; as a citizen, she or he has the right to expect that the society will cater for those needs in circumstances of deprivation or disability.

If Marshall spoke little of "democracy" as such, it is because the burden of his work was concerned with welfare systems and the welfare state. The welfare state, in his argument, becomes part of the general extension of democratization. Yet mechanisms of political democracy tend in his writings to be taken for granted rather than directly explored.

Marshall wrote at a period during which it seemed to almost everyone, supporters and critics alike, that the welfare state would continue its upward trajectory. Hayek was thought of by most as an eccentric and marginal thinker; neoliberalism, as it later became, might have been a gleam in his eye but was hardly even dreamed of by anyone else. Over the past twenty or so years, of course, welfare systems have been the subject of sustained attack from the neoliberal Right. Some of the policies and programmes that Marshall believed would allow disadvantaged individuals to live a full and rewarding life have been seen by the neoliberal critics as producing precisely the opposite. Such critics have attacked welfare rights as promoting dependency and apathy. Far from ensuring that the underprivileged have a full place in the wider society, according to them one of the consequences of the rise of the welfare state has been the creation of an excluded underclass.

The collapse of the Marshallian vision, if such has indeed occurred, cannot be laid solely at the door of neoliberalism. Rather, the neoliberals provided an – unsound – interpretation of wider changes effecting not only welfare institutions but many other aspects of modern societies also. Marshall concentrated his attention upon Britain. He did not give much attention to transnational events or structures, but it is to these events and structures we must look to explain the difficulties of the welfare state today. Marshall did not, and could not, have anticipated some of these developments. But neither do his writings give much purchase upon either the expansion of democratic concerns in the present day or the troubles that democracy at the same time is experiencing.

Just as Marshall's thinking about citizenship and the welfare state had its origins in the UK, so in some part did neoliberalism, in the shape of what came to be called Thatcherism. Neoliberal doctrines, in one guise or another, however, have been influential worldwide. At the same time, there has occurred something of a global expansion of democracy, expressed not only in the fall of Communism but in the decline of authoritarian or military governments in other areas. In the sense of liberal democracy, democratization seems to have become something of a global process today. On the other hand, in the heartlands of liberal democracy, the Western capitalist states, liberal democratic institutions appear to be suffering from stresses and strains as substantial as those affecting the welfare state. Many of the population have become evermore distrustful of politicians, alienated from political participation and unable to identify with any existing political party.

Set against the general background of Marshall's work, a number of questions can be asked in this situation: 1. What accounts for the renewed importance of democratizing processes? 2. What are the main mechanisms of democracy — should democracy be equated with liberal democracy? 3. What connections might exist between problems of democratic organization today and problems facing the welfare state?

For reasons already mentioned, Marshall did not really explore the attractions or the limitations of liberal democracy. He was conscious of both, to be sure, and he believed that to establish a strong welfare system without democratic parliamentary institutions would lead to authoritarianism. Marshall does not appear to have seen the cultural foundations of liberal democracy as particularly problematic. Others, however, have done so and some of these include scholars who have drawn extensively upon Marshall's work on citizenship. For such authors the advantages of liberal democracy compared to other types of political order are obvious; the emergence of sound liberal democratic institutions is inevitably a long-term process. For a properly functioning liberal democracy depends upon a wider civic culture — not just the civic rights that Marshall so ably analyzed, but a more diffuse political culture conducive to the regular succession of political parties and to non-coercive government.

Such a view of democracy provides a rationale for the spread of democratization in current times, but also suggests that newly democratizing states will have great problems in establishing well functioning democratic institutions. I shall refer to this position as the "fragile flower" theory of democratization. It equates democratization with liberal democracy in the context of the nation-state.

According to the fragile flower theory of democracy, if liberal democratic institutions are spreading into many countries it is because liberal democracy is manifestly superior to any other type of political system. Two cheers for democracy, as E. M. Forster said: democracy might be imperfect but it is still superior to any alternatives and can be seen by everyone to be so with the disintegration of Soviet Communism. Democracy, however, is a plant that needs fertile conditions in order to grow. It needs soil that has been laid down across the generations and like any other fragile sapling needs constant nurturance. The fragile flower theory of democracy is also a catching-up theory: for democratization to be successful in areas such as Asia, Africa or Latin America, the conditions that have led to the successful development of democratic institutions in the Western countries have to be duplicated. Since democracy is a fragile flower these conditions are problematic: there cannot be any relatively sudden transition to democratic organization.

Most who have taken such a view have accepted a general association between the development of the democratic civic culture and the progression of capitalistic or market institutions. Markets do not create or sustain democracy in and of themselves. They are the natural complement to democratization, since they cultivate individualism and freedom of choice, even if marketization cannot in and of itself create the cultural conditions necessary for stable democratic life.

The fragile flower theory is fairly simple and it is intuitively attractive, making sense as it does both of the spread of democracy and of the conditions for its success. There are good reasons, nevertheless, to be somewhat cautious about it. First, there do seem to have been historical circumstances in which liberal democracy has been established almost overnight and where it has persisted in a stable fashion. Thus Germany and Japan were both authoritarian states that, largely through the intervention of the victorious powers after the Second World War, established liberal democratic institutions that took an instant hold. Secondly, the theory presumes events not fully explained – including especially the fall of Soviet Communism – in order to interpret the spread of democratization. Although there were protest movements in the East European countries, the Soviet Union was not brought down by any sort of "democratic deficit". Thirdly, the theory does not cast any light upon the troubles of liberal democracy in those countries that have well developed democratic institutions. The apparently global triumph of liberal democracy is accompanied by a process of strain or decline. Why should this be so?

The importance of liberal democracy cannot be gainsaid. Even those on the political left who might once have tended to downplay its significance now accept this. To explore its nature, and its current popularity, however, perhaps we need more than the fragile flower theory. Instead of such a view, what I would propose might be called the sturdy plant theory. The sturdy plant theory is not a catching-up theory of democracy; and it places current processes of democratization in the context of wider changes sweeping through not only the industrialized countries but most of the word as a whole. Such a view does not identify democracy *tout court* with liberal democracy. The very spread of liberal democratic institutions can be understood as part of the same processes that, in their heartlands, tend to compromise or challenge them.

Democracy is perhaps a sturdy plant that can in fact take root in what was previously quite stony soil; it does not necessarily depend upon a long-established civic culture, but rather upon other structural conditions that on occasion can be put in place rather quickly. It is always probably vulnerable, but may have more inherent strengths than other competing types of political system or legitimation.

We should situate democratization in the context of a number of very basic social changes. The first of these is by now very well known and, over the past few years at least, has become as much debated as has democracy. This is the impact of globalization. While the term has been used a lot it has not to my mind always been adequately conceptualized or understood. Western capitalism has always had an expansionist character, well known from the writings of Marx and others. In that sense the impact of Western society has long tended towards globalization.

This, however, is a phenomenon of the long term. Over the past four or five decades or so, I would argue there has taken place an intensifying and a reshaping of globalizing processes. We should understand by globalization not simply economic change and not simply the emergence of large-scale global systems. Globalization is best understood as being about the transformation of space and time, particularly the expansion of what I would call "action at distance" in our lives. The intensifying of globalization over the recent period has been strongly influenced not only by the worldwide expansion of economic markets but also by developments in transportation and in electronic communication.

Globalization in this contemporary period still expresses the dominance of Western power; but it has become much more decentred. Not only in the "Easternization" of Western industry but in many other respects too there is no longer a clear centre to globalization processes. Globalization increasingly intrudes into the core of day-to-day life and causes profound shifts in the texture of everyday experience. Globalizing processes are complex, ambivalent and contradictory; they produce an accentuating of local identity, alter the conditions even of personal identity and transfigure many forms of localism. They also generate new institutions. Global money markets, operating on a 24-hour basis, supply an interesting and important illustration. Such money markets are a recent development and depend upon global systems of satellite communication that make possible the instantaneous transmitting of information across the globe. Yet such money markets, of course, have a very direct influence upon individual lives and personal capabilities.

The second set of changes is intimately bound up with globalizing processes: these changes are to do with the impact of de-traditionalization. For some two centuries modernity created something of an effort-bargain with tradition. The philosophers of Enlightenment set themselves against tradition; one of the dominant impulses of modern society, with its heavy reliance upon science and technology, is the overcoming of fixed legacies from the past. Yet modernity in some large part accommodated itself to tradition and vice versa. On the level of the large-scale, new ideologies were invented or re-invented with a heavy shot of tradition including, for instance, various kinds of religious belief and symbolism. Just as important, was the persistence of what can be termed infrastructural traditions – traditions of everyday life. In respect of gender, the family, kinship, sexuality and other domains, traditions became altered but also reconstructed during the course of the nineteenth and early twentieth centuries.

De-traditionalization in the current period stems from two main sources: one is the impact of social movements of various types. Thus the feminist movement, for example, actively sought to place in question traditionalized or taken-for-granted aspects of the position of women and gender identity more generally. Tradition encompasses what has been called a "silent power": it forecloses options at the same time as it supplies guidelines to conduct. When questions that are latent in tradition are brought in to the public domain they have to be discursively justified. Traditional ways of doing things give way to actively promoted and debated courses of action.

Globalizing processes tend to be de-traditionalizing because they bring together a diversity of newly visible worlds and ways of life. Anyone who persists with a traditional way of doing things cannot but be aware that many other alternative life practices exist. A world of cultural cosmopolitanism of this sort is not one where tradition necessarily disappears. Almost to the contrary, tradition often is reconstructed and achieves a new dynamism. Yet it cannot take the forms it once did.

A particularly important aspect of de-traditionalization is the emergence of fundamentalism. In a few short years we have become accustomed to the idea that there are tensions between fundamentalism and democracy. Indeed in the shape of political extremism, ethnic purification and assertive religious dogma, fundamentalisms of various sorts are perhaps the chief enemy of democratic dialogue. Marshall gives no attention at all to this phenomenon. And this is not in any way surprising: for the rise of fundamentalism is actually a quite recent occurrence, reflecting the global changes here being discussed.

Although the term "fundamentalism" dates from around the turn of the century, it has only come into common currency over about the last 20 years. The widespread introduction of a term in this way where none previously existed, or where its use was marginal, virtually always suggests the arrival of a new social phenomenon. Fundamentalism can be understood as a reaction to radical de-traditionalization – a reaction to the expansion of modernity but also an attempt to defend tradition as authentic and as having its own indigenous claims to truth. Fundamentalism seeks to defend tradition in the traditional way in a world that is increasingly globally cosmopolitan; in so doing it purifies tradition, often in an aggressive fashion and at the same time often links into the new modes of global electronic communication.

Fundamentalism is complex and I would not want to oversimplify its character. By and large, however, it can be said that fundamentalism can emerge in any domain subject to de-traditionalization. Fundamentalism is essentially a means of authenticating tradition and therefore is not specifically linked to religion. Fundamentalism is in

72

some sense in genuine dialogue with the presuppositions of industrial capitalist civilization. It poses the question: "Can we live in a world where nothing is sacred?" Fundamentalism is not always dangerous to others, but can easily become so. For it implies a refusal of dialogue, a justification of tradition that resists discursive engagement with others.

The third cluster of changes affecting the contemporary world is connected to increasingly high levels of social reflexivity. "Reflexivity" refers here to the active engagement with diverse sources of incoming knowledge or information that is an inevitable part of living in a de-traditionalized social environment. Ulrich Beck has justly spoken of the retreat of fate in our lives as intimately bound up with de-traditionalizing influences. When social roles were relatively fixed, for example, it was the fate of most men to expect to leave school or college and go out to work until age 65, followed by a period of retirement. Most women could anticipate a life of domesticity, centred upon children and the home, even if a substantial proportion of women were always also in paid work. Anatomy is no longer destiny and gender is no longer fate. In most areas of social life, whether they be affluent or less privileged, most people have to take a variety of life decisions that cannot be settled by appeal to past tradition. They must make such decisions, some way or another, in the context of diverse information sources and malleable knowledge claims.

A world of heightened social reflexivity is one infused with diverse forms of expertise, but where at the same time expertise becomes fragmented. It is a world of active involvement yet one that is puzzling and often opaque.

Where these various sets of changes take hold, a variety of institutional consequences follows. In the area of social and economic organization, for instance, the old bureaucratic hierarchies, which once were seen by Weber and others as the height of social efficiency, start to become beleaguered and ineffective. A reflexive citizenry, living in a world where fate is in retreat, is loath to accept the sorts of labour discipline characteristic of earlier periods. What seemed to Weber an inexorable process, submission to bureaucratic dominion, becomes contested and vulnerable. Institutions that seemed so solid as to be unshakeable do not look so at all when suddenly placed in question. Both the fact and the ideology of bureaucratic hierarchy begin to cede place to an emphasis upon the small-scale and upon bottom-up decision-making.

An increasingly active, reflexive citizenry both demands democratization and at the same time becomes disenchanted with politics. Political authoritarianism has scarcely disappeared and indeed this is all too evident in different parts of the world. Yet the counterpressures are also increasingly strong. Authoritarian regimes become vulnerable for much the same reason as bureaucratic organizations of the Weberian type become social dinosaurs. Calls for "flexibility" and "social involvement" are no doubt often ideological; yet where fate no longer rules it is difficult for political authoritarians to effectively rule either. The result is not necessarily enhanced democracy. Such a situation, in some contexts at least, can lead to social disintegration and the virtual impossibility of effective government of any kind.

The consequences for established democratic systems are mixed. The advance of globalization links local and regional systems to events and processes that bypass the national state. Many events that affect people's lives either happen above the level of the nation-state or in the area of what Ulrich Beck calls "sub-politics" – domains of social and technological change in everyday life. It is not only the political or sociological observer who notices these things. They become to some degree the common currency of everyone and form part of their own reflexive awareness of and reaction to contingent events.

Disenchantment with politics within the democratic societies in some part reflects the visible discomfort experienced by political leaders. To sustain legitimacy such leaders must make promises and must assert their capability to control or alter the existing framework of events. Yet the mass of the citizenry can see quite well that these promises have little chance of being effective. I do not think that political disaffection is the only consequence that can flow from such a situation, nor is it the case that the arena of national politics inevitably loses all its effectiveness. On the more positive side, there are possibilities for "the democratizing of democracy" that both promise greater democratic involvement for many and which also address the issue of generating effective political power.

The democratizing of democracy involves various elements. These include an attack upon various forms of political patronage. It is not by chance that corruption cases have come to the fore in many diverse political settings around the world. Such corruption is not necessarily a recent development. Rather, the enhanced "social visibility" of the political domain means that influences that were once concealed, or even thought generally acceptable, now come into public view and are actively condemned. The democratizing of democracy also implies the downward and upward devolution of power. We do not know as yet what institutional forms such devolution is likely to assume, if it can be realized. Neither existing forms of local government, nor existing supranational organizations, seem fully up to the task. There are real possibilities of developing forms of democratic participation that might enhance local decision-making, as many proponents of a "revived civil society" have proposed. In the contemporary world, however, local and global happenings are often directly tied to one another. We have to search for democratic forms that are able to grapple with the new connections of the local and the global.

Nobody knows where this situation will lead. Yet the very intensity of recent debates about democracy, involving proposals for forms of democratic organization once thought to be either obsolete or unavailable in a large-scale society, points to a transformed agenda. Participatory democracy was long ago written off by Weber, Schumpeter and others as irrelevant and unrealizable in the settings of modern social life. Yet with the social transmutations now occurring, including especially the downwards devolution of power, schemes of participatory democracy have again been widely canvassed. In the short space available to me here, I do not propose to look at the diversity of schemes of democratic renewal now being discussed. I want to mention only one mechanism of democracy, which I hold to be particularly important in the social circumstances I have analyzed.

Whether one speaks of liberal democratic institutions or other forms of democracy, democracy involves two partly separate dimensions. One is the representation of interests. Democratic institutions provide a means whereby a variety of interests can find expression and where there is some means of organizing to represent those interests. But democracy also means the chance to have one's say. It means, in other words, the possibility of dialogue. Liberal democratic institutions plainly provide various contexts in which dialogic engagement is possible – in parliaments, congresses and in other public media. Perhaps the most interesting attempt to reinterpret liberal democratic mechanisms in recent years – that associated with the idea of deliberative democracy – depends upon the idea of resolving issues through dialogue. As usually understood, deliberative democracy falls far short of Habermas's ideal speech situation. In empirical situations of dialogue, it will often be the case that controversial issues cannot be directly resolved; yet discussion can allow us to agree to disagree and therefore be a powerful medium for tolerance and conciliation.

Dialogic democracy, or its possibility, should not be seen as limited to formal contexts of democratic participation. Mechanisms of dialogic democratization need to be established – and to some extent are developing – in a number of other major arenas of social life, both local and more global.

The background to the emergence of dialogic democracy in such contexts is again the sweeping changes diagnosed above. We live now in a much more intensely cosmopolitan world than even three or four decades ago. Cosmopolitanism and difference were until relatively recently often preserved through geographical segregation. Different groups, cultures and regions co-existed in some part through sheer geographical separation. In an age of instantaneous global communication, geographical separation loses much of its meaning and its social significance. Different groups and cultures are brought much more directly into relation with one another and global cultural diasporas of all kinds form a routine part of the daily experience of individuals who may be separated geographically by many thousands of miles.

New possibilities, indeed demands, for communication and symbolic exchange thus emerge. At the same time, the relation between dialogue and potentialities for social or political violence become especially tensionful. Fundamentalisms, with their assertion of the integrity of "purified" traditions, readily step into the spaces where dialogic relations are ill-formed or lacking.

In all settings of communicative contact communication can move in two possible directions. On the one hand, as we know both from the literature of global diplomacy and from that of much more intimate personal relationships, communication can be a means of the fruitful exploration of difference. Getting to know the other, whether an individual, group or culture, better can serve to increase one's self-knowledge, heighten communication with the other, and initiate a virtuous circle of mutual understanding. On the other hand, degenerate cycles of communication produce a diametrically opposite effect: dislike feeds on dislike or, worse, hate feeds on hate. Whether assessing conflicts in marriage, or violence between religious or ethnic groups, it is important to recognize that, like love, hatred does not exist in a "fixed quantum". Vicious group conflicts, involving the most extreme forms of barbarism, can develop in situations where there was previously a reasonable degree of co-existence between the groups or communities involved. It is not too fanciful to draw a parallel with personal life here. In marriage tolerance or love, when a relationship deteriorates, can turn into an elemental hatred. A sobering finding of the literature on emotional relationships is that very often the things which attracted one individual to another in the first place – certain traits of personality and behaviour – become those most despised or reviled if the relationship enters a negative communication spiral.

The formation of mechanisms of dialogic democracy in the transnational sphere is a matter of the first importance. As yet we can only dimly foresee what such mechanisms might be. Advocates of "cosmopolitan democracy", such as David Held, have argued that parliamentary institutions or congresses can be stretched above the level of the nation-state so as to create regional and international assemblies, such assemblies having a direct tie to the United Nations. Yet we might have to look for somewhat more unorthodox models of dialogic engagement than this, although I shall not pursue this issue here.

In the domain of "sub-politics" there are at least two arenas in which mechanisms of dialogic democratization become important or vital. One concerns the ever more pervasive role of science and technology in our daily lives. The relation of science to tradition in Western society is an interesting and tangled one. On the face of things, as the prime progenitors of enlightenment, science and technology set themselves radically against tradition. Yet for a long while science itself was a sort of tradition in modern society. That is to say, science remained fairly insulated from the wider lay community and scientists got on with testing their findings relatively independently of the broader population. With the acceleration of social change, and the role of technological innovation in creating such acceleration, this insulating barrier breaks down. Science is no longer regarded by the majority as sacrosanct, as having the status of unquestioned authority. In a reflexive social universe, where the essentially sceptical nature of scientific method becomes revealed to view, lay individuals have a much more dialogic involvement with science and technology. Not only do they "talk back" to science, they routinely engage with its claimed findings.

Individuals diagnosed as HIV positive, or suffering from AIDS for instance, are sometimes in the forefront of scientific research concerned with their malady. They do not just accept what "the doctor" tells them, but conduct an active interrogation into the current state of scientific and technological knowledge. They don't wait for the "normal" processes of long-term testing that a more insulated scientific community used to take for granted. Many issues and problems stem from this situation, including forms of commercial exploitation of the needy or desperate. But in such dialogic engagement there is the promise of greater democracy – the opportunity to forge constructive dialogues between those who produce scientific knowledge and those whose lives are affected by that knowledge.

Another prime context for the advance of dialogic democracy is that of personal life: in the spheres of sexual relations, marriage, the family and friendship. All of these areas of social activity have been subject to de-traditionalizing processes. De-traditionalized personal relations fall within the category of what I term the "pure relationship". The pure relationship is an ideal typical form. Actual contexts of action approximate to it only in greater or lesser degree. The pure relationship is a relationship that is lived for its own sake: it is one that in principle depends upon personal integrity and gaining the active trust of the other. Pure relationships necessarily are dialogic because they do not draw upon traditional ways of doing things or relating to others.

We can speak of the advance of dialogic democracy in the various contexts of personal life to the degree to which certain communicative conditions are fulfilled. These conditions are readily apparent in the therapeutic literature dealing with personal or emotional life. There is a remarkable similarity between what a good relationship is like, as diagnosed in the literature of therapy and self-help, and the properties of formal democracy in the political sphere. A good relationship, in brief, is one in which each individual accepts that the other is independent and equal; problems in a relationship are settled through discussion, rather than coercion or violence; the relationship is an open and mobile one, corresponding to the changing needs of each partner, and negotiation and compromise are central. These traits could very well be taken as constitutive of a democratic polity, at least in the sense of deliberative democracy.

Two cheers for democracy – this theorem applies not only to liberal democracy but to all the other contexts of actual or possible democratization. Democracy is not a panacea: it is a means of enabling individuals to live together in conditions of mutual communication and mutual respect. Imperfect though it might be, a "democracy of the emotions" in personal life is likely to prove just as consequential as the development of democracy in the more public sphere. As with other contexts of dialogic democratization, the tension between communication and violence is particularly important, yet problematic. It is not yet clear how far dialogic democracy will develop or whether in these spheres as in others, forms of fundamentalism, perhaps linked to generic violence, will surface.

I have strayed some way by now from the ideas of T. H. Marshall. Can we bring such a discussion back to focus more squarely on questions of citizenship and the welfare state? There is no doubt that we can. It has often been said that Marshall's account of citizenship rights has been made redundant by the very effects of globalization. To be a citizen, in any meaningful sense, is to be a citizen of a nation-state; and the nation-state is being outflanked by the combined forces of globalism and localism. It is true that citizenship for us cannot carry exactly the weight that Marshall wanted it to bear; yet analyzing various possibilities of the democratizing of democracy does allows us to pursue themes that Marshall raised and to elaborate upon them in the context in which we now find ourselves.

A grasp of the problems facing the welfare state, and its likely future, is fundamental to assessing Marshall's long-term intellectual legacy. What Marshall took to be enduring aspects of welfare institutions now look distinctly shaky. Marshall's perspective is dated in a number of respects, but it would be as much a mistake to accept the critiques of the welfare state offered by the neoliberals, as it would be to hold that the origins of its troubles are to be traced to a fiscal crisis. Welfare dependency, at least among some groups and in some situations, is surely a reality; and the fiscal strains of the welfare state are apparent enough. However, I would look at the stresses currently affecting welfare institutions in terms precisely of the social changes that have been the core focus of my discussion in this chapter.

The welfare institutions with which Marshall was preoccupied developed at a time when most social lifestyles were more stable than they are today and where life continued to be lived largely as fate. Welfare systems were thus established on the presumption that the state can guarantee against various categories of risk, each being treated as akin to risks of nature. One might be or become poor, fall ill, become disabled, or be divorced: the state can step in to protect those who are affected by such hazards. In the more active, reflexive, yet disturbingly unsettling world of today, these assumptions do not make sense in the way they once did. Divorce, for instance, is not something that now only affects a minority and it is not something that simply "befalls" individuals. The problem is not solely, or perhaps even primarily, how to fund welfare institutions: it is how to re-order those institutions so as to make them mesh with the much more active, reflexive lives that most of us now lead. And here new thinking about citizenship has to be integrated with a reappraisal of democracy and its possibilities.

CHAPTER 5

# T. H. Marshall and ethical socialism

## A. H. Halsey

## Introduction

When Professors John Smith and John Martin first wrote to me in
1983 about the inauguration of these lectures, I had just finished writing an appraisal of T. H. Marshall's life and work for *Sociology* (Halsey
1984), the journal sponsored by the British Sociological Association of
which Marshall had been the most distinguished president. I have no
reason to revise that appraisal and indeed was much gratified by the
reaction to it from my sociological colleagues. I came then to praise
Marshall, not to bury him, and I want to do the same in this chapter
despite painful awareness of the extent to which Marshall's writing and
my appreciation of it have been remarkably heavily dated by the subsequent political debate. Norman Dennis and I gave T. H. Marshall an
honoured place among *English ethical socialists* when we published our
book under that title in 1988. With Tony Blair as the leader of the
Labour Party in the 1990s, we have seen a return of Marshall's ideas
to the centre of the political stage. Marshall was in one sense the
outstanding sociological interpreter of British Butskellism, the subtle
advocate of the British version of the welfare state, legitimizing it by
placing it in the long march of British developmental history. In his
view, as in that of most analysts of the modern western Europe political democracies, the market has a necessary place in welfare-capitalism. Both the Berlin Wall and the British Labour Party's Clause Four
have faded into history.

He wrote:

> I am one of those who believe that it is hardly possible to
> maintain democratic freedoms in a society which does not
> contain a large area of economic freedom and that the incen-
> tives provided by and expressed in competitive markets make
> a contribution to efficiency and to progress in the production
> and distribution of wealth which cannot, in a large and com-
> plex society, be derived from any other source.

Neither Marshall nor any of the rest of us fully realized at that time
how far the recrudescence of economic liberalism had the power to
shift the balance between welfare and market principles through governmental action in a democratic society. Before that time it was
hardly conceivable that an occupant of No.10 Downing Street would
even rhetorically announce an intention of eliminating "socialism"
from the political agenda.

Nevertheless, writing in the early 1970s, Marshall demonstrated, I
think, his firm grasp of the central issue. Looking back over developments in the post-war period he saw that the democratic-welfare-
capitalist society had been expected to bring with it consensus over
basic issues and values. But even the most cursory glance at the history
of western Europe during the 1960s showed that it did not. He wrote:

> Though the principles and practices of democracy, capitalism
> and welfare were the objects of much criticism, this did not
> reflect battles being waged between them, but dissatisfaction
> with the whole of which they were parts. Materialism, profit-
> seeking, quantity-worship and growth-mania are not charac-
> teristics of capitalism, but permeate the whole of modern
> technological mass society. Bureaucratic excesses and rigid-
> ities are not a political malady only but are found also in the
> economy, the universities and even in welfare. The transfor-
> mation sought by the more purposeful and less destructive
> sections of those voicing our present discontents is one of
> attitudes and values rather than of basic structure, though
> institutional changes are sought as a means to this end, as
> is also the protection of the physical environment. I see no
> reason why their aims should not be achieved – if they can be

achieved at all – within a social framework that includes representative government, a mixed economy and a welfare state. The only alternative is something more totalitarian and bureaucratic, and that is not at all what the more novel and significant elements in the movement of protest are seeking. (Marshall 1981: 120–21)

Then in his very last writing just before he died in 1981, he noted that:

there is a disposition today, when considering what more should be done, to imagine that the desired effect can be obtained by attaching a framework of scaffolding of welfare services alongside the market economy, matching its operation and engaged to patch cracks, fill holes, press wounds and generally to make up, as far as is considered necessary, for the inability of the economy to meet its social obligations. Already there is too much of this, and to put still greater reliance upon it would lead to the gradual degradation of the welfare principle. There will always be casualties to be cared for and it will be part of welfare's task to care for them, but, it is to be hoped, more as a personal social service than as poor relief. Welfare fulfils itself above all in those services that are its own in every sense – health, education, the personal social services and, with increasing emphasis, community services for the preservation and development of the physical, social and cultural environment. It is by strengthening these that the civilised power of welfare can be most effectively increased. (Marshall 1981: 135)

It is this passage and the last, now unfashionable, affirmation that dates Marshall. Yet I want to take it up for it places Marshall in a tradition – the tradition of ethical socialism that is now in retreat, which has been diminished, is being diminished, and ought to be strengthened. So I shall try to locate Marshall in the ethical socialist tradition. I want only to pause before doing so to give a contemporary empirical context in the form of a generalization about the distributions that result from market and welfare institutions in western Europe political democracies.

If we divide the nation into households and order the households into quintiles by income it typically turns out as follows. The top fifth of households take about half of total market income and the bottom fifth approximate to zero. Then if we look at welfare benefits the mirror image appears – the bottom fifth get half and the top nothing (actually not quite nothing because educational grants in particular tend to go to the better-off families). But then putting all income together, because market incomes typically make up over three-quarters of all the income generated, the net result is a markedly unequal distribution of income between families in democratic-welfare-capitalist society. The British case illustrates the generalization and is shown in Table 5.1 from the latest official statistics.

Trends in the decade since Marshall wrote have been towards greater inequality. Between 1979 and 1991 the original or market income of the bottom fifth of UK households dropped as a share of all market income while the top fifth moved up. The redistributive activity of the state modified this inequality but did not change the direction of the movement. The bottom group had net incomes after

**Table 5.1** Distribution of disposable household income (percentages).[1]

| United Kingdom | Quintile groups of individuals | | | | | |
|---|---|---|---|---|---|---|
| | Bottom fifth | Next fifth | Middle fifth | Next fifth | Top fifth | Total |
| Net income before housing costs | | | | | | |
| 1979 | 10 | 14 | 18 | 23 | 35 | 100 |
| 1981 | 10 | 14 | 18 | 23 | 36 | 100 |
| 1987 | 9 | 13 | 17 | 23 | 39 | 100 |
| 1988–9 | 8 | 12 | 17 | 23 | 39 | 100 |
| 1990–1 | 7 | 12 | 17 | 23 | 41 | 100 |
| Net income after housing costs | | | | | | |
| 1979 | 10 | 14 | 18 | 23 | 35 | 100 |
| 1981 | 9 | 14 | 18 | 23 | 36 | 100 |
| 1987 | 8 | 12 | 17 | 23 | 40 | 100 |
| 1988–9 | 7 | 12 | 17 | 23 | 41 | 100 |
| 1990–1 | 6 | 12 | 17 | 23 | 43 | 100 |

[1] The unit of analysis is the individual and the income measure is net equivalent household income, explained in the original source, Appendix, Part 5: Households below average income and equivalisation scales.
*Source: Social Trends* **24**, 77, 1994, reporting data from Department of Social Security.

housing costs amounting to 10 per cent of the whole in 1979 reduced to 6 per cent in 1990–1 while the top fifth raised their share from 35 to 43 per cent.

I use this example simply to illustrate that T. H. Marshall's concern about the capitalist or market share in its balance with the other two spheres of welfare and democracy is more, not less, problematic a decade after he expressed it.

Let me turn now to the tradition in which he was writing.

## Ethical socialism

Ethical socialism is a radical tradition that makes heroic claims on and for persons and on and for the society that nurtures them. It offers and demands both a code of conduct for individuals and a guide to social reform towards a society of optimal conditions for the highest possible moral attainment of every person. Its credibility rests neither only on an intellectually adequate and morally compelling prescription of private individual virtue nor only on a benign blueprint for the social conditions of virtue. It has to pass both tests because it is a tradition that ultimately denies any distinction between the moralities of private and public behaviour.

The tradition is thus prescriptive of both individual action and social organization. It asserts consistent principles of responsibility and altruism – for the individual from conscience, for society through democracy. Conscience in the European context derives from the Judaic-Christian moral inheritance. Democracy in the same context has evolved as universal opinion mobilized by subscribers to this traditional conscience who apply it to politics. The underlying theory of human nature is that people live by ends as well as means. It posits free will and a self-consciousness that enables a man or woman to distinguish between and aspire beyond immediate desires or appetites towards the rational realization of a fully developed self. The underlying theory of society is of complex relationships constraining but also sustaining the exercise of choice to move in innumerable ways from the world as it is to a koinonia of equal respect for every morally free person within it.

"But wait", the reasonable critic will say, "can this really be realistic morals and practical politics for the twenty-first century?" The

85

challenge is fair. Norman Dennis and I tried to answer it in our book (1988) by examining the tradition, its success and failures, and finally its relevance to contemporary Britain. We do so in the main by reviewing the personal values and social analyses of certain outstanding English writers who have lived and expounded the culture and politics that we advocate. T. H. Marshall is a late child of the tradition we describe.

## The great names

Our selection is not complete but neither is it arbitrary. We see R. H. Tawney as the great modern master of ethical socialism. He offered the most complete expression of the tradition we seek to understand. In him the tradition reaches its highest point of personal accomplishment and its most comprehensive range of argument. Much of what he had to say had been developed by L. T. Hobhouse, the first Professor of Sociology in Britain, under whom Tawney undertook his first researches at the London School of Economics. Although their message was similar and reached an increasingly receptive public until about the time of Tawney's death in 1962, as the master rose to fame his precursor passed into oblivion. Yet it remains true that Hobhouse provided the philosophical and empirical underpinning for many of the assertions the truth of which Tawney felt able to take for granted and thus to propagate with clarity and confidence. In the twentieth century the London School of Economics was the principal channel through which ethical socialism was conveyed by Tawney's contemporaries and successors, notably R. M. Titmuss, but certainly also T. H. Marshall and the generation of sociologists shortly after the Second World War influenced by his theory of citizenship.

Ethical socialism, however, was the exclusive product of neither academics nor the twentieth century. In order to demonstrate that the attitudes and ideas of ethical socialism are deeply rooted in English culture we deal with two famous figures from very different centuries and backgrounds: Thomas More, the sixteenth-century statesman responding to an England on the threshold of capitalist agriculture, and William Cobbett, the ploughboy turned pamphleteer, commenting indefatigably on an England in the throes of the Industrial Revolution. As a reminder that the tradition flourished mightily outside the universities we deal also with the work of Marshall's contemporary George Orwell.

Whether directed at academicians or activists our method is socio-logical. We try in each case, and at greater length for Tawney, to analyze the political engagement of an individual in the way that Max Weber recommended for the understanding of all social action. We ask what ends were sought as possible and desirable, what the actor took to be true about the circumstances in which we lived, what means he proposed as effective to move his country from its past and present to or towards the preferred future, and what state of affairs ensued when his efforts had been exhausted. In what way and in these terms we can offer an understanding of how and how far ethical socialism has informed the lives and transformed the environment of some remark-able champions of a social ideal.

They are not, to repeat, the whole tradition, which has its radical and its conservative enemies and false friends to the Left and the Right. And their experience has been widely scattered over the his-tory of agrarian and industrial Britain. So their preoccupations have varied with circumstances. What they have in common is a steady gaze in search of common wealth. In modern political language they have all sought an optimal combination of liberty, equality and fraternity.

## The tradition defined

Socialism, like Marxism or Liberalism, is an inevitably imprecise concept because it refers to an ideology of many dimensions all of which vary in significance under different historical circumstances. As cultures and social structures change words change their meanings, political taxonomies are defied. The history of socialism is marked with simplistic identification of the concept with, for example, collec-tivism or statism or common ownership of property. In historical real-ity divisions within have been as bitter and crucial as conflict between socialism and its competing ideologies. And many individual socialists, not only those we discuss in our book but also others such as Robert Owen, William Morris or G. D. H. Cole, could at least partially be claimed for the ethical socialist camp.

There is no formal doctrinal constitution of ethical socialism. The emphases of the tradition shift according to social conditions as our exemplars have been chosen to illustrate. But four common factors make up the totality of the tradition, their combination varying to produce the uniqueness of each individual representative. First, second and third are positive commitments to liberty, equality and fraternity. Marshall exhibited all these three commitments in his writing and his life. And fourth in listing, though first in importance, is a shared belief in the power of moral character to perfect a person and ennoble a nation. Marshall wrote little or nothing directly about personal character. His great contribution was, however, to clarify the social conditions of citizenship that foster the development of responsible citizens.

Belief in moral commitment informs the distinctive attitude of ethical socialists to the meaning of liberty, equality and fraternity. It perhaps fits less well to Marshall, for it abhors idleness and is suspicious of intellectuals. On the other hand it gives libertarianism a markedly individualistic flavour and an anti-historic slant – both characteristics of Marshall's outlook. And it distrusts the bureaucratic state, is aware of enemies to freedom on the Left as well as the Right and is implacably opposed to totalitarianism from either of these directions. It gives egalitarianism a pronounced emphasis on the importance of respect and dignity rather than material equality. It gives fraternity a no less distinctive sense of history, love of country, dislike of violence and above all a faith in the good sense of ordinary people. Accordingly it favours parliamentary government while seeking also to extend the democratic principle to participatory citizenship in all spheres of public and especially industrial life. Again Marshall appears as the sympathetic interpreter of movements that made progress in the world he knew.

If these are the elements of the tradition we can also specify the characteristics of its outstanding exponents. The first is egalitarianism. Whatever their circumstances all ethical socialists have had a hatred of inequality at the centre of their social thought and political action. A passion for social equality is a necessary if not sufficient condition for membership of the ethical socialist tradition. But there have been other socialists and other egalitarians.

"We hold", wrote Thomas Jefferson (1743–1826), "these truths to be self-evident; that all men are created equal and independent . . .". No natural scientist qua scientist could do other than dismiss such a statement as either meaningless or empirically false. Equality for a mathematician is a concept of some complexity, in relation, for example, to identity or correlation, but one of no moral significance. In politics by contrast the debate about equality adds to the mathematician's complexity the further complications of moral argument. Equality refers to the principles on which human society ought, as well as might, be based. Jefferson's was a moral declaration, not an empirical description. The practical question is whether, and in what sense, social, political and economic equalities are possible. The answer is tentative, requiring the determination of the origins of inequality, the significance of inequality and the viability of action intended to establish equality. All three aspects are disputed.

Traditional discussion of the origins of inequality turned on a crude distinction between nature and society. Modern recognition of cultural evolution complicates that distinction and tends to substitute a more elaborate matrix out of the consequences of interaction between genetic and environmental material and cultural influences. But in neither simple nor sophisticated discussion is there denial of natural inequalities, the Jeffersonian declaration notwithstanding. Men are not clones, and Mendelian genetics guarantees variation. Dispute, however, continues in important areas of scientific ignorance. For example, there is not adequate scientific evidence to settle the dispute between those who believe in the genetic basis of differences between ethnic or racial or class groups in educational attainment or performance in intelligence tests, and those who hold such differences to be socially created. Resolution of such disputes is, in principle, possible through the further advance of empirically tested theories of the interaction between heredity and environment.

Meanwhile dispute about the significance of natural differences continues its long history. Plato confidently argued from natural to political inequality. Hobbes expressed the opposite view in 1651:

> Nature hath made man so equall, in the faculties of body, and mind; as that though bee found one man sometimes manifestly stronger in body, or of quicker mind than another; yet when all is reckoned together, the difference between man, and man, is not so considerable, as that one man can thereupon claim to himselfe any benefit, to which another may not pretend, as well as he. (Hobbes 1934: 63)

Hobbes's formulation still defines the debate. Egalitarian claims, especially with respect to race and gender, are more strident now than they were in the seventeenth century, and we would now say that Hobbes was making empirical propositions from both genetics and sociology, the one referring to natural differences and the other (about claiming and pretending) referring to the social psychology of man's perceptions of social rights. But the central assertion is fundamentally about the values that ought to be reflected in the actual relations of men and women in society.

In this sense the debate, turning as it does on ethical priorities between such values as equality, liberty and fraternity may never be finally resolvable. There have been, to be sure, notable recent contributions to greater conceptual clarity as to the meaning of terms. John Rawls (1971) adopts the device of the "original position" – an "if so" story of the rational choices that might be expected from an individual contemplating different societies with known different equalities or inequalities of positions but an unknown placement for the contemplator – to illuminate the problems of value choice. Brian Barry (1973) takes the discussion further to demonstrate how a small adjustment to Rawls's social and psychological assumptions opens the possibility of a crucial shift of preference towards egalitarian rather than liberal forms of society. But no amount of conceptual clarification, sophisticated or erudite, solves the problems of evaluation. In discussing the ethical socialists we shall be looking for a convergent evaluation of what is possible and desirable in modern society.

Meanwhile we can note the provenance of different priorities. One mundane but momentous perspective recurs down the ages, recognition of mortality. Thus Horace (65–8 BC) wrote: "Pale death kicks his way equally into the cottages of the poor and the castles of kings." And James Shirley (1596–1666) reminds us that:

> Death lays his icy hand on kings
> Sceptre and crown
> Must tumble down
> And in the dust be equal made
> With the poor crooked scythe and spade. (Shirley 1646)

This attitude is integral to Christian social teaching that dominated the evaluation of equality at least until the eighteenth century. It was not that natural inequalities between individuals were denied so much as deemed irrelevant in discussing the rights and wrongs of dictatorship or democracy, freedom or slavery. Christians were not only "equal before the Cross" but, as the early Church Fathers insisted, would, if they eschewed sin, live like brothers without inequalities of property and power. Sin, since the fall of Adam, had created earthly inequality. Political inequality might be necessary to protect order and restrain evil, but it did not arise, as Plato imagined, from natural inequality. Political inequality in Christian tradition must be endured but by no means implied a necessary respect or admiration for the rich and the powerful. On the contrary, position in the next world was typically held to be threatened by privilege in this. "He hath put down the mighty from their seat and hath exalted the humble and meek", says the *Magnificat*.

The break with Christian attitudes of submission to inequality dates from the eighteenth century with the decline of religious belief and the beginnings of a secular optimism with respect to the possibility of social transformation. Ethical socialism spans the ancient and modern conceptions of social equality. We try to show in our book that the ethical socialists, including Orwell who formally disavowed Christian belief and T. H. Marshall who lost his faith at Cambridge, are each in their different way people crucially influenced by both the Christian ethic and belief in at least the possibility of social progress. They are all pilgrims to a New Jerusalem.

Egalitarianism as a movement is commonly associated with Rousseau. But Rousseau, though believing that the evils of unfreedom and inequality were socially created, was a remorseless pessimist. He held that freedom was impossible except in a community of equals, but held out no hope of social transformation towards equality. In this sense he was a child of Christianity and if the early socialists (Fourier, Proudhon, Saint, Simon, Robert Owen, William Thompson) were his intellectual children they were also crucially different in entertaining the hope of progress. Modern egalitarianism derives from this form of sociological optimism and it was encouraged by, if by no means identical with, either the Hegelian idealist or Marxist materialist theories of the inevitability of social transformation. Hegel's elaborate analysis of the relation between masters and slaves, and Marx's development of it into a prediction of the future history of the working class hold out the possibility of a community of equals.

However, ethical socialism does not presuppose either the Hegelian or the Marxist theory of history. It proceeds on assumptions of openness or voluntarism as opposed to necessitous history. We postulate as a second condition of membership in the ethical socialist tradition this refusal to espouse historicism. We emphasize this second condition, which is met most closely and explicitly by Tawney and Marshall, because of its moral implications. Free men and women to be free must make their own history in however difficult circumstances. And socialism is not inevitable, nor irreversible if attained. At the same time anti-historicism is by no means a conspicuous feature of the outlook of all the writers we discuss. Hobhouse, heavily influenced by Hegel, has been, however unfairly, dismissed as a liberal historicist; and Orwell came close at one stage of his life to believing in the ineluctable coming of socialism.

These debates are the substance of a crucially practical aspect of the equality problem – the viability of deliberate social action aimed at reducing inequality. Marshall's theoretical approach deserves special emphasis here because it avoids both liberal evolutionist determinism and the alternative Marxist historicism. Marshall's interpretation of the development of citizenship in advanced industrial societies shows in the case of Britain how the basic equality of membership in a society that is rooted in the civil rights established in the eighteenth century was extended to include political rights in the nineteenth century and certain social rights in the twentieth century, when citizenship and class have been at war as opposing principles of social distribution (Marshall 1950). Marshall's analysis also brings out the important truth that the forces that influence the distribution of life chances are neither mechanical nor irreversible. Class displaced feudal status with formal equality of market relations as well as ushering in new inequalities of social condition. Citizenship promotes unequal rewards as well as equal rights, for example, state scholarships to selective university admission and universal political franchise. More generally, it may be noted that no social goal, equality, efficiency, liberty, order or fraternity, may be regarded as absolute. Public policies are perforce compromises aiming at optimal balance between desired ends.

Criticism of the ethical socialist view of equality is often advanced by economic liberals who assume an immutable occupational hierarchy, postulating a *de facto* necessity for some jobs to be more distasteful, unrewarding, and injurious to health than others. Given that life chances are largely determined by the individual's occupation, a hierarchy of social advantage seems to be inescapable and equality, as opposed to equality of opportunity, therefore unobtainable. But, ethical socialists reply, a less inegalitarian society is not sociologically impossible.

More's *Utopia* (1988) pointed the way out of the economic inequality of rank and station in Tudor society, albeit through compulsory labour service in the fields of an agrarian society. Cobbett's optimism about individual energy and intelligence convinced him that ordinary families would establish a community of equals in sufficiency if released from the tyranny of corrupt government and its "place men". Hobhouse derived from Alfred Marshall and J. A. Hobson a bourgeois version of the theory of surplus value that would be used to create a dominantly equal society by a benign state resolved to redistribute the surplus to its rightful owners.

In our own still highly inegalitarian society it is not difficult to imagine a wide range of counteracting social policies. Apart from progressive taxation and levies on wealth there could, for example, be national service specifically designed to direct the advantaged to a period of distasteful labour. The obvious rejoinders are lodged in the name of liberty and economic efficiency, again emphasizing the relativist character of claims for any social principle. Value choice is always the nub of the issue.

Another objection to egalitarianism is the alleged obstacle of genetic differences between races and classes of which Jensen (1972) has been an outstanding proponent. As to classes, and against Jensen's marshalling of the evidence from studies of twins reared apart, there is the opposed conclusion of Schiff (1982) from his studies of cross-class adopted children in France. As to race, it has to be said that we do not yet have the techniques or the data to measure definitively the genetic and environmental influences on race-IQ differences. Nor does the answer really matter, for there are more important issues of equality and justice in present-day society that do not have to wait upon further advance in the social sciences.

Certainly the writers we discuss did not wait for social scientific resolution of issues in social biology. They advocated and acted with confidence for two reasons that may be postulated as a third and fourth characteristic of the ethical socialist outlook – a sense of history and a theory of personality and society that places moral motivation as the mainspring of individual conduct and social organization. All our authors interpret their age as one of transition. Even Thomas More, though medievally Christian in his belief that the only really important transition was for the individual to the next world, and for the collective in the second coming, had an acute sense of historical deterioration in his England and of historical continuities and discontinuities with the Hellenic age that were being rediscovered by his fellow humanists.

But the fourth criterion is paramount. Socialism can only be built on moral character and history is a never-ending struggle to develop the altruism of individuals, to mould social institutions in its image and to pass on its tradition to each new generation. This essential theory of human nature is interpreted contextually according to the social experience of each devotee. But its vision of an improvable if not perfectable person is always there. Moral commitment can surmount any material obstacle. More discovered this truth among the Carthusian monks of the Charterhouse, Cobbett on his *Rural rides* (1936), Orwell in anarchist Barcelona, Hobhouse observing trade unionists at Toynbee Hall, Tawney with working men in tutorial classes at Rochdale, Marshall watching imprisoned sailors in a German prison camp.

## The making of ethical socialists

In their excellent book on the life and thought of the British Idealists – the colleagues and followers of T. H. Green (Bosanquet, Ritchie, Wallace, Caird, Haldane) – Andrew Vincent & Raymond Plant (1984) have sympathetically but sadly traced the opposition to the metaphysic of Green's theory of citizenship. This debate is not my direct concern any more than Marshall's sociology was more than marginally theirs in the period they discuss. But leaving aside for the moment the general question of the social and philosophical origins of ethical socialist belief, it is instructive to look at the lives of the heroes with whom we deal in our book from the point of view of how their own moral characters were shaped, bearing in mind especially T. H. Green's attempt to ground a theory of society in the ordinary consciousness of personality and ordinary people.

This general project is common to ethical socialists. In More it takes the form of moral appeal to the conscience of Christendom – the "communion of saints in every age". In Cobbett it is the conviction of a cultural patrimony of commonsense, competence and commitment to individual freedom among Englishmen from time immemorial. For Hobhouse, Tawney, Orwell and Marshall it is that distinctive if imprecise phrase from the British political lexicon – common decency.

Yet all except Cobbett of those writers have social origins in the advantaged strata of British society. They may therefore be compared in their biographical excursions, which brought them into serious contact with the mass of their common compatriots. In every case it seems that there was a personal experience of negotiating social marginality.

The young Tom Marshall as I have described him "knew nothing of working-class life, and the great industrial north was a nightmare land of smoke and grime through which one had to travel to get from London to the Lake District" (Marshall 1973: 88). Before the great trauma to his class of the outbreak of war in 1914, as his sister describes him, he was "a charming and clever nineteen-year-old, my mother's favourite child and destined for the Foreign Service . . ." (Partridge 1981: 42). It was at this point, in the spring of 1914, that the easy unfolding of a conventionally successful career was arrested and turned to new direction. He spent the next four years as a civilian prisoner of war in a camp outside Berlin, having been sent to Weimar to learn German. He received, one might say, an abruptly involuntary and unconventional pre-education in sociology. Marshall recognized his enforced sojourn at Ruhleben as "undoubtedly the most powerful formative experience of my early years" (1973: 89). His attitude to the world around him was "deeply affected by having lived through this real-life social experiment". (For a detailed account of Ruhleben, see Ketchum (1965) and Marshall's review (1967b).)

Ruhleben was also an enforced escape for Marshall from the narrow social confines of his upbringing in the English bourgeois intelligentsia. A prison camp being non-producing cannot be a class society in the ordinary sense. But the merchant seamen and fishermen, the "camp proletariat", introduced Marshall to familiarity with an unfamiliar subculture of class. As J. Davidson Ketchum described it, "without its seafarers Ruhleben would have been a very different camp, softer, less virile, top-heavy with intellectuals. It was their courage that set the first high standards, and their healthy philistinism that kept the cultural life in balance" (1965:126).

Of course, in a formal academic sense, it was an unknowing intro-duction to his future profession, just as was the medieval history that he studied at Cambridge under the tutelage of Gaillard Lapsley, and that which gave him his first acquaintance with the study of social systems as understood by Vinogradoff, Maine and Maitland. Marshall's later conception of capitalism, socialism and democracy was built on the foundations of the analytical construction of estate society fash-ioned by these historians. The greater significance of Ruhleben lay in personal confrontation of an unexpected, uncharted, to-be-con-structed world. It is a widely observed characteristic of most, if not all, notable sociologists that they negotiate social marginality. The gener-alization rests on a commonplace: disjunctive personal experience is likely to induce curiosity about society. Sociologists have typically lived and moved between at least two social worlds, be it Jewish and gentile, rural and urban, colonial and metropolitan, or some other margin of national, ethnic or class identity. For Marshall at Ruhleben it was a temporary marginality thrust upon a most unmarginal young man.

At all events the experience was morally and intellectually crucial, generating in him a new dimension of social sensibility reaching beyond the civilities of his upbringing in the style of life of Victorian London and Edwardian Cambridge. Superficially and initially, however, it was not so. Marshall returned to Cambridge to compete successfully for a Trinity Fellowship on the basis of a dissertation on seventeenth-century guilds, suggested by Clapham. He formed an understanding of post-feudal or post-estate society, especially in Eng-land, and most especially from the point of view of the legal basis of the institutions of class and status that interacted to produce equalities and inequalities.

He was thus embarked on what would have been a career entirely appropriate to a young man of his class, as a Cambridge historian. But he soon made a diversion, at least temporarily, from the normal path of the don into another encounter with working-class people. He stood as a Labour candidate for a safe Conservative constituency in Surrey at the General Election of 1922.

I mentioned too that Tawney and Orwell followed different paths from similar origins. Both were sons of Empire and followed the pattern of upbringing that was characteristic of the imperial upper-middle class. Eric Blair was conventionally launched and habituated during his first 25 years. He was sent to a private preparatory school in Sussex at the age of eight until he was thirteen and then on to Eton for four-and-a-half years via a term at Wellington. And thence, not yet out of his teens, back to the Indian Imperial Police in 1922 to be trained in Burma.

Thus Eric Blair was, in any social and statistical sense, an extraordinary English man. The vast majority of English men born at the beginning of the twentieth century were in fact born in England and into the familistic culture of the English working class. He was born overseas and never underwent the normal experiences of English family life. He hardly saw his father before the latter retired in 1912. He spent most of his childhood in the peculiar institutional life of the dormitory houses of schools designed to bring up the metropolitan and imperial classes. His was an upbringing not in a family or even a nation so much as in a ruling-class network in which he was a subordinate rather than a dominant member.

Raymond Williams (1971) puts great emphasis on the background we have described of atypicality with respect to class and family so as to dramatize the translation of identity from Eric Blair to George Orwell. Williams makes a distinction between on the one hand the imperial and the domestic (England in the context of Empire and England as a parochial island); on the other hand he distinguishes between the ruling class and the working class. Eric Blair belonged to the imperial ruling class. Orwell could have gone in three possible directions. He could have gone native in Burma (imperial working class). He could have rejected the Empire but remained in the dominant class as a don or teacher or writer or in some other island-based profession (domestic ruling class). In fact Orwell emerged pseudonymously out of excursions into the domestic working class. As V. S. Pritchett put it, "he might be described as a writer who has 'gone native' in his own country" (in Phelps 1947).

From the time he returned on leave from Burma in 1927, Blair sought a life as a writer and affiliation with the exploited and the ordinary, away from imperialism and from the ruling class. He spent time in spikes, lodging houses and hotel kitchens, living with tramps and hop pickers, and washing dishes. Out of it came his *Down and out in Paris and London* (perhaps better described under its French title, *La Vache enragée*). Discussing its publication with his agent in 1932, he asked for it to be published under a pseudonym and gave a list that included his preference for George Orwell – the reference being to a river in Suffolk near his parents' home. Blair the person continued in his family, his marriage and some of his literary and professional connections. But George Orwell the writer, journalist and developing moralist was now established.

Tawney's father was the Principal of Presidency College – a senior position in education in the Indian Empire at the height of its security and success (Pressnell 1956: 55–6). The confident sense of benign historic mission felt by such servants of Empire is remote to us now (cf. Woodruff 1953). Others of Tawney's class became socialists through the experience of rejecting the imperialist culture in Eastern service. Tawney's exact contemporary Leonard Woolf did so gently out of Ceylon (Woolf 1980: vol. I, 133–301), the younger Eric Blair did so dramatically as George Orwell out of Burma. It was a culture Tawney never embraced. He was sent to England to be reared in the conventional mode of his class – a preparatory school at Weybridge, followed by Rugby and Balliol. The cult of the English gentleman in his generation was as strong and as laden with commitment to public service at home and abroad as it was ever to be. John Henry Newman had defined it as a "cultivated intellect, a delicate taste, a candid, equitable, dispassionate mind, a noble and courteous bearing in the conduct of life" (Newman 1903: 112). Alfred Marshall (1925) had looked forward confidently in 1873 to its dissemination to the working class. Tawney was to live its ethos and to work for its realization in the British Labour movement.

The Oxford definition of a gentleman in Tawney's youth was in effect of a class that denied class. Its ideal was a moral character and outlook that preferred public service to private commerce, asceticism to social display. Social obligation was the corollary of privilege. Ruskin, T. H. Green, and Arnold Toynbee were among its founders; Christians and socialists like Scott Holland or Sidney Ball were among its proselytes. The most famous Master of Tawney's college, Benjamin Jowett, had urged idealistic undergraduates to go and "find their friends among the poor" (Barnett & Barnett 1915: 27). Edward Caird, Master in Tawney's day, urged both Tawney and Beveridge in 1903 to discover why poverty co-existed with so much wealth in England. Tawney responded positively, as did Hobhouse, Beveridge, Attlee, and Gaitskell. He lived for three years at Canon Barnett's Toynbee Hall during his Oxford days and after.

# The theory of citizenship

If Marshall is important to our further understanding, it is not so much because he offers yet another personal example of one born to advantage who lived and worked to better the lot of his less fortunate compatriots. He was indeed a private cultivator of friendship and a dutiful public servant: but exculpation from middle-class guilt, if present at all in his conduct of life, was certainly never dramatized in the manner of an Arnold Toynbee or a George Orwell. His significance for us is that he offered a theory of ethical socialism, conceptualized as citizenship, which is sociologically more defensible than the Hobhousian theory of progress, for while it gives due weight to the autonomously moral, it corrects Hobhouse's overemphasis on it.

In Marshall's sense of the term, all the writers we have reviewed have in common a search for the theory and practice of citizenship. The word citizenship is often narrowly associated with the ideology of the French Revolution, but carries older radical concerns than those of nineteenth-century and twentieth-century socialists, and with languages of class anterior to that disseminated by Marx and Engels. In T. H. Marshall both citizenship and class receive an analysis that advances their historical and sociological usefulness. Marshall, unlike T. H. Green, Bosanquet and Hobhouse, was able to explain the development of both the welfare state and class inequality in terms of the progress of society through the moral sense of the individual.

Marshall's work is also of more immediate political significance for the interpretation of the post-war period and for the debate over welfare-state capitalism led by economic liberals since the mid-1970s. By adding a social dimension to the Idealist theory of citizenship advanced by T. H. Green, the Oxford school in the second half of the nineteenth century eventually had a spectacular and divisive impact on liberalism in British theory and practice. Its impact on the twentieth century Labour Party was also impressive. But its validity was disputed and undermined by criticism of its metaphysic. It always had the debilitating weakness in political argument that its propositions could not be falsified by empirical enquiry. For those who accepted the Christian faith it had few problems as a general guide to social obligation. But few modern philosophers accept its metaphysic and few practical politicians can agree with Green that it can be rooted in the implicit social consciousness of ordinary people.

99

Moreover social, especially Marxist, historians such as Gareth Stedman Jones (1983) or John Foster (1974) challenge or reject the account of ordinary consciousness that the ethical progressivists (George Eliot, Arnold Toynbee, L.T. Hobhouse) offered. Writers in the ethical socialist tradition have, to be sure, found that decency, the habit of solidarity, the conviction that "we are here for a purpose beyond egotistical fruitful response to political leadership of the right calibre" (Clarke 1978: 5–6). And Gladstone's populism managed to run the democratic Liberal Party by keeping class issues out of politics. "The Gladstonian style of politics made a transcendental appeal to conscience, but one seldom directed towards social evils at home" (Clarke 1978). In the twentieth century as a restricted franchise moved towards universal adult suffrage, industrial economy towards high productivity, and industrial society towards suburban mobility and prosperity, the problem of citizenship became more, not less difficult. The bases of social integration in Christian belief, national and imperial success, localized kinship and the collective self-help institutions of the urban proletariat were all to decay. Erosion was slow and could be reversed, as during the Second World War when a form of siege socialism knit the nation together, widened social sympathies and gave popular appeal to the possibility of a future classlessness. In the remarkable history of wartime social services, R. M. Titmuss (1950) argued a logic of social solidarity, class reconciliation and communal altruism in response to external military threat. Total war with its food rationing, conscription and evacuation justified the limitation of individualism and demonstrated the practicality of social planning. Tawney (1950), reviewing Titmuss, saw the whole experience as a universal socialist education. T. H. Marshall is the outstanding interpreter and advocate of the central development of an alternative social solidarity – the welfare state.

# CHAPTER 6

# The uses of history in sociology: reflections on some recent tendencies

## John H. Goldthorpe

### I

To take up again the question of the uses of history in sociology may well appear regressive. For to do so implies, of course, making a distinction *between* history and sociology that would now be widely regarded as untenable. Thus, for example, Philip Abrams, in his highly influential book, *Historical sociology*, has advanced the argument that since "history and sociology are and always have been the same thing", any discussion of the relationship of one to the other must be misguided; and Abrams in turn quotes Giddens to the effect that "There simply are no logical or even methodological distinctions between the social sciences and history – appropriately conceived."[1]

As Abrams is indeed aware, the position he adopts is in sharp contrast with that which would have been most common among sociologists two decades or so previously. At this earlier time, sociologists were for the most part anxious to differentiate their concerns from those of historians. For example, much use was made of the distinction between "idiographic" and "nomothetic" disciplines. History was idiographic: historians sought to *particularize* through the description of singular, unique phenomena.[2] Sociology was nomothetic: sociologists sought to *generalize* through formulating theories that applied to categories of phenomena. However, all this was in the period before the British sociological community (anticipating Sir Keith Joseph) lost its nerve over the idea of "social science" – before, that is, the so-called "reaction against positivism" of the late 1960s and 1970s created a new mood in which political radicalism went together with intellectual conservatism.

My first contribution to the debate on "history and sociology" dates back to this prelapsarian time, and was in fact a *critique of* the idiographic–nomothetic distinction.[3] My remarks were not especially well received by either historians or sociologists, and this present contribution may, I fear, prove similarly uncongenial. For what I would now think important is that attempts, such as that of Abrams and Giddens, to present history and sociology as being one and indistinguishable should be strongly resisted.[4]

To avoid, if possible, being misunderstood, let me stress that I do not seek here to re-establish the idiographic–nomothetic distinction, or at least not as one of principle. I do not believe, for example, that sociologists can ever hope to produce theories that are of an entirely transhistorical kind; nor that historians can ever hope to produce descriptions that are free of general ideas about social action, process and structure. However, good grounds do still remain for refusing to accept the position that any distinction drawn between history and sociology must be meaningless.

To begin with, I would argue that the idiographic–nomothetic distinction is still pertinent if taken as one not of principle but of *emphasis*. Historians do – quite rightly – regard it as important that dates and places should be attached to the arguments they advance as precisely as possible; as E. P. Thompson has aptly remarked, "the discipline of history is above all a discipline of context".[5] Sociologists – no less rightly – believe that they are achieving something if the time and space co-ordinates over which their arguments apply can be widened. And from this, one use of history in sociology is immediately suggested. History may serve as, so to speak, a "residual category" for sociology, marking the point at which sociologists, in invoking "history", thereby curb their impulse to generalize or, in other words, to explain sociologically, and accept the role of the specific and of the contingent as framing – that is, as providing both the setting and the limits – of their own analyses.[6]

However, it is not on such issues that I wish here to concentrate. My aim is rather to focus attention on another major difference between history and sociology that has, I believe, been much neglected but which carries far-reaching implications for sociological practice. This difference concerns the nature of the evidence that the two disciplines use or, more precisely, the way in which this evidence comes into being.[7]

As a trainee historian at University College London in the 1950s, I underwent a standard catechism on method, which began with the question: what is a historical fact? The answer that had to be given was: a historical fact is an inference from the relics. This answer struck me then – and still strikes me – as the best that can be given, and as one of considerable significance. What the answer underlines is the obvious, but still highly consequential, point that we can only know the past on the basis of what has physically survived from the past: that is, on the basis of the relics – or of what may be alternatively described as the residues, deposits or traces – of the past.[8]

These relics are of very different kinds. They may, for example, be simply natural remains, such as bones or excrement; or again, artefacts, such as tools, weapons, buildings or works of art. But of most general importance are what one might call "objectified communications": that is, communications in some written form and, especially, "documents" of all kinds. Whatever their nature, it is these relics, and only these relics, that are the source of our knowledge about the past. Statements about the past – historical "facts" – are inferences from the relics, and can have no other basis. In short: no relics, no history.

So far as the practice of history is concerned, there are two points about relics that it seems important to recognize: first, they are *finite* and, secondly, they are *incomplete*. The relics that exist are just a limited selection of all that could have survived – a sample, so to speak, of a total universe of relics, where, however, neither the properties of the universe nor of the sample are, or can be, known.[9] The relics of a given period may diminish, by being physically destroyed, but they cannot increase.

It is true of course that not all the relics that exist at any one time are known about. Historians have always the possibility of discovering "new" relics, of adding to the known stock: and it is indeed an important part of their *métier* to do so. It is also true that from any set of relics, the inferences that can be made are *infinite*. The "facts" that the relics yield will tend to increase with the questions that historians put to them and, in turn, with the range of the problems historians address and with the development of their techniques of enquiry. However, none of this alters the situation that the relics themselves, in a physical sense – what is *there* to be discovered and interrogated – are finite and are, to repeat, a selection, and probably only a quite small and unrepresentative selection, of all that could have survived. It must therefore be the case that limitations on the possibilities of historical knowledge exist simply because it is knowledge of the past – because it is knowledge dependent on relics. There are things about the past that never can be known simply because the relics that would have been essential to knowing them did not in fact survive.

Historians, we may then say, are concerned with *finding* their evidence from among a stock of relics. In contrast – and this is the difference I want to stress – sociologists have open to them a possibility that is largely denied to historians. While sociologists can, and often do, draw on relics as evidence, in just the same way as historians, they can, in addition, *generate* evidence. This is of course what they are doing when they engage in "fieldwork". They are producing, as a basis for inferences, materials *that did not exist before.*[10] And it is, I would argue, such generated evidence, rather than evidence in the form of relics – in other words, evidence that is "invented" rather than evidence that is discovered – that constitutes the main empirical foundations of modern sociology.

The immediate reason for this difference in the way in which historical and sociological evidence comes into being is obvious: historians work "in the past", while sociologists *can also* work "in the present". However, behind this immediate reason lies the difference of emphasis that I earlier referred to: sociologists do not seek to tie their arguments to specific time and space co-ordinates so much as to test the extent of their generality. Thus, if a sociologist develops a theory intended to apply, say, to all industrial societies, it will be only sensible at all events to *begin* the examination of this theory through research conducted in contemporary rather than in past industrial societies; and hence through research that permits the generation of evidence rather than imposing a reliance upon relics.

If, then, there is here, as I would wish to maintain, a major difference between history and sociology as forms of disciplined enquiry, what follows from it for the uses of history in sociology? The main implication is, I believe, clear enough. Because sociologists have the possibility of producing their own evidence – over and above that of exploiting relics – *they are in a position of advantage that should not be disregarded or lightly thrown away.* In other words, sociologists should not readily and unthinkingly turn to history: they should do so, rather, only with good reasons and in full awareness of the limitations that they will thereby face.

Here again I am, I suspect, in some danger of being misunderstood. Let me therefore at once add that I do not in any way seek to suggest that sociology is in some sense a "superior" discipline to history: rather, I am concerned to bring out just how difficult history is – since, as will later emerge, I believe that some sociologists have clearly failed to appreciate this. Nor do I suppose that generated evidence, in contrast to that in the form of relics, is unproblematic. I am well aware that it too must always be critically viewed as regards its completeness as well as its reliability and validity, and indeed that in these latter respects special problems result precisely from the processes of generation. However, what I do wish to emphasize are the very real advantages that are gained where the nature and extent of available evidence is not restricted by the mere accidents of physical survival; where, moreover, the collection of evidence can be "designed" so as to meet the specific requirements of the enquiry in hand; and where questions of the quality of evidence can always be addressed, as they arise, by generating yet further evidence through which to check and test the original.[11]

## II

To develop these arguments, I now turn to particular cases. To begin with, it may be helpful if I give an example of what I would regard as a mistaken – one might say, perverse – recourse to history on the part of a sociologist. I take here Kai Erikson's book, *Wayward Puritans*, which is a study of social deviance within the seventeenth century Puritan community of Massachusetts Bay.

In his preface, Erikson states his aims clearly. He begins with certain hypotheses about social deviance drawn from a Durkheimian position, and he aims to examine two hypotheses in particular: first, that some amount of deviance is functional for a community in helping it to define its moral and social boundaries, and thus in preserving its stability; and secondly, that, because of this functionality, deviance within any community will tend to be at a fairly constant level over time. Erikson then proposes to take Massachusetts Bay as a case study:

> The purpose of the following study is to use the Puritan community as a setting in which to examine several ideas about deviant behaviour. In this sense the subject matter of the book is primarily sociological, even though the data found in most of its pages are historical.

And, he goes on:

> The data presented here have *not* been gathered in order to throw new light on the Puritan community in New England but to add something to our understanding of deviant behaviour in general, and thus the Puritan experience in America has been treated in these pages as an example of human life everywhere.[12]

Judged in the light of this statement, *Wayward Puritans* is, I would argue, a failure – and indeed a necessary failure – because of its reliance on historical materials. The hypotheses that Erikson starts from are not seriously examined, and could not be, simply because Erikson does not have the evidence needed for this among the relics at his disposal.

Thus, as regards the first hypothesis, on the functionality of deviance, Erikson draws largely on court records, indicating the response of the authorities to anti-nomianism, Quakerism and alleged witchcraft. But he has little evidence of how *the community at large*, as distinct from the authorities, reacted to such deviance or, for that matter, to its treatment by the authorities. In other words, he has no adequate basis on which to determine whether, in consequence of the deviance he refers to, there was, or was not, a stronger definition of the moral and social boundaries of the community. So far as popular perceptions and evaluations are concerned, he is without means of access.

Likewise, in treating the second hypothesis, on the constant level of deviance, Erikson has to rely on official crime statistics, which, for well known reasons, give only a very uncertain indication of the actual level of social deviance, and are influenced in their trend by a variety of other factors. However, unlike the sociologist of deviance working in contemporary society, Erikson cannot investigate in any detail the processes through which the official statistics were constituted, nor can he collect data of his own that could provide alternative estimates – as, say, through some form of "victim survey".

To be sure, the hypotheses that Erikson addresses are not ones that would be easily tested under any circumstances. But, given that they derive from a theory that pretends to a very high level of generality, there is all the more reason to ask why Erikson should impose upon himself the limitations that must follow from choosing a historical case. Why should he deny himself the possibility of being able to generate his own evidence, to his own design, and under conditions in which problems of reliability and validity could best be grappled with? Any sociologist, I would maintain, who is concerned with a theory that *can* be tested in the present should so test it, in the first place; for it is, in all probability, in this way that it can be tested most rigorously.[13]

I would now like to move on to consider cases where the recourse of sociologists to history *would* appear to have the good reasons that, I earlier maintained, should always be present. Here my aim is to illustrate what such reasons might be, but also – when they are acted upon – the difficulties that may be expected.

Sociologists, one might think, will most obviously need to turn to history where their interests lie in social change. However, it should be kept in mind that a recourse to the past – or, that is, to the relics thereof – is not the only means through which such interests may be pursued: life course, cohort or panel studies, for example, are all ways of studying social change on the basis of evidence that is, or has been, collected in the present. Sociologists, I would argue, are compelled into historical research only where their concern is with social change that is in fact historically defined: that is, with change not over some analytically specified length of time – such as, say, "the life-cycle" or "two generations" – but with change over a period of past time that has dates (even if not very precise ones) and that is related to a particular place. Sociologists have a legitimate, and necessary, concern with such historically defined social change because, as I have earlier suggested, they wish to know how widely over time and space their theories and hypotheses might apply.[14]

One illustration of what I have in mind here is provided by Michael Anderson's book, *Family structure in nineteenth century Lancashire* (1971). Anderson is concerned with the hypothesis that in the process of industrialization, pre-existing forms of "extended" family and kinship relations are disrupted. Specifically, he is interested in whether or not this hypothesis holds good in the British case – that of the "first industrial nation". Thus, to pursue this issue, Anderson aims to examine just what was happening to kinship relations in Britain at the time when, and in the place where, the "take-off" into industrialism is classically located. In contrast, then, with Erikson, Anderson has a quite clear rationale for turning to historical research.

A second illustration is provided by Gordon Marshall's book *Presbyteries and profits* (1980). Marshall is concerned with the "Weber thesis"– that a connection exists between the secular ethic of ascetic Protestantism and "the spirit of capitalism". In the long-standing debate on this thesis, the case of Scotland has several times been suggested as a critical one, in that, in the early modern period, Scotland had a great deal of ascetic Protestantism – that is, Calvinism – yet showed little in the way of capitalist development. Marshall's aim is then to re-examine the Scottish case for the period from around 1560 down to the Act of Union of 1707. Marshall points out that Weber himself always emphasized that his argument on the role of the Protestant ethic in the emergence of modern capitalism was intended to apply only to the early stages of this process: once a predominantly capitalist economy was established, its own exigencies – in the workplace and market – would themselves compel behaviour generally consistent with the "spirit of capitalism" without need of help from religion. Again, then, Marshall, like Anderson, has obviously good grounds for his recourse to history.

Now before proceeding further, I should make it clear that I have the highest regard for the two studies to which I have just referred. Both make signal contributions to the questions they address; and, for me, they stand as leading examples of how in fact historical sociology should be conceived and conducted. I say this because I want now to go on to emphasize the severe limitations to which the analyses of both authors are subject: *not* because of their deficiencies as sociologists, but simply because of the fact that they were forced into using historical evidence – forced into a reliance on relics – rather than being able to generate their own evidence within a contemporary society.

The relics on which Anderson chiefly relies are the original enumerators' books for the censuses of 1841, 1851 and 1861. On this basis, he can reconstruct household composition according to age, sex and kinship relations, and he can also to some extent examine the residential propinquity of kin. But this still leaves him a long way short of adequate evidence on the part actually played by kinship in the lives of the people he is studying and on the meanings of kinship for them. He attempts to fill out the essentially demographic data that he has from the enumerators' books by material from contemporary accounts. But these would, I fear, have at best to be categorized as "casual empiricism" and at worst as local gossip or travellers' tales. Titles such as *Walks in South Lancashire and on its borders, A visit to Lancashire in December 1862* and *Lancashire sketches* give the flavour.

Anderson is in fact entirely frank about the problem he faces. "It must of course be stressed", he writes, "that just because interaction with kin occurred it is no necessary indication that kinship was important. The real test, which is quite impossible in any precise way in historical work, would be to examine the extent to which kinship was given preference over other relational contacts (and the reasons for this preference), and the extent to which contacts with kin fulfilled functions which were not adequately met if kin did not provide them".[15]

The point I want to make here would perhaps best be brought out if one were to compare Anderson's study of kinship with one carried out in contemporary society – let us say, for example, Claude Fischer's study of kinship and of other "primary" relations in present-day San Francisco, *To dwell among friends*.[16] The only conclusion could be that the latter is greatly superior in the range and quality of data on which it draws, and in turn in the rigour and refinement of the analyses it can offer. And this point is, of course, not that Fischer is a better sociologist than Anderson but that he has an enormous advantage over Anderson in being able to generate his own data rather than having to rely on whatever relics might happen to be extant.

Turning to Marshall, one finds that he has problems essentially the same as those of Anderson. One of Marshall's main concerns is that Weber's position should be correctly understood – following the vulgarizations of Robertson, Tawney, Samuelson and other critics, and in this respect Marshall makes two main points. First, Weber was not so much concerned with the influence of official Calvinist doctrine on economic activity as with the consequences of *being* a believing Calvinist for the individual's conduct of everyday life – consequences that the individual might not even fully realize. In other words, Weber's thesis was ultimately not about theology but subculture and psychology. Secondly, Weber's argument was that the Protestant ethic was a necessary, but not a sufficient cause of the emergence of modern capitalism; there were necessary "material" factors also – such as access to physical resources and to markets, the availability of capital and credit, etc.

Thus, Marshall argues, in evaluating the Weber thesis, it is not enough to look simply for some overt association between theology, on the one hand, and the development of capitalist enterprise on the other. What is required is more subtle. It is evidence that believing Calvinists, on account of their acceptance of a Calvinist world view, were distinctively oriented to work in a regular, disciplined way, to pursue economic gain rationally and to accumulate rather than to consume extravagantly – so that, *if* other conditions were *also* met, capitalist enterprise would then flourish.

Marshall's position here is, I believe, entirely sound. But it leads him to problems of evidence that he can in fact never satisfactorily overcome despite his diligence in searching out new sources and his ingenuity is using known ones. And the basic difficulty is that relics from which inferences can systematically be made about the orientations to work and to money of early modern Scots are very few and far between.

In other words, what is crucially lacking – just as it was lacking for Anderson and indeed for Erikson – is material from which inferences might be made, with some assurance of representativeness, about the *patterns of social action* that are of interest within particular collectivities. As Clubb has observed, the data from which historians work only rarely allow access to the subjective orientations of actors *en masse*, and inferences made in this respect from actual behaviour tend always to be question-begging.[17] And Marshall, it should be said, like Anderson, sees the difficulty clearly enough. He acknowledges that it may well be that "the kind of data required in order to establish the ethos in which seventeenth-century Scottish business enterprises were run simply does not exist" – or, at least, not in sufficient quantity to allow one to test empirically whether Calvinism did indeed have the effect on mundane conduct that Weber ascribed to it.[18]

## III

Let me at this point recapitulate. I have argued that history and sociology differ perhaps most consequentially in the nature of the evidence on which they rely, and that this difference has major implications for the use of history in sociology. I have presented a case of what, from this standpoint, must be seen as a perverse recourse to history on the part of a sociologist; and I have now discussed two further cases where, in contrast, such a recourse was justifiable, indeed necessary, given the issues addressed, but where, none the less, serious difficulties arise because of the inadequacy of the relics as a basis for treating these issues.

To end with, however, I would like to move on from these instances of sociologists resorting to history in the pursuit of quite specific problems to consider – with my initial argument still in mind – a whole *genre* of sociology that is in fact *dependent upon history in its very conception*. I refer here to a kind of historical sociology clearly different to that represented by the work of Anderson or Marshall, and which has two main distinguishing features. First, it resorts to history because it addresses very large themes, which typically involve the tracing out of long-term "developmental" processes or patterns or the making of comparisons across a wide range of historical societies or even civilizations. And secondly, it is based largely or entirely not on inferences from relics but rather on "history" in the sense of what historians have written – or, in other words, not on primary but on secondary, or yet more derivative, sources.

The idea that sociologists might proceed by taking the results of historical research as their main empirical resource in developing wide-ranging generalizations and theories is not of course a new one. It was in fact a nineteenth-century commonplace. Its plainest expression was perhaps provided by Herbert Spencer when he wrote that, for him, sociology stood to works of history "much as a vast building stands related to the heaps of stones and bricks around it", and further, that "the highest office which the historian can discharge is that of so narrating the lives of nations, as to furnish materials for a Comparative Sociology".[19]

From the end of the nineteenth century, this understanding of the relationship between history and sociology met with severe criticism and rather rapidly lost support. Historians had indeed never taken kindly to the idea that they should serve as some kind of intellectual under-labourers; and sociologists became increasingly interested in developing their own methods of data collection.[20] However, in more recent times, a notable revival of what might be called "grand historical sociology" has occurred. This was led by the appearance in 1966 of Barrington Moore's *The social origins of dictatorship and democracy*, and

111

then consolidated in the USA by the subsequent work of Immanuel Wallerstein and Theda Skocpol, and in this country by that of Perry Anderson, with other authors such as John Hall and Michael Mann following in the wake.[21] What I would now wish to argue is that the practice of these authors does in fact raise again all the difficulties inherent in Spencer's programme, and that the use of history in sociology as exemplified in their work is problematic in a far more fundamental way than in any of the studies earlier considered.

The authors in question would certainly not wish to represent their position in terms similar to those of Spencer. They would rather incline to the idea that history and sociology are one and indivisible; and, instead of viewing historians *de haut en bas*, they would surely wish to include them in the joint enterprise as equal partners.[22] None the less, the fact remains that grand historical sociology in its twentieth-century form, just as in its nineteenth, takes secondary historical sources as its evidential basis, and must therefore encounter the methodological difficulties that are entailed even though its exponents have thus far shown little readiness to address, or even acknowledge, them.

The root of their predicament is richly ironical. The revival of grand historical sociology can be seen as one expression of the "reaction against positivism" within the sociological community to which I referred at the start; and yet its practitioners' own *modus operandi* — the use they seek to make of secondary sources — must depend upon what is an essentially positivistic conception of *historiography* — to which they would, I suspect, be reluctant to give any explicit support.

The catechism that I was put through as an undergraduate had a clear objective. It was to prompt a rejection of the view that the past — or at least certain well documented aspects of the past, such as "high" politics — could in principle be reconstructed, fact by fact, so that the distinction between history in the sense of what actually happened in the past and history in the sense of what is written about the past might be elided. Against this "positivist" conception of historiography — as it was indeed labelled[23] — it was urged upon us that historical facts could not be cognitively established as a collection of well defined items or entities, each independent of the rest, which, when taken together, would then dictate a specific and definitive version of the past. Rather, historical facts should be recognized as no more than "inferences from the relics"; and inferences that had always to be weighted, so to speak, according to the security of their grounding, which were often interdependent – that is, stood or fell together – and which were of course at all times open to restatement, whether radically or through the most subtle changes of nuance.

Now, to repeat, I very much doubt if grand historical sociologists would wish to take up the defence of positivist historiography as against this latter view. But it is difficult to see how, *in practice*, they can avoid *assuming* an essentially positivist position. For even if the procedures they follow in producing their sociology do not actually require the elision of the two senses of history, they still cannot afford to recognize a too indeterminate relation between them.

Grand historical sociologists have to treat the facts, or indeed concatenations of facts or entire "accounts", that they find in secondary sources *as if they were* relatively discrete and stable entities that can be "excerpted" and then brought together in order that some larger design may be realized. In anti-positivist vein, Carl Becker has expressly warned that historical facts should not be thought of as possessing "solidity", "definite shape" or "clear persistent outline", and that it is therefore especially inapt to liken them to building materials of any kind.[24] But the very procedures of grand historical sociologists push them back, willy-nilly, to Spencer's idea of using the stones and bricks of history to construct the great sociological edifice – and constructional metaphors do indeed reappear. Thus, for example, one finds Skocpol remarking that "primary research" – that the comparativist "has neither the time nor (all of) the appropriate skills to do" – "necessarily constitutes, in large amounts, the foundation upon which comparative studies are built".[25]

However, I would then wish to respond that the constructions that result are likely to be dangerously unsound. In particular, I would argue that in grand historical sociology the links that are claimed, or supposed, between evidence and argument tend to be both *tenuous* and *arbitrary* to a quite unacceptable degree.

As regards the first charge, it is, I would suggest, instructive to consider some fairly specific argument advanced by a grand historical sociologist, and to note the "authorities" that are invoked as providing its factual basis; then, to work back from these citations – through perhaps other intermediate sources that are involved – until one comes to direct references to relics of some kind. What, I believe, one will typically find is that the trail is longer and harder to follow than one might

113

have expected, and that, not infrequently, it reaches no very satisfactory end.

For example, in *Social origins of dictatorship and democracy*, Moore spends several pages reviewing aspects of English economic history over the late medieval and early modern periods, and then concludes as follows:

> In the light of this general background there would seem to be little reason to question the thesis that commercially minded elements among the landed upper classes, and to a lesser extent among the yeomen, were among the main forces opposing the King and royal attempts to preserve the old order, and therefore an important cause, though not the only one, that produced the Civil War.[26]

However, if one actually examines the sources that Moore cites, both before and after this passage, the grounding of his argument is very far from apparent. Indeed, it is quite unclear just what is the evidence, at the level of relics, in the light of which there would be "little reason to question" the thesis that Moore advances. In the "authorities" referred to – the main ones are Tawney's *The agrarian problem of the sixteenth century*, his essay on "The rise of the gentry" and Campbell's *The English yeoman* – there is in fact remarkably little "evidence" bearing in any direct way on the crucial link that Moore seeks to establish between economic position and political action.[27] And such as there is cannot be regarded as evidence in the sense that relics themselves are evidence or, for that matter, the data of a social survey are evidence. Rather, what one has are series of inferences, often complex and indeed often quite speculative, which are drawn from relics that are manifestly incomplete, almost certainly unrepresentative, and in various other ways problematic – as the authors in question are very well aware. In other words, such "facts" as are here available cannot be understood as separate, well defined "modules", easily carried off for sociological construction purposes, but would be better regarded simply as strands in heavily tangled, yet still often rather weak skeins of interpretation.

In effect, then, what grand historical sociologists seem to me to be generally doing is not developing an argument on the basis of evidence – in the manner of "primary" historians or again of sociologists working on their "own" research data – but, rather, engaging in interpretation that is of, at least, a second-order kind: that is, in interpretation of interpretations of, perhaps, interpretations. And in consequence, I would maintain, the connection between the claims they make about the past and relics that could conceivably serve as warrant for these claims is often – as in the passage from Moore that I have quoted – quite impossibly loose. Following the practices that are here illustrated, history must indeed become, in Froude's words, "a child's box of letters with which we can spell any word we please".[28]

As regards my second charge, that of arbitrariness, the idea of historiography as a matter of inferences from relics that are finite and incomplete is again directly relevant. It follows from this that historians working on the same topic, and indeed on the same relics, may quite reasonably come to quite different conclusions – as of course they may for other reasons too. But it further follows that there may be little or no possibility of their differences ever being resolved because the relics that would be necessary to settle the disputed issues simply do not exist. For grand historical sociologists, this then raises a major problem: where historians disagree, and may have perhaps to remain in disagreement, *which* secondary account should be accepted? By what criteria should the grand historical sociologist opt for one of two, or more, conflicting interpretations?

Thus, to return to Moore and his treatment of the economic and social origins of the English Civil War, the question one may ask is: why, on this notoriously controversial matter, and one plagued by a lack of relevant evidence, does Moore choose largely to follow what has come to be thought of (not altogether fairly) as the "Tawney" interpretation rather than any of its rivals? By the time Moore was writing, it should be said, the idea that the "rising", commercially oriented gentry were key actors in the parliamentary opposition to the King and his defeat in the Civil War was in fact fast losing ground among English historians, both to interpretations that gave the leading role to other socio-economic groupings and, more importantly, to ones that questioned whether political allegiance in the Civil War period had any close association at all with economic position and interest.[29]

The answer to the question I have posed is, I believe, as obvious as it is unsatisfactory. Moore favours the interpretation that fits best with his overall thesis of the "three routes to modernity"; in other words,

115

that which allows the English Civil War to be seen as an instance of a successful "bourgeois revolution". However, he still fails to present any serious case for this choice. Supportive sources simply receive accolades, such as "excellent analysis" or "unsurpassed account", while less congenial ones are disparaged as "conservative historiography".[30]

This clearly will not do. But if mere tendentiousness is not the solution, what is? In the end, of course, any rational way of evaluating a secondary source must involve some judgement on the inferences made from the primary sources – that is, from the relics. But once this is recognized, the methodological bind in which grand historical sociologists find themselves becomes only more apparent. Their large designs mean, they tell us, that they cannot themselves be expected to work directly from the relics but must rely on the studies of specialist authorities. However, they are then either forced into positivistic assumptions concerning the "hardness" and "solidity" – and also the "transportability" – of the evidence that these works can yield; or, if they accept that what these sources provide is no more than rival complexes of inference and interpretation, then they must explain how they propose to choose among them *without knowledge of* the primary sources.[31]

Since I have been so critical of the methodological basis of grand historical sociology, I should, before finishing, consider what its exponents have themselves had to say on the matter. In fact, as I have already implied, they have said remarkably little. Methodological issues tend to be raised, if at all, in the early pages of their books, but then only to be dealt with in a quite perfunctory – and unconvincing – manner.[32] However, there is one statement by Skocpol, from the concluding chapter of the collection she edited, *Vision and method in historical sociology*, which is of interest in several respects.

Skocpol writes as follows:

> Because wide-ranging comparisons are so often crucial for analytic historical sociologists, they are more likely to use secondary sources of evidence than those who apply models to, or develop interpretations of, single cases . . . From the point of view of historical sociology . . . a dogmatic insistence on redoing primary research for every investigation would be disastrous; it would rule out most comparative-historical research. If a topic is too big for purely primary research – *and*

116

if excellent studies by specialists are already available in some profusion – secondary sources are appropriate as the basic source of evidence for a given study. Using them is not different from survey analysts reworking the results of previous surveys rather than asking all questions anew.[33]

I would note, first of all, about this passage how clearly it shows the pressure that bears on grand historical sociologists to move towards the positivistic, Spencerian programme – "excellent" historical studies by specialists can be "the basic source of evidence" for the wide-ranging sociologist. And also revealing is the reference to "redoing primary research" – as if it were apparent that the same result as before would necessarily emerge.

Secondly, I would point out that Skocpol is quite mistaken in the analogy she seeks to draw with survey-based research. The "secondary analysis" of survey data to which she refers is different from the grand historical sociologist's use of secondary sources, precisely because it does entail going back to the "relics": that is, at least to the original data-tapes and perhaps also to the original questionnaires or interview schedules. And it is then these materials that serve the secondary analyst as evidence – *not* the interpretations of the original analyst, which may be, and indeed often are, disputed. Thus, a closer parallel would be between the secondary analyst of surveys and the historian who again works through and reinterprets a body of source materials discovered and initially analyzed by a predecessor.

Thirdly, I would remark that by way of providing a rationale for the methodology of grand historical sociology, Skocpol has little at all to offer. Apart from her – mistaken – *tu quoque* argument directed at survey researchers, all she in fact says is that it would be "disastrous" for grand historical sociologists if they were to be forced back to primary sources – which is scarcely a way of convincing sceptics.

What is actually of greatest interest is what Skocpol goes on to acknowledge in the paragraph that immediately follows the one from which I quoted: namely, that "it remains true that comparative historical sociologists have not so far worked out clear, consensual rules and procedures for the valid use of secondary sources as evidence" and further, that in this respect "varying historiographical interpretations" is one obvious problem to be addressed. "Certain principles", Skocpol believes, "are likely to emerge as such rules are developed." But, one must conclude, so far at least, grand historical sociology is *not* significantly rule-governed; its practitioners enjoy a delightful freedom to play "pick-and-mix" in history's sweetshop.[34]

# IV

To sum up, then, I have argued that the view that history and sociology "are and always have been the same thing" is mistaken and – dangerously misleading. Sociology must, it is true, always be a historical discipline; sociologists can never "escape" from history. It is therefore highly desirable that they should be historically aware – by which I mean, aware of the historical settings and limits that their analyses will necessarily possess, even if they may never be precisely determined. But history and sociology can, and should, still be regarded as significantly different intellectual enterprises. A crucial source of the difference, I have sought to show, lies in the nature of the evidence that the two disciplines use – in the fact that historians have for the most part to rely on evidence that they can discover in the relics of the past, while sociologists have the considerable privilege of being able to generate evidence in the present.

As regards, then, the use of history in sociology, what I have sought to stress is that sociologists should not underestimate, or readily give up, the advantages that they can gain from having evidence that is "tailor made", whereas historians have usually to "cut their coats according to their cloth". Where sociologists are compelled into historical research by the very logic of their inquiries, then, I have suggested, they must be ready for a harder life – for research typically conducted, as one historian has put it, "below the data poverty line".[35] They must not only learn new techniques but also to accept new frustrations; in particular, those that come from realizing that issues of crucial interest are, and will probably remain, beyond their cognitive reach. Historical sociologists such as Anderson and Marshall have learnt well; and much of what they can in turn teach us stems from their sensitivity to just what manner of inferences the relics available to them can, and cannot, sustain. In contrast, grand historical sociologists seem to me to have, so far at least, shied away from the major intellectual challenges that historiography poses, and to have traded implicitly on a conception of it that I doubt if they would wish openly to defend.

Until, then, they do meet the challenges before them, and provide a coherent methodology for their work, the question must remain of how far this does possess a real basis in the relics of the past or merely an illusory one in a scattering of footnotes.

# Notes

In addition to being delivered as the 1989 Marshall Lecture at the University of Southampton, versions of the paper were also given at seminars at the Universities of Oxford, Exeter and Stockholm, and I benefited greatly from comments by participants. Further thanks are due to Klas Amark, Robert Erikson, Stephen Mennell, Patrick O'Brien and, especially, Gordon Marshall and Lucia Zedner.

[Editor's note: Following the original publication of this chapter in the *British Journal of Sociology* in 1991, the journal received several submissions responding to the critique of "grand historical sociology" contained in it, and subsequently published a symposium debate on the subject of "The uses of history in sociology" in the March 1994 issue, consisting of articles by Joseph M. Bryant (1994), Nicky Hart (1994), Nicos Mouzelis (1994) and Michael Mann (1994) with a reply by John Goldthorpe (1994). The notes that follow here are as in the original version in the *British Journal of Sociology*, 1991.]

1. Abrams 1980: x; Giddens 1979: 230.
2. The distinction originates in the *Methodenstreit* in nineteenth-century German universities. For a brief discussion, see Collingwood 1946: 165–83. An interesting example of its use in the period referred to in the text, with the aim of differentiating yet at the same time showing the complementarity of history and sociology, is Bierstedt 1959: 95–104.
3. Goldthorpe 1962: 26–9, reprinted in Bulmer 1983: 162–74.
4. Clearly, my position has in important respects changed since the time of my earlier paper – as a result, I would like to think, of my having had much more experience, whether first- or secondhand, of research into societies both past and present. However, both history and sociology, and the typical orientations of their practitioners, have also changed. Today, interdisciplinary, or rather a-disciplinary, enthusiasm would seem to me to have gone much too far, at least on the sociological side. And I find it of interest that a similar view has also been taken from the side of history by a distinguished practitioner who is by no means unsympathetic to sociology: see Stone 1987a,b.
5. Quoted in Stone 1987a: 31.
6. This use of history is that with which I have in fact been most concerned in my own work on comparative social mobility. The classic programme for a comparative macro-sociology is that set by Przeworski & Teune 1970, which has as its ideal objective "the replacement of the names of nations with the names of variables". In so far as, in explaining cross-national variation in social

structure or process (e.g. in mobility rates and patterns), the sociologist is forced into invoking institutional or cultural features, or indeed events, as specific features of national histories, then *pro tanto* the Przeworski–Teune programme must fall short of realization. (Cf. Erikson & Goldthorpe 1987: 54–77,145–66.)

7. For pertinent but brief comments by previous authors, see Marshall 1963: 38 esp.; and Bell & Newby 1981: 5–19.

8. I was myself put through the catechism by G. J. Renier, a remarkable teacher, whose book *History: its purpose and method* (1950) was our main text and is now unduly neglected. Also influential was Collingwood, *The idea of history* (1946), especially the Epilegomena.

9. Cf. Murphey 1973; Clubb 1980: 13–24.

10. The one instance of which I am aware in which historians likewise generate their evidence is when they engage in "oral" history. Here too, though, it may be noted that problems of survival, and in turn of representativeness, are of large importance.

11. Another way of putting much of this is to say, as does Clubb (1980: 20), that "The source materials upon which historians must rely are virtually by definition 'process produced'" and that they are, moreover, "the residual process-produced data that have survived the ravages of time". Clubb notes that historians occasionally have at their disposal data that were collected for social scientific purposes, and that this is likely to be a more common situation for future historians. However, he then rightly comments that ". . . we can also imagine that historians in the future will regard these data as no less process produced in this case by the process of social research as archaically practiced in the mid-twentieth century – and will bemoan the fact that the wrong data were collected, the wrong questions asked, and that underlying assumptions and methods were not better documented".

12. Erikson 1966: vii–viii, emphasis in original.

13. Skocpol treats Erikson's intentions as being "characteristic of historical sociologists who apply general models to history". See Skocpol 1984: 364. There can of course be little value in such a procedure unless there are *independent* grounds for believing that the models have some validity. But it should in any event be noted that Erikson himself is clear that his concern is (see text) "to examine several ideas about deviant behaviour" – for which he does not appear to claim any prior validity.

14. It may also be argued that sociologists have a legitimate recourse to history where their concern is with phenomena such as revolutions, major economic crises, mass panics or crazes, etc., which not only happen rather infrequently but are in any event more amenable to investigation in retrospect than as they occur. I am not fully convinced by this argument but, for present purposes, it is not necessary to contest it. Nor do I take up here a concern with history displayed by some sociologists that I would most certainly regard as illegitimate: that is, a concern with "theorizing" history so as, it is hoped, to secure a

cognitive grasp on its "movement" or "logic". I have written critically else-where on the persistence of such historicism: see, e.g. Goldthorpe 1971: 263–88, and Goldthorpe 1979.

15. Anderson 1971: 62.

16. Fischer 1982.

17. Clubb 1980: 20.

18. Marshall 1980: 35.

19. Spencer 1904, vol. II: 185 and Spencer 1861: 29.

20. An early but cogent, and, I suspect, highly influential, attack on Spencer by a pre-eminent historian was Maitland 1911. Note also Collingwood's critique of the last phase of "scissors-and-paste" historiography, that of the "pigeon-holers", whose approach was: "Very well: let us put together all the facts that are known to historians, look for patterns in them, and then extrapolate these patterns into a theory of universal history" (1946: 263–6). On the sociological side, the late nineteenth and early twentieth centuries saw of course the beginnings in Britain of sample survey methods and a growing interest in other means of data collection. (Cf. S. & B. Webb 1932.)

21. Moore 1966; Wallerstein, 3 vols, 1974, 1980, 1989; Skocpol 1979; Anderson 1974a, b; Hall 1985; Mann 1986. It might be argued that this "new wave" of grand historical sociology was in fact led by S. N. Eisenstadt's study, *The politi-cal systems of empires* (1963). But Eisenstadt's influence would seem to have been clearly less than that of Moore chiefly, I suspect, because his highly academic structural functionalism accorded far less well with the prevailing mood of the later 1960s than did the *marxisant* tone and explicitly "radical" commitment of Moore's work.

22. Thus, for example, in the collection of essays edited by Skocpol, *Vision and method in historical sociology* (1984) consideration is given to the work of histo-rians such as Marc Bloch, Charles Tilly and E. P. Thompson alongside that of authors such as Eisenstadt, Moore, Wallerstein and Anderson. Admirers of Bloch, in particular, might well be led to ask "Que diable allait-il faire dans cette galère?"

23. See, for example, Collingwood 1946: 126–33. Then, as apparently later (cf. Carr 1961, Ch.1), the classic expositors of such positivism in historiography were taken to be von Ranke and, in Britain, Lord Acton.

24. C. Becker, "What are historical facts?" in Meyerhoff (ed.) 1955: 120–37.

25. Skocpol 1979: xiv.

26. Moore 1966: 14.

27. Tawney 1912, and Tawney 1941, reprinted with a "Postscript" in Carus-Wilson 1954; Campbell, 1942. It must be emphasized that none of these three studies is in fact concerned with the Civil War in any direct way, and that references to it occur only rather incidentally.

28. Froude 1884, vol.I: 21.

29. An essay important for its catalytic effect was Hexter 1958 and then in an enlarged version in Hexter 1961. For a more recent critique of "social change

explanations" of the English Civil War – but certainly not one that could be dismissed as sociologically unsophisticated – see Clark 1986, ch.3 esp.

30. See, for example, Moore 1966: 6, 14 and the Appendix. In the Appendix, "A note on statistics and conservative historiography", Moore takes up the difficulties posed for his interpretation of the Civil War by D. Brunton & D. H. Pennington's *Members of the Long Parliament* (1954), which, as Moore notes, led Tawney himself to acknowledge that the division between Royalists and Parliamentarians within the Long Parliament "had little connection with diversities of economic interest and social class". Moore then tries (pp. 511–12) to rework Brunton & Pennington's statistics to save what he takes to be Tawney's thesis against Tawney's own abandonment of it – but succeeds only in providing a nice example of the ecological fallacy.

It might be added here that the treatment of the English Civil War by both Wallerstein and Anderson is no more satisfactory. Wallerstein, who claims that "contrapuntal controversial work" is a positive advantage for his enterprise (1974: 8), reviews a wider range of literature than Moore but by an eirenical *tour de force* still ends up where he wants to be: i.e. able to claim that the English Civil War, though not a direct struggle between classes, none the less resulted from the formation of an agricultural capitalist class that the old aristocracy was forced to accommodate and in part to merge with, thus leading to the early creation in England of a "national bourgeoisie" (see esp. 1974: 256, 269, 282, 297). It must, however, be pointed out that of the "authorities" whom Wallerstein cites, at least as many would reject this conclusion as would accept it.

Anderson, in contrast, refers to only a very limited number of secondary (or tertiary) sources and then, effectively disregarding all controversy, blandly asserts (1974b: 142): "English Absolutism was brought to a crisis by aristocratic particularism and clannic desperation on its periphery; forces that lay historically behind it. But it was felled at the centre by a commercialized gentry, a capitalist city, a commoner artisanate and yeomanry: forces pushing beyond it. Before it could reach the age of maturity, English Absolutism was cut off by a bourgeois revolution." Once more, it must be emphasized that it is essentially the interpretation of the English Civil War as a "bourgeois revolution" that has been challenged by "revisionist" historians over the last two decades or more.

My own judgement would be that the revisionists have indeed succeeded in undermining the supposed evidence for such an interpretation. But, further, I would doubt that even if there *were* a valid "social change explanation" of the English Civil War, adequate relics could be found to allow its validity to be demonstrated. What Hexter remarked (1961: 149) apropos the initial Tawney versus Trevor-Roper debate is likely to remain the last word: "And what such masters of the materials of seventeenth century history and of historical forensics cannot prove when they set their minds to it, is not likely ever to be proved."

31. Where historians themselves draw on secondary sources, as for example, in situating their own primary research or in writing "surveys" of a field, issues of the availability, quality, etc. of sources are typically discussed. Moreover, in the latter case at least, and likewise in the writing of textbooks, authors are not under pressure to defend a particular interpretation but can present a review of different positions. Grand historical sociologists, in contrast, usually cannot afford such even-handedness; they need to use – that is to choose among – secondary sources as evidence for or against a particular thesis. Furthermore, the central theses argued for by authors such as Moore, Wallerstein and Anderson are ones that they themselves clearly see as being politically highly consequential, so that questions of how far their use of secondary sources is politically influenced, and of what checks on political bias *they* would believe appropriate, inevitably arise.

32. See, e.g. Moore 1966: x–xi; Skocpol 1979: xiv–xv; Anderson 1974a: 8; Mann 1986: vii–viii, 3–4, 31–2.

33. Skocpol 1984: 382.

34. Unlike Skocpol, the other authors earlier cited do not even appear to recognize the need for a methodology. Their main justification for grand historical sociology would seem to be simply that it gives "the broad view" and is thus a necessary complement to "specialist" history. Thus Moore writes (1966: xi): "That comparative analysis is no substitute for detailed investigation of specific cases is obvious." But he goes on: "Generalizations that are sound resemble a large-scale [*sic*] map of an extended terrain, such as an airplane pilot might use in crossing a continent. Such maps are essential for certain purposes just as more detailed maps are necessary for others." Moore's cartography inspires no more confidence than his historiography. Assuming that in the above he means "small-scale" not "large-scale", a small-scale map, useful for an "extended terrain", is dependent for its accuracy on the detailed surveying from which it is built up. And likewise, as a "cliometric" and a "conventional" historian have written together, "the quality of an historical interpretation is critically dependent on the quality of the details out of which it is spun. Time and again the interpretation of major historical events, sometimes of whole areas, has been transformed by the correction of apparently trivial details" (See Fogel & Elton 1983: 125.)

It should also be said that the methodology of grand historical sociology has attracted little attention from writers concerned with the methodology of the social sciences in general. One essay by Johann Galtung (1979) may be noted, though its contribution to practice does not seem large.

35. Clubb 1980: 20.

# CHAPTER 7

# Ruling class strategies and citizenship

## Michael Mann

### Marshall's theory

Novel, important and true ideas are rare. Such ideas that are then developed into a coherent theory are even scarcer. T. H. Marshall is one of the very few to have had at least one such idea, and to develop it. That is why it is important to understand and to improve upon his theory of citizenship.

Marshall believed that citizenship has rendered class struggle innocuous; yet citizenship is also in continuous tension, even war, with the class inequalities that capitalism generates. He identified three stages of the struggle for, and attainment of, citizenship: *civil*, *political* and *social*. Civil citizenship emerged in the eighteenth century. It comprised "rights necessary for individual freedom – liberty of the person, freedom of speech, thought and faith, the right to own property and to conclude valid contracts, and the right to justice". Political citizenship emerged in the nineteenth century: "the right to participate in the exercise of political power, as a member of a body invested with political authority or as an elector of the members of such a body". The third stage, social citizenship, developed through the twentieth century: "the whole range from the right to a modicum of economic welfare and security to the right to share to the full in the social heritage and to live the life of a civilized being according to the standards prevailing in the society". It is what we mean now by the welfare state and social democracy.

Through these stages the major classes of modern capitalism, bourgeoisie and proletariat, institutionalized their struggles with the *ancien régime* and with each other. Citizenship and capitalism were still at war, Marshall declared, but it was institutionalized, rule-governed warfare. Such was the model developed in his famous 1949 lecture, *Citizenship and social class* (1963). It has continued to seem true and important. Major sociologists like Reinhard Bendix, Ralf Dahrendorf, Ronald Dore, A. H. Halsey, S. M. Lipset, David Lockwood and Peter Townsend have acknowledged his influence (e.g. Lipset 1973, Lockwood 1974, Halsey 1984). It remains strong today (see, for example, the recent admiring work by Turner 1986). This is for a good reason: Marshall's view of citizenship is essentially true – at least as a description of what has actually happened in Britain.

There is one rather remarkable feature of *Citizenship and social class*. It is entirely about Great Britain. There is not a single mention of any other country. I write Great Britain rather than United Kingdom, because there is no reference to Northern Ireland, which would not fit well into his theory. Did Marshall regard Britain as typical of the capitalist West as a whole? He does not explicitly say so. Yet the most general level of the argument explores the tension between economic inequalities and demands for popular participation, both generated everywhere by the rise of capitalism. This certainly implies a general evolutionary approach, and indeed he does intermittently use the term "evolution". In his book *Social policy* (1975), evidence from other countries is only introduced to illustrate variations on a common, British theme. Finally, others have used his model in explicitly evolutionary theories of the development of modern class relations (e.g. Dahrendorf 1959: 61–4). Flora & Heidenheimer (1981: 20–21) have observed that general theories of the modern welfare state have been dominated by British experience, chronicled especially by Marshall and Richard Titmuss.

## Six counter-theses

I wish to deviate from this Anglophile and evolutionary model in six ways.

1. The British strategy of citizenship described by Marshall has been only one among five pursued by advanced industrial

countries. I call these the *liberal, reformist, authoritarian monarchist, Fascist* and *authoritarian socialist* strategies.

2. All five strategies proved themselves reasonably adept at handling modern class struggle. They all converted the head-on collision of massive, antagonistic social classes into conflicts that were less class-defined, more limited and complex, sometimes more orderly, sometimes more erratic. Thus evolutionary tales are wrong. There has been no single best way of institutionalizing class conflict in industrial society, but at least five potentially durable forms of institutionalized conflict and mixes of citizen rights.

3. In explaining how such different strategies arise, I will stress the role of ruling classes. By "ruling class" I mean a combination of the dominant economic class and the political and military rulers. I do not mean to imply that such groups were unchanging or even united – indeed the degree of their cohesion will figure importantly in my narrative. But I do imply the pair of general explanatory precepts expressed in (4) and (5) below.

4. Influence on social structure varies according to power. As a ruling class possesses most power, its strategies matter most. In fact, many anciens régimes could survive the onslaught of emergent classes with a few concessions here and there. Neither the bourgeoisie nor the proletariat has been as powerful as has been argued by the dominant schools of sociology, liberal, reformist (like Marshall) and Marxist. Indeed, ruling class strategies tended to determine the nature of the social movements generated by bourgeoisie and proletariat, especially whether they were liberal, reformist or revolutionary. This argument has also been made by Lipset (1985: Ch. 6).

5. Tradition matters. We generally exaggerate the transformative powers of the Industrial Revolution. That revolution was preceded by centuries of structural change – the commercialization of agriculture, the globalization of trade, the consolidation of the modern state, the mechanization of war, the secularization of ideology. If *anciens régimes* had learned to cope with these changes, they could master the problems of an industrial society with traditional strategies, updated. If not, they were usually already vulnerable and internally divided before the actual bourgeois or proletarian onslaught. Others have also stressed the survival of

tradition through the Industrial Revolution – classically Moore (1966) and Rokkan (1970), more recently Mayer (1981) and Corrigan & Sayer (1985).

6. The durability of regime strategies has been due less to their superior internal efficiency than to geopolitics – and specifically to victory in world wars. The geopolitical and military influences on society have been considerable but neglected in sociological theory. However, they have recently been receiving the attention they deserve (e.g. Skocpol 1979; Mann 1980, 1986; Giddens 1985; Hall 1985; Shaw 1987).

Let us approach the historical record with these six theses in mind. What were the traditional regime strategies used to cope with the initial rise of the bourgeoisie?

## Absolute and constitutional regimes

We can divide the regimes of pre-industrial Europe into approximations to two ideal types, absolute monarchies and constitutional regimes (for a fuller elaboration see Mann 1993).

By 1800 the principal absolutists were Russia, Prussia and Austria. Their monarch's formal *despotic* powers were largely unlimited (Mann 1984). Citizenship was unknown. The rule of law supposedly operated, but personal liberties, and freedom of the press and association could be suspended arbitrarily. Indeed, any conception of universal rights was restrained by the proliferation of particularistic statuses, possessed by corporate groups – estates of the realm, corporations of burghers, lawyers, merchants and artisan guilds. Yet the real, *infrastructural* powers of the monarchs were far from absolute. They required the co-operation of the regionally and locally powerful. Repression was cumbersome and costly, and far more effective if used together with "divide-and-rule" negotiations with corporate groups. The monarch's crucial power was tactical freedom: the capacity to act arbitrarily both in conducting negotiation and in using force. It is important to realize that these three characteristics – arbitrary divide-and-rule, selective tactical repression and corporate negotiations – survived intact into the twentieth century.

Britain and the United States were the main constitutional regimes. There civil citizenship was well developed. Individual life and property were legally guaranteed, and freedom of the press and of association were partially recognized – they were "licensed" under discernible rules. Political citizenship also existed, though it was confined to the propertied classes who "virtually represented" the rest. Social citizenship was as absent here as in absolutist regimes. All this was well understood by Marshall.

Not all regimes were either predominantly absolutist or constitutional. Some formerly absolutist regimes had experienced revolution or serious disorder, and were now bitterly contested between constitutionalists and reactionaries: France after 1789, Spain and several Italian states. In others absolutism and constitutionalism merged through less violent, more orderly conflict: principally the Scandinavian countries.

Capitalist industrialization changed much, but we can nonetheless see the initial imprint of these four types of regime: absolutist, constitutional, contested and merged. Let us follow this in more detail, concentrating in turn on the USA, Britain and Germany.

## From constitutionalism to liberalism – the USA and Britain

In Britain and the USA the rise of liberalism strengthened civil and political citizenship. The rule of law over life, property, freedom of speech, assembly and press was extended, as was the political franchise. But any social citizenship remained equivocal. The regime provided basic subsistence to the poor out of charity and a desire to avoid sedition. But provision came from local worthies and private insurance; and legislation encouraged rather than enforced. Subsistence was not a right of all, but the result of a mixture of market forces, the duty to work and save, and private and public charity. The state was not interventionist or "corporatist": interest group conflict was predominantly left to the economic and political market places, its limits defined by law. However, collectivities could legitimately exploit their market powers, and the regime devised rules of the ensuing game. Under liberalism individuals and interest groups, but not classes, could be accommodated within the regime. Repression, now fully institutionalized, was reserved only for those who went outside the rules of the game.

Such was one basic strategy of dealing with the rise of the bourgeoisie. But could it cope with the working class? The two main cases, the United States and Britain, coped differently.

In the USA labour was eventually absorbed into the liberal regime. A broad coalition, from landowners and merchants down to small farmers and artisans, had made the revolution. White, adult males could not be easily excluded from civil and political citizenship. By the early 1840s all of them, in all states, possessed the vote – 50 years earlier than anywhere else, 50 years before the emergence of a powerful labour movement. Thus the political demands of labour could be gradually expressed as an interest group *within* an existing federal political constitution and competitive party system. As Katznelson (1981) has shown, workers' political life became organized more by locality, ethnicity and patronage than by work, unions or class. In the sphere of work there was severe and violent conflict, between unions and employers aided by government and the law courts. But here too the ruling class eventually came to accept the legitimacy of unions in essentially liberal terms; while the Wagner Act allowed unions to negotiate freely, Taft-Hartley compelled them to act only as the balloted representatives of their individual members.

The USA gives us the truest picture of what would have happened to class conflict without the politics of citizenship. If class struggle had only concerned the Marxist agenda, of relations of production, labour processes, and direct conflict between capitalists and workers, then liberal regimes would have dominated industrial society. As the (white) working class was civilly and politically inside the regime, it had little need for the great ideologies of the proletariat excluded from citizenship: socialism and anarchism. American trade unions became like other collective interest groups exploiting their market power. If workers did not possess effective market powers, they would be outside this liberal regime and tempted by socialism and anarchism. But they could be repressed – with the consent of labour organizations accepting the rules of the game. Consequently, neither class nor socialism has ever appeared as a fundamental organizing principle of power in the United States. Those groups who in other countries constituted the core of the labour and socialist movement – male artisans, heavy industrial, mining and transport workers – became predominantly interest groups inside the liberal regime, while the unskilled, those in other sectors, females and ethnic minorities were left outside.

Liberalism was thus the first viable regime strategy of an advanced industrial society. It still dominates the United States, and is also found in Switzerland. In these countries social citizenship is still marginal. Economic subsistence and participation is provided overwhelmingly out of the economic buoyancy of their national capitalisms, from which the large majority can insure themselves against adversity. Below that, there are welfare provisions against actual starvation, though they vary between states and cantons, are often denied to immigrant workers, and are sometimes provided only if the poor show their "worth". It is closer to the eighteenth-century Poor Law than to what Marshall meant by social citizenship. Its social struggles remained defined by liberalism. If civil and political citizenship could be attained early, before the class struggles of industrialism, then social citizenship need not follow. The most powerful capitalist state has not followed Marshall's road. It shows no signs of doing so.

But Britain strayed from liberalism towards reformism, as Marshall depicted. Britain's initial struggle for liberal political citizenship was more of a class struggle, waged predominantly by the rising bourgeoisie and independent artisans. However, the British constitution has not excluded classes or status groups as systematically as have most constitutions of continental Europe. The franchise before 1832 was extraordinarily uneven; then, until 1867, it passed through the middle of the artisan group; between 1867 and 1884 it grew to include 65 per cent of the adult male population. In 1918 all adult males and many females were included, and in 1929 all females. Hence at any particular point in time emerging dissidents – petty bourgeois radicals, artisan and skilled factory worker socialists, feminists – have been partially inside, partially outside the state. Thus liberalism and socialism have both remained attractive ideologies. Indeed, perhaps only the splits in the Liberal Party consequent on the First World War may have ensured that a joint liberal/reformist ideology would be carried principally by an independent Labour Party, rather than through Lib–Lab politics. Britain has enshrined the rule of both interest groups and classes, jointly. The labour movement is part sectional interest group, part class movement, irremediably reformist, virtually unsullied by Marxist or anarchist revolutionary tendencies.

Britain is thus a mixed liberal/reformist case. The state remains liberal, unwilling to intervene actively in interest-group bargaining – it has incorporated the lower classes into the rules of the game, not into the institutions of "corporatism". Yet social citizenship has advanced somewhat beyond the American level. The state guarantees subsistence through the welfare state, but this meshes into, rather than replaces, private market and insurance schemes. Thus its major social struggles are fought out in terms of an ideological debate, and a real political pendulum, between liberalism and social democracy. In reaction to the Thatcher Government's liberal strategy, the reformist strategy is now becoming more popular again.

## Contested and merged regimes – France, Spain, Italy, Scandinavia

In France, Spain and Italy, reactionaries (usually monarchist and clerical) and secular liberals struggled over political citizenship for most of the nineteenth and twentieth centuries, with many violent changes of regime. Citizenship remained bitterly disputed, though there was undoubtedly some secular progress in the Marshallian direction. As radical bourgeoisie, peasantry and labour were erratically but persistently denied political citizenship, these developed competing excluded ideologies. Sometimes they rejected the state, as in anarchism and syndicalism; sometimes they embraced it, as in Marxist socialism. The fierce competition between anarcho-syndicalism, revolutionary socialism and reformist socialism was not solved until after the Second World War, for reasons I mention later.

In several other countries the absolutist/constitutional struggle proceeded to more peaceful victory for a broad alliance between bourgeoisie, labour and small farmers. Over the first four decades of this century they achieved civil and political citizenship, and proceeded furthest along the road to social citizenship. The absolutist inheritance, never violently repudiated (unlike in France), provided a more corporatist tinge to regime negotiations that still endures. The Scandinavian countries are the paradigm cases of this route, less affected by the dislocations of war than any other. This second road, a corporatist style of reformism, corresponds closely to Marshall's vision (more so than the British case does). Its social struggles are avowedly class ones, but they are managed by joint negotiations, and constrained more by pragmatic that ideological limits. Continuing reform, it is agreed, will be limited primarily by the growth record of each national economy.

But to investigate properly the absolutist legacy suggests a methodology of examining the "purer" and longer-lasting cases of absolutism, in Russia, Austria, Japan and especially in Prussia/Germany.

## From absolutism to authoritarian monarchy – Germany, Austria, Russia, Japan

The absolutist regimes entered the nineteenth century with two conflicting predispositions. First, monarch, nobility and Church were unwilling to grant *universal* citizen rights to either bourgeoisie or proletariat, since that would threaten the particularistic, private and arbitrary nature of their power. Secondly, despite their despotic appearance, they were pessimistic about their infrastructural capacity to overcome determined resistance with systematic repression. When it became obvious that neither the bourgeoisie nor the proletariat would go away, the regimes not only cast around for other solutions to maintain their power – they also realized that to incorporate these rising groups would "modernize" the regime and increase its Great Power status. The most successful regime in Europe was Wilhelmine Germany, on which I will therefore concentrate. The literature for this discussion is enormous and often controversial. In addition to works cited later, see Calleo (1978: 57–74) and the various essays in Sheehan (1976).

German absolutists were willing to concede on civil citizenship. Often this did not seem like "concession" at all. *Ancien régime* members were major property-holders, gradually using their property more capitalistically. They were not opposed to the spread of universal contract law and guarantees of property rights – including the liberal conception of freedom of labour. Recent Marxists have observed that classical liberalism, combining capitalism with democracy, has not often appeared subsequently: much civil can exist with little political citizenship (e.g. Jessop 1978). Blackbourne & Eley (1984) have demonstrated this case with respect to nineteenth-century Germany: liberal legal rights (civil citizenship) were achieved through a consensus between the Prussian regime and the bourgeoisie over what was needed to modernize society.

Absolutist regimes also favoured a minimal social citizenship. Their ideology and particularistic practices were already paternalist.

133

Particular groups like artisans or miners often had their basic wages, hours and working practices guaranteed by the state. When state infrastructural powers expanded, after about 1860, so could a minimal social citizenship. As is generally recognized today, Bismarck and Kaiser Wilhelm, and not liberals or reformists, were the founders of the welfare state, though it is true that they did not take it very far (Flora & Alber 1981).

The sticking-point was over political citizenship. Real parliaments could not be conceded; democrats could not be allowed absolute freedoms of the press, speech or assembly. Gradually, however, the more astute monarchists institutionalized a workable political strategy. The regime conceded a parliamentary shell but weighted the franchise, rigged ballots and only allowed elected representatives limited powers alongside an executive branch responsible to the monarch alone. Thus the bourgeoisie, even the proletariat, could be brought within the state but could not control it. By this sham political citizenship they were "negatively incorporated", to use Roth's (1963) term.

The tactics were divide-and-rule: negotiate with the more moderate sections of excluded groups, then repress the rest; play off incorporated interest groups and classes against each other; and preserve a vital element of arbitrary regime discretion. In the hands of a Bismarck the discretion could be used quite cynically: Catholics, regionalists, National Liberals, classical liberals, even the working class, would be taken up, discarded and repressed according to current tactical exigencies (see the brilliant biography of Bismarck by Taylor 1961). Divide-and-rule was corporatist and arbitrary – both qualities inherited from absolutism. Groups and classes were integrated as organizations into the state, rather than into rule-governed market places. The state could alter the rules by dissolving parliament, restricting civil liberties and selecting new targets for repression. By these means authoritarian monarchism emasculated the German bourgeoisie, dividing it among Conservative, National Liberal, Catholic and regionalist factions, all vying for influence within the regime. By 1914 the German bourgeoisie was finished as an independent political force (as Max Weber so often lamented). Only a small radical rump was prepared to ally with the excluded socialists against the regime.

The proletariat was treated more severely. Though the regime became somewhat internally divided, and though different Länder also varied (with liberals arguing that concessions to labour unions would detach them from socialism), in the end the authoritarians proved to be the heart of the regime. Apart from a brief period (1890–94) under the Chancellorship of Caprivi, a liberal Prussian general, the politics of conciliation never carried the court – and the Kaiser dismissed Caprivi rather than make concessions to labour. The regime was essentially united and so could respond with a clear strategy. The German working class could elect representatives to the Reichstag, but these were excluded from office or influence on the regime. Unions were permitted, but – even after the anti-socialist laws were repealed in 1889 – their legal rights were unclear. The state could exploit legal uncertainties or invoke martial law to repress strikes, meetings, marches, organizations and publications. It did so arbitrarily, according to its traditions.

Faced with a strategy largely of civil and political exclusion, labour responded predictably. It followed the Marxist Social Democrats, ostensibly revolutionary but geared up in practice to fight the elections. Most activist workers joined the socialist unions, committed to SPD rhetoric, but able to make reformist gains in some industries and localities. But to be a reformist brought frustration, because of regime intransigence. By 1914 Karl Legien, the crypto-reformist leader of the socialist unions, had carefully built up a measure of autonomy from the SPD. But he was forced to confess that reform was impossible without a fundamental change in the state. The working class was largely outside political citizenship. It responded with a flawed revolutionary Marxism – extreme rhetoric, practical caution and a leadership, conscious of the isolation of the movement, concentrating on electoral politics.

How frightened was the regime of the socialist threat? In the 1912 election the SPD achieved its greatest success, capturing a third of the votes, and becoming the largest single party in the Reichstag. The regime was taken aback but quickly recovered. The Chancellor, Bethmann-Hollweg, used the Red Scare against his major enemy at the time, which was the Right, not the Left. He exploited the fears of the propertied classes to finally push through an income tax, long desired by the regime, long resisted by the agrarian landlords. (Kaiser 1983: 458–62 makes this argument, against the more traditional view of writers like Berghahn 1973 that the regime feared the Left and militarized society to counter its threat.) Authoritarian monarchy was still successfully dividing-and-ruling and modernizing at the onset of the First World War.

Each of the authoritarian monarchies provided its variation on this German theme. I discuss them briefly in order of their success, beginning with Japan, the most successful.

The Japanese monarchy itself had less freedom of action. Instead a tightly knit Meiji elite, modernizing but drawn from the traditional dominant classes, used the monarchy as its legitimating principle. The Meiji Revolution represented an unusually self-conscious regime strategy of conservative modernization. After a careful search around Western constitutions, the German constitution was adopted and modified according to local need. (Bendix 1978: 476–90 gives a succinct summary of the Meiji strategy.) It is worth adding that forms of organization from liberal/reformist countries were also borrowed where they could fit into an authoritarian mould – notably French army and British navy organization. Authoritarian monarchy became rather more corporate, less dependent on the personal qualities of the monarch, than in Europe – an apparent strengthening of the strategy.

Less successful was Russia, whose regime generally favoured more repression and exclusion, yet vacillated before modern liberal and authoritarian influences from the West. Two periods of regime conciliation (1906–7 and 1912–14) enabled the emergence of bourgeois parties of compromise and labour unions run by reformists. But each time the subsequent return to repression cut the ground from under liberals and reformists. They could promise their followers little. Many became embittered and moved leftward. Socialist revolutionaries took over the labour and peasant movements and even some of the bourgeois factions (see, e.g., on the workers' movement, Bonnell 1983, Swain 1983). Divisions and vacillation at court prevented successful emulation of the German model. The *ancien régime* still possessed the loyalty of the nobility and propertied classes in general, but its modernization programme began to disintegrate from within (as Haimson 1964, 1965 classically argued). The regime lacked a corporate core of either liberal or conservative modernizers. Stolypin, the architect of the agrarian reforms designed to recruit rich and middling peasant support, was the potential conservative saviour of the regime, yet his influence at court was always precarious. The divided regime became buffeted by the personal irresoluteness of Nicholas and the reactionary folly of Alexandra. When monarchy begins to depend on the personal qualities of its monarchs, it is an endangered species. Russia represented the opposite pole to Japan within the spectrum of authoritarian monarchy – no corporate regime strategy, much depending on the monarch himself. On the other hand, economic and military modernization was proving remarkably successful in pre-war Russia. Could the regime find a comparably coherent political strategy? In 1914 the answer was not yet clear. Though regime weaknesses had begun to create what later proved to be its revolutionary gravediggers, their influence was still negligible in 1914.

The least successful case was Austria (became the Dual Monarchy of Austria-Hungary in 1867), uniquely beset by nationality conflicts as well as class struggle across its variegated lands. (Historical sociologists have tended to ignore Austria, except in relation to nationalism. For a narrative that enables us to piece together most of the complex relations between regime, classes and nations, see Kann 1964.) The monarchy attempted divide-and-rule on both fronts at once, but was faced by defections among *ancien régime* groups (Hungarian and Czech nobilities) as well as the hostility of bourgeois liberal nationalism. As the monarchy faltered, some peculiar alliances developed. After 1867 the most loyal and dominant groups in the two halves of the Dual Monarchy were the German nobility and bourgeoisie and the Hungarian nobility. But the monarchy found their support unwelcome because it alienated all the other nationalities these two exploited. After 1899 the Marxist SPD rejected nationalism as a bourgeois creed, thereby becoming to its surprise the major *de facto* supporter of the transnational monarchy. The monarchy belatedly converted to parliamentary institutions similar to Germany's (universal suffrage to parliaments whose rights were subordinate to the monarchy's) and tried to reach out to exploited nationalities and even classes. But noble and bourgeois nationalists, not the proletariat, made the parliaments unworkable, and they were dissolved. This authoritarian monarchy could not even retain the loyalty of the whole *ancien régime*, let alone incorporate the bourgeoisie. By 1914 the regime consisted of the monarchy, the army and the largely tactical support of various national and class groupings. Its corporate solidarity was probably the weakest of the four cases.

The four cases reveal considerable variation in regime strategy and success. The crucial criteria of success were to maintain the corporate coherence of the *ancien régime*, and to modernize by incorporating sections of the bourgeoisie. It is outside the scope of this chapter to attempt to explain why some regimes did much better than others at these tasks. However, regimes seem not to have prospered or faltered because of the strength in general class and numerical terms of bourgeoisie and proletariat. In these terms the rising classes in Germany were initially the most threatening, those of Japan the least threatening, with Austria and Russia somewhere in between. This is not the same ordering as for regime success. The bulk of the explanation of success would seem to lie among the traditional regimes and classes, not among the rising classes.

At its most coherent, authoritarian monarchy provided a distinctive mixture of citizen rights – a fair degree of civil citizenship, minimal social citizenship, limited political citizenship, the whole varying by class and tactically undercut by an arbitrary monarchy and court-centred elite. Its social struggles were part ideological class struggle, part incorporated interest-group jostling, erratically violent yet institutionalized nonetheless. Was this the third viable strategy for advanced industrial societies? Could it have survived the working-class pressure indefinitely? But for the fortunes of war, would it still survive today in three of the four greatest industrial powers in the world, a united Germany, a Tsarist Russia and an Imperial Japan? We cannot be sure because these regimes collapsed in war. But let us consider four supports for this counter-factual possibility.

First, in its own time Wilhelmine Germany was not idiosyncratic. Its emerging institutions were better-organized versions of the European mainstream. As Goldstein (1983) has shown, the combination of selective repression and sham parliaments was the late-nineteenth-century norm, not well developed liberalism, still less reformism. For this reason German institutions were much copied, especially by Austria and Japan.

Secondly, by the time of their entry into the decisive war, 1914 (or 1941 in the case of Japan), the authoritarian monarchies were already becoming great industrial powers. Germany had overtaken Britain and France and was matched only by the United States. Japan and Russia were industrializing rapidly and successfully; and Russian economic resources, then as now, made up in quantity what they lacked in quality (quantitative indices of the economic strength of the Great Powers can be found in Bairoch 1982). Authoritarian monarchy was surviving into advanced industrial societies in Germany and Japan, still had a reasonable chance in Russia, and was obviously failing only in Austria, where nations, not classes, provided the main threat.

Thirdly, we must beware a too homogeneous view of industrial society and its class struggles. The main reason the working class was not so threatening was its limited size. National censuses conducted between 1907 and 1911 show Britain to be exceptional. Only 9 per cent of its working population was still in agriculture, compared to 32 per cent in the USA, 37per cent in Germany and more than 55 per cent in Russia. Among the major powers, only in Britain were more working in manufacturing than in agriculture (Bairoch 1968: Table A2 has assembled the census data). Outside Britain, labour needed the support of peasants and small farmers to achieve either reform or revolution. It achieved this partially in the "contested" cases of France, Italy and Spain, and more sustainedly in the "mixed" cases of Scandinavia. But in Germany, Japan and Austria it failed dismally. Socialism was trapped in its urban–industrial enclaves, outvoted by the bourgeois–agrarian classes, and repressed by peasant soldiers and aristocratic officers. Authoritarian monarchy could continue to divide-and-rule and selectively repress provided it could manipulate divisions between agrarian and bourgeois classes, and motivate them both with fear of the proletariat. Few twentieth-century socialists have broken this strategy – Lenin being the obvious exception.

Fourthly, the numerical weakness of labour has continued, though in changed form. The rise of the "new middle class" and of the "service class", the re-emergence of labour market dualism, and the increasing size and variety of service industries soon introduced new differentiations among the employed population, just as agriculture declined. Successful labour movements in the post-war period, like those of Scandinavia, have managed to repeat their earlier populist strategy (Esping-Andersen 1985). They have recruited white-collar workers and new economic sectors into the Social Democratic movement, just as they earlier recruited bourgeois radicals and small farmers. But could labour movements that had already failed to attract the bourgeoisie or farmers, as in Germany or Japan, now do better among newer groups? It is surely more plausible to conceive of divide-and-rule, selective repression strategies, wielded by arbitrary authoritarian monarchies, surviving successfully today in Germany and Japan, and possibly also in Russia and constituent parts of Austria-Hungary.

I conclude that the third strategy, authoritarian monarchy, could probably have survived into advanced, post-industrial society, providing a distinctive, corporately organized, arbitrary combination of

139

partial civil, political and social citizenship. This was not envisaged by Marshall, or indeed by any modern sociologist.

## Fascism and authoritarian socialism

The First World War resulted in two further strategies, Fascism and authoritarian socialism. Nazi Germany and the Soviet Union are their exemplars. Both used more repression, using the infrastructural capacities of the twentieth-century state, and proclaiming violent legitimating ideologies. In practice, as in all regimes, repression had to be combined with negotiation. Both regimes delineated out-groups with whom they would not negotiate: for both, anyone providing principled opposition; for the Nazis labour leaders, socialists, Jews and other non-Aryan groups; for the Soviets, major property owners. But other interest groups – never acknowledged as antagonistic classes – could join the regime, establish cliques within and clients without, and bargain and jostle in time-honoured absolutist style. Now social struggles were not openly acknowledged at all. But within the regime they would continue, flaring into intermittent life with purges, riots and even armed factional struggle.

Neither regime provided civil rights; neither provided real political citizenship (though they provided the institutions of sham corporatism and socialism). Yet they moved furthest towards social citizenship. Fascism's move was hesitant: full employment and public works programmes were not greatly in advance of others of the time (and were partially an outcome of a more important policy goal, rearmament). But had the regime survived the war, its encroachments on capitalism would surely have extended the state's role in guaranteeing subsistence. The Soviet regime has gone much further, proud of its programme of social citizenship. The state formally provides the subsistence of all (though the reality, with private peasant plots and black markets, is less clear cut).

Of course, German Fascism was deeply unstable. But this was due to the restless militarism of its leaders in geopolitics, not to its class strategy. Indeed, this was remarkably successful in a short space of time. The proletariat was suppressed more completely than any of the regimes discussed so far would have believed possible. Its leaders were killed or exiled; its organizations disbanded or staffed by the regime's paramilitary forces; its masses silenced, seemingly with the approval of other social classes. The bourgeoisie was emasculated even more effectively than the Wilhelmine regime had managed. The liberals were killed or silenced, the rest kept quiet or loudly voiced their support. Ruthlessness was no longer hidden by scruple. Thus Fascism might have offered a fourth, chilling resolution to class struggle in advanced societies. Its main test would have been the next one: could it take on capital too? It was already beginning to do this by subordinating economic profit to militarism. This proved its downfall – but not at the hands of domestic social classes, who fought loyally for the Nazi regime down to its last days.

The stability of the fifth solution, authoritarian socialism, cannot be in doubt. The Bolsheviks and their ruling successors soon cowed the bourgeoisie, and gradually domesticated the labour movement. The trade unions were converted into apolitical welfare state organizations (sometimes headed by ex-KGB men). It took almost 50 years for the institutionalization to be complete. But once in place, it appears no less stable than other enduring types of regime.

## The impact of war and geopolitics

I have described five viable regime strategies and mixtures of citizenship: liberalism, reformism, authoritarian monarchy, Fascism and authoritarian socialism. Yet industrial society today has lost some of this variety. Authoritarian monarchy and Fascism no longer exist. Why? Is it because of their inherent defects or instability? I have already suggested not.

There is an alternative explanation. To paraphrase a famous epitaph on the Roman Empire – these regimes did not die of natural causes, they were assassinated. Of course, Fascism and authoritarian socialism were also born out of assassination. But for the fortunes of the First World War, authoritarian monarchy might be alive today, while Fascism and authoritarian socialism might never have been born. But for the fortunes of the Second World War, Fascism might dominate the world today. True, it is difficult to see American liberalism being overthrown by the German, Austrian and Japanese alliances. But Europe and Russia might well have had viable futures under very different regimes.

Of course, proof of this argument would require disposing of the reverse causality: regime type might have determined the role of war. This could have happened in two stages. Certain regimes – obviously the more authoritarian ones – may have been more militaristic and provoked the world wars; yet they may have been less effective at fighting them. The first stage has validity. The Nazis and Japanese did aggress in the Second World War; and, in a more confused, stumbling way, the authoritarian monarchies did start the First World War. But is the second stage of the argument valid? Were liberalism, reformism and authoritarian socialism better suited to mass mobilization warfare? The ideologies of the victors suggest the answer "yes". I have only time here to give fragmentary evidence, but my answer is "no".

In both wars the German army fought better than its enemies, who continuously needed numerical superiority to survive. German civilians also loyally supported their regimes to the end. Both points hold also for the Japanese in the second war. The Eastern Front in the first war offers further shocks to the liberal/reformist perspective. Authoritarian monarchy Russia outfought the by now semi-authoritarian monarchy of Austria-Hungary, whose troops in turn outfought the by now largely liberal regime of Italy. Indeed, when in 1917 the Austro-Hungarian armies against Russia collapsed, they were stiffened by Prussian officers and NCOs and then began to get the upper hand (Stone 1975). The Central and Axis powers were correct in their view that the fortunes of war turned less upon citizenship than on efficient military organization. Unfortunately for them, military efficiency became overweighted by numbers. Numbers resulted principally from the alliance system – how may powerful states were on each side? Authoritarian monarchy and Fascism were defeated by superior geopolitical alliances, not by their domestic socio-political structure.

After 1945 this result was deliberately rammed home by the victors, careful not to repeat the mistakes of the peace treaties of 1918 (see Maier 1981). Eastern Europe was made safe for authoritarian socialism by the Red Army. Western Europe and Japan were more subtly made safe for liberal/reformist regimes (though Japan's regime does not fit happily into this categorization, because of the survival of many authoritarian traditions). In western Europe the authoritarian Right was eliminated by force, the revolutionary Left had the ground cut from under it by reforms and economic growth offered to governments and industrial relations systems of the Centre and Centre-Left.

142

By 1950 the contest was over. A cross between Marshallian citizenship and American liberalism dominated the West, less through its internal evolution than through the fortunes of war. It still dominates today.

Marshall's general argument was that industrial society institutionalized class struggle through mass citizenship. This seems true. All regimes have guaranteed *some* citizen rights. But they have done so in very different degrees and combinations. It is a more complex and less optimistic overall picture than he envisaged. But for the logic of geopolitics and war – including the sacrifices of his own generation – it might have been a very different and infinitely more depressing picture in Europe.

Sociologists are prone to forget that "evolution" is usually geopolitically assisted. Dominant powers may impose their strategies on lesser powers; or the lesser may freely choose the dominator's strategy because it is an obviously successful modernization strategy. This means that what "evolves" depends on changing geopolitical configurations.

Let me quote Ito Hirobumi, the principal author of the Meiji constitution of 1889:

> We were just then in an age of transition. The opinions prevailing in the country were extremely heterogeneous, and often diametrically opposed to each other . . . there was a large and powerful body of the younger generation educated at the time when the Manchester theory was in vogue, and who in consequence were ultra-radical in their ideas of freedom. Members of the bureaucracy were prone to lend willing ears to the German doctrinaires of the reactionary period, while, on the other hand, the educated politicians among the people having not yet tasted the bitter significance of administrative responsibility, were liable to be more influenced by the dazzling words and lucid theories of Montesquieu, Rousseau and similar French writers.

I have taken this quotation from Bendix (1978: 485) who uses it in support of a general evolutionist model of how Western ideals of popular representation supplanted monarchy everywhere. He rightly notes the importance of "reference societies", more advanced societies to which modernizers could point with approval. But the quotation reveals that at the end of the nineteenth century there were at least three – Britain, France and Germany – and this reflected a real balance of power among several great powers. No single power could impose its will on others (outside its colonial or regional sphere of influence). Modernizers could choose from among several regime strategies. That is far less the case today. The Soviet and Anglo-American strategies were imposed – in the East by force, in the West by assisting certain political factions and subverting others. The two strategies have worked in their different ways for 40 years, and are now backed by the economic, ideological, military and political resources of two hegemonic superpowers. Eastern Europe is still held down by force. In the western European periphery, deviant regimes in Portugal, Spain and Greece have succumbed to the Anglo-American vision of modernization desired increasingly by their domestic elites. In the Third World there is more variety of choice, because most countries are more insulated from both Western and Eastern blocs, but the choices tend to be around the two models provided by the superpowers.

Geopolitics has also provided a second recent change: the emergence of nuclear weapons. Warfare at the highest level would now destroy society. Therefore, the war-assisted pattern of change dominant in the first half of the century cannot be repeated. The emergence of the superpowers and of nuclear weapons both indicate that the future of citizenship will be different from its past. Our assessment of its prospects must combine domestic with geopolitical analysis.

# CHAPTER 8

# Full employment, new technologies and the distribution of income

## James Meade

My old friend Tom Marshall was a great sociologist. I am an economist with no experience of social administration or theory, and I feel that the best way in which I can pay my tribute to my old friend in this series of lectures instituted in his memory is simply to tackle an economic problem that has far-reaching social implications, one in which Tom Marshall and I shared an interest and which was often a topic of conversation between us.

Tom was above all interested in the social problems and values of what may be called the Mixed Society, a society based on the three principles of political democracy, economic market capitalism and social welfare; a mixture of which he thoroughly approved but which, as he argued, called often for workable compromise arrangements between the rights and obligations that each of these three principles implied. (For a comprehensive review of Marshall's work in this field, see Reisman 1984.) I have always been interested in the search for workable compromise arrangements in the Mixed Economy in order to obtain the best possible package of economic efficiency, freedom of choice, decent distribution of income and participation in decision-making.

The social problems of the Mixed Economy are not identical with the economic problems of the Mixed Economy. But there is clearly much overlap. Economic freedom and efficiency have much to do with market capitalism; the distribution of income has much to do with the welfare state; and participation in decision-making has much to do with democracy. I have accordingly chosen as a topic for my lecture a problem whose solution depends upon these interconnections in the Mixed Economy.

My thesis is a simple, straightforward one. I am of the opinion that in the sort of Mixed Society–Mixed Economy in which we live and in which people like Tom Marshall and I have seen so much merit, there is now need for a fundamental shift of attitudes and reform of institutions; much less emphasis must be put upon using prices, and in particular upon using the price of labour, as a major instrument for achieving a fair and acceptable distribution of income; much more emphasis must be put upon the setting of prices so as to obtain a full and efficient use of resources and in particular of labour; and much more attention must be paid to measures other than price and wage-setting in order to achieve a fair and acceptable distribution of income and property. I believe that this necessary shift of emphasis demands far-reaching changes in economic institutions and in social and political ideas.

It is the recent experience of stagflation, that is to say, of economic stagnation combined with the threat of a runaway inflation, which has led me to this conclusion. Tom Marshall's main thoughts and writings on the Mixed Society were formulated in the Golden Age of a quarter of a century after the Second World War when we enjoyed full employment without excessive inflation. There were, of course, many important social problems; but he wrote of these on the tacit or express assumption of the continuation of full employment without runaway inflation, an assumption that he shared with the great majority of economists during those years. Many of us were conscious of the threat of inflation, but most of us assumed that some way would be found of controlling inflation without the massive depression and unemployment that we are in fact experiencing.

What then has gone wrong? The fundamental nature of our predicament is easily described. For a quarter of a century after the Second World War we enjoyed a period of full employment with a high level and rate of growth of our standards of living such as we had never before enjoyed in our history, and we combined this with only a very moderate inflationary rise of money prices and costs. During the last decade we have experienced a rapid rise of unemployment and a very sharp fall in economic activity combined with a very high rate of price inflation.

This has confronted all governments with what may be called the dilemma of stagflation. If we increase the demand for goods and services by means of Keynesian expansionary financial policies, we may reduce unemployment but at the cost perhaps of a renewed explosive inflation of prices; if we follow Mrs Thatcher and restrain money expenditures, we can hope, as she has done, to fight the inflation but at a cost of massive unemployment.

The development of the social policies, institutions and attitudes that lie at the root of this problem can be very well illustrated by three outstanding features of the policies of the post-war Labour Government of 1945, namely, Full Employment, the Welfare State, and Free Collective Bargaining. First, the Attlee Government was committed to the adoption of monetary and fiscal policies to ensure a high level of effective demand for the products of labour so as to maintain Full Employment – what we may label the contribution of Keynes. Secondly, the Attlee Government built a set of humane and caring institutions that we may call the Welfare State and with which we may properly connect the name of Beveridge. Thirdly, Free Collective Bargaining by strongly organized independent labour unions was to be recognized and further developed as the method for setting wages at rates that ensured a high standard of living for the worker.

The commitment of the government to the maintenance of a high and stable level of employment marked a revolution in political ideas. For a quarter of a century after 1945, unemployment was held down to a figure varying between 1 and 3 per cent, as compared with the interwar range of between 10 and 25 per cent. This most desirable and successful development had, however, the important side-effect of encouraging the idea that, since it was the government's responsibility to maintain employment, little or no attention need be paid in formulating and pressing wage claims to any possible adverse effects of high wage costs upon the demand for labour and so upon the level of employment.

This attitude has undoubtedly been encouraged by the building of a humane welfare state. I am not suggesting that the structure is a perfect one, and indeed it will be part of my later argument that, as a means for redistributing income, it needs much further development. Unemployment can still lead to real deprivation. But if one compares the position of the unemployed in the 1930s with the position today, the contrast is indeed striking. The grinding poverty and complete destitution of the 1930s no longer occurs. I myself regard such a change as a most desirable one, but it has an important side-effect on our wage-setting institutions. Anxieties about possible effects of wage claims on levels of employment are reduced, and there is less possibility of undercutting of agreed rates of pay by a desperate search for work at any cost by the unemployed.

But with the introduction and development of policies for Full Employment and for Social Welfare, free collective bargaining between independent, highly organized bodies of employers and employees becomes a most inappropriate and dangerous method of setting rates of pay. So long as Full Employment was successfully maintained by Keynesian financial policies, workers were apt to formulate wage claims without much concern about their possible effects on employment, even though they might aim at standards of real pay that were overambitious in view of the real productivity of their work. Employers did not resist such claims with great determination in view of the general belief that, in order to maintain full employment, the government would in one way or another ensure that money expenditures were sufficiently increased to cover any increased costs of production; prices were then raised to cover costs. As a result, money wage claims were further increased to cover the consequential rise in the cost of living, and the explosive inflationary spiral was completed. At this point Mrs Thatcher or some other determined person is elected to restrain demand in order to fight inflation instead of expanding demand in order to maintain employment. There follows a reduction in inflation at the cost of mass unemployment.

There are deep roots in history for our highly emotive reactions to any criticism of this inappropriate and disastrous system of wage-setting by what is called "Free Collective Bargaining" but which I, taking advantage of the richness of the English language, will translate into " Uncontrolled Monopoly Bargaining". For the first two-thirds of the nineteenth century, the workers had in effect no representation in Parliament. The only method of asserting a claim on the community's real income was by the industrial action of organized bodies of workers who, in response to exploitation by employers, would ensure by monopolistic counteraction that no-one, even though he or she might be unemployed, would offer to work at a lower rate of pay. It is, I think, possible greatly to admire and to sympathize with this heroic chapter of historical struggle by the underdog for the establishment of free institutions for Uncontrolled Monopoly Bargaining without allowing this overhang of history to blind oneself to the deficiencies of the system in the totally different circumstances of today.

In the bad old days there was no alternative method. But the existence of parliamentary democracy now makes possible redistribution through fiscal and similar measures, methods that will not simply collapse in the disappointments of runaway inflation. One of the great "ifs" of history is what might have happened if the Chartists had been successful in the middle of the last century. Would the consequential much earlier opening up of the possibility of redistribution through parliamentary democracy rather than by direct industrial action mean that our emotional commitment to the sacredness of Uncontrolled Monopoly Bargaining would now be markedly less?

As an aside, I ask the question whether this unfortunate historical need for the underdog to rely wholly on free trade union action to the exclusion of democratic parliamentary methods may not at this moment be of necessity repeating itself in Poland.

I do not mean that there is no proper place for trade union organization. Production must be conducted on a large enough scale to be efficient. This means that one employer or employing body (such as a firm or company) employs many workers. In conditions of imperfect competition, this opens the way for great inequality of bargaining power unless the many workers combine to confront the single employer with a single seller of labour. For this, if for no other reason, trade union organization is most desirable and I am not arguing that the way to cope with our present predicament is simply to bash the unions. However, the function – indeed the proper function – of a trade union leader in bargaining with the employer is to attain the best possible conditions for the employed members of his union whose interests he represents.

During a period of economic recession such as we have been experiencing in the last few years, the result is moderation in wage claims. As the demand for the products of an enterprise falls, the jobs of those in employment are threatened, and wage claims by those who are not yet unemployed are restrained in fear that they will price themselves out of their existing jobs, But when recovery comes and the demand for the products of an enterprise is expanding, the existing workers in employment are faced with a choice. Should the greater expenditure on their products be taken out in the form of a higher wage for those in employment or in the form of an expansion of the numbers employed at the current wage rate? There is a basic conflict of interest between the monopolistically organized insiders who are interested in wage rates that maximize their income per head and the unorganized outsiders whom I will call the unemployed black school leavers from Brixton, and whose real interests lie in wage rates that will expand employment opportunities. I am not necessarily arguing against Collective or Monopoly Bargaining, but I am arguing that, as in the case of other monopolies, society has a duty to ensure that the prices that are set are such as to promote output and employment rather than to ensure high gains to privileged insiders.

There is, I think, a growing realization of the inadequacies of Uncontrolled Monopoly Bargaining as a method of fixing wages. One radical proposal is to get rid of the wage-fixing problem by getting rid of wages and transforming the pay of workers into a share of the total value of the net output of the business in question. Reform in this direction covers a multitude of different arrangements stretching from minor profit-sharing arrangements to full-scale labour-owned, labour managed co-operatives.

I cannot possibly treat this immense subject at all fully in this chapter. Changes along these lines imply greater participation in decisions affecting working life, greater sharing of the profits that can be made by running a business efficiently and successfully, and a breaking down of barriers between "them" and "us". On these grounds I personally would warmly welcome developments on these lines. But here the professor of the dismal science enters his caveat – I do not believe that they are an answer to the problem of providing full employment without inflation. Indeed, I think that they may intensify that problem.

The point is a very simple one that I illustrate with the following very simple numerical example. We imagine a firm that might employ 98, 99, 100 or 101 workers. As it employs more workers and produces more output, the value of output per head of the working force falls.

This relationship will be typical of the actual market position of any firm in our free enterprise society. As long as a firm can hire unemployed labour at a given wage rate that is less than the value of output per employee, it would always pay it to take on more workers and produce more if the value of output per head did not decline.

At some point, however, either because of diminishing output per head as more and more workers are crowded on to the existing plant

**Table 8.1**  Employment, output and value added.

| Number employed | Value of output per head £ | Value of total output £ | Value added by additional employment £ |
|---|---|---|---|
| 98 | 100.20 | 9.819.60 | 0 |
| 99 | 100.10 | 9,909.90 | 90.30 |
| 100 | 100.00 | 10,000.00 | 90.10 |
| 101 | 99.90 | 10,089.90 | 89.90 |

or, more probably in modern conditions, because it would have to cut the selling price of its product in order to expand its sales, the value of output per worker will start to decline as employment is increased.

Suppose in our example that the weekly wage was £90. In this case it would pay the firm best to stop at an employment level of 100. Column 3 of Table 8.1 shows the total value of the firm's output and is derived simply from multiplying employment by value of output per head. Column 4 shows how much will be added to the total value of the firm's output by employing one additional worker. Thus, by increasing employment from 98 to 99, column 4 shows that £90.30 will be added to the firm's total revenue from its sales. So long as the addition to its total revenue is greater than the wage of £90 that represents the additional cost of production, the firm will increase its profit by expanding output. In my illustrative case it would pay it to stop at employment of 100: to take on 101 instead of 100 workers would now add only £89.90 to its revenue, that is less than the extra wage cost of £90.00.

At this employment level of 100 the total value of output is £10,000 and the wage-bill is £9,000 (i.e. 100 workers at £90.00 a worker). The workers will be getting 90 per cent of the firm's output. Suppose then that the wage system were abolished and that agreement was reached between the employers and workers that the workers should receive always 90 per cent of the total value of the firm's output. At the existing level of employment of 100 there would be no change in profits or in the pay of workers.

But the employers would now have an incentive to expand output and employment. Since they would receive 10 per cent of the value of the firm's output, they would wish to go on expanding as long as the additional employment added anything to the total value of the firm's output. A share system in which the employers retained the decisions about employment, output and sales would be expansionary. (See Weitzman 1984, to whom I am greatly indebted.)

But, alas, the same share system in which the workers took the decisions about employment, output and sales would be contractionary and not expansionary. Suppose an elderly worker is retiring from the workforce, leaving only 99 colleagues in employment. The value of total output will, it is true, have fallen from £10,000 to £9,909.90; but the value of output per head will have risen from £100.00 to £100.10, with a rise in the individual worker's share from £90.00 to £90.09. The remaining workers will have an incentive to let the scale of operations contract so long as this causes a rise in the value of output per head.

If, therefore, extensive participation in decision-making is to be combined with the profit-sharing developments, there is a serious danger of introducing contractionary motives into any given market situation and thus increasing the difficulty of attaining full employment and making even more pronounced the conflict between employed "insiders" and unemployed "outsiders".

There are two lines of answer to this problem. The first is an idealistic approach whereby labour co-operatives are set up and managed, as I believe to be the case in the Mondragon experiment (Thomas & Logan 1982), with the object of providing as much employment as possible at a given rate of reward rather than with the object of maximizing the income per head of the co-operators. One applauds this. But I hope that I am not being over-cynical in holding the view that this altruistic attitude to the outsiders cannot be assumed to work as the basic motivation throughout a free competitive economy, whether the individual firms are comprised of capitalist wage-paying enterprises or labour co-operatives or other forms of labour–capital partnerships.

The second and realistic approach is much less attractive; it consists in accepting an inegalitarian principle in rates of reward to workers. Consider my simple numerical example. Taking on a 101st worker will add £89.90 to the firm's total revenue. Suppose that some unemployed outsider would be only too glad to get a job at £80.00 a week. This would leave an additional £9.90 to be divided between profits and the pay of the 100 workers who were already in employment and whose rewards could therefore be ever so slightly increased. Arrangements could be made whereby everybody – the profit-makers, the existing workers and the outsider – could be better off, provided that the principle of equal pay for equal work was abandoned and new-comers from outside were admitted on less favourable terms than existing insiders, even though they were to work with equal efficiency at the same job at the same workbench. I have myself outlined else-where in some detail the way in which inegalitarian labour–capital partnerships of this kind might be organized (Meade 1982: Ch. 9).

I myself believe that if partnerships between labour and capital are to become a really important element in our society, this inegalitarian principle will inevitably find a place in their development, as indeed it already does in many professional partnerships. If so, the fact that this implies unequal pay for equal work would greatly strengthen my gen-eral thesis that it is extremely important to shift the emphasis away from rates of pay on to other measures for attaining a fair and accept-able distribution of income.

Before I can come on to any cheerful discussion of the alternative constructive ways in which one might tackle these problems of distri-butional justice, I have one more sad duty to perform as professor of the dismal science. There is no doubt that we are now entering a period of extremely rapid and basic technological change that will have a dramatic effect in increasing the productivity of labour. As I have been arguing that our troubles are due to wage claims that out-strip the workers' productivity, it may at first sight appear that a new industrial revolution that increases output per head must at least help to solve our problems. This may be the outcome; but, alas, it is not at all certain.

Consider an office or factory with a given amount of capital equip-ment and a given number of workers both before and after the techni-cal change. The capital equipment will take a new form: tapes, word processors and computers instead of filing cabinets, typewriters and leather-bound ledgers; and robots instead of conventional machine tools. Average output per unit of capital equipment and average out-put per unit of labour would both have risen in the same proportion as total output, if the total amounts of capital and of labour had remained unchanged. But in this case what would have happened to the relative importance at the margin of capital equipment and of labour? It is pos-sible, though by no means certain, that the nature of the inventions is such as to make the new forms of capital equipment very close and very efficient substitutes for labour, in which case the office or factory would be able to produce its new output at a lower cost by dismissing many workers and replacing them with a small additional amount of capital equipment. In a free-enterprise regime in which labour became less productive at the margin relative to the capital equipment, workers would be dismissed and replaced by the more productive equipment, unless the cost-price of labour (i.e. the wage rate) was lowered relative to the cost of employing capital equipment (i.e. the rate of return on capital funds), with a consequential shift of distribution of income from earnings to income on property.

The process of introduction of the new technology will, of course, have very important temporary effects in shifting demand from one type of occupation to another and in stimulating the replacement of the old equipment with the new. I am not concerned in this chapter with these very important temporary phenomena, but with the longer-run effects that may be apparent after the disturbances and extra activities of the change-over have come to an end.

The ultimate outcome will depend not only upon the nature of the new technologies as they are developed and applied but also upon many complicated interactions between different parts of the economy and upon many features of probable behaviour in response to the new conditions. This is *par excellence* a field in which co-operative work between technologists, economists and sociologists is desirable, and it is encouraging to know that such work is going ahead in many institutions and universities. Much can be achieved by such research, but the possible changes are so great, so complicated, and as yet so uncertain that for a long time it will be impossible to do more than guess the answer to my basic economic question: Will Men become at the margin much less important relatively to Machines, not merely in one or two striking but exceptional cases, but on the average over all activities in the economy? There is one feature of the new technologies that does give one a certain sense of unease. Basic features of the new technologies are to provide machines with memories and with flexible intelligent or semi-intelligent powers of receiving, analyzing and responding to outside data, and that to a layman does sound like turning them into close and efficient substitutes for men. Perhaps machines are now destined to replace men's brains as well as their brawn and thus to raise the value of capital equipment relative to that of labour. If this were to happen, there would be two possible lines of response.

In the first place, the wage rate might be allowed to fall relatively to the return on capital equipment. This would reduce the cost of relatively labour-intensive products and processes. If this went far enough, such products and processes might be expanded at the expense of the more capital-intensive processes to the extent necessary to provide full employment. In this case full employment would be maintained but at the expense of a very unequal distribution of income. The ownership of property is much more concentrated than the ownership of the ability to work. A relative rise in the profits going to the relatively few rich owners of the capital equipment and a relative fall in the wages of labour would, to take a childish example, be compatible with a full employment society in which the rich owners of the robots employed a large number of poorly paid butlers and other servants.

A second, and with our present institutional arrangements a more probable, outcome would be on the following lines. The workers in the various industries, seeing the average output per worker being immensely raised and seeing the greater part of this going to the profits of the owners of the capital equipment, would through trade union or similar action insist that the wage rate was raised at least in line with the rise in average productivity, so that the price of labour was not allowed to fall relatively to the yield on capital. In this case, if technological developments were of the relatively labour-saving kind that I have discussed, it would not pay producers to employ as much labour as before with the available amount of capital equipment. There would be a limited amount of well paid, perhaps very highly paid, employment of a few persons to look after the robots; the rest of the labour force would be unemployed – or possibly in a few cases acting as poorly paid butlers to the few highly paid workers who were in employment or to the not-quite-so-rich owners of the capital equipment. The problems of what I have described as the conflict of interests in the labour market between the insiders and the outsiders would be intensified; a large part of the available workers would have joined the black school leavers from Brixton.

I have described these two possible scenarios in childishly stark and simple imagery. Things will not happen quite like that. But I hope that my two fables will serve to make clear the two sorts of development that might occur to a greater or smaller degree. Neither of them is at all attractive. Surely there must be a better way of organizing our institutions so that new technologies that could enable everyone to have a higher standard of living than before will not threaten to lead to either of these disastrous situations. My answer would be to attempt to devise wage-setting institutions that would allow the real wage rate to fall to the extent necessary to provide employment opportunities to all who sought them, but to combine this with fiscal and other institutions that ensured that directly or indirectly everyone enjoyed a fair share of the profits earned on the robots, computers and tapes, and indeed on property in general.

In these circumstances, the setting of the real wage at a level low enough to provide employment opportunities to all who sought them does not, of course, imply that employment will be on as big a scale after the technological improvements as it was before them. The technological improvements will have greatly increased real income per head and the fiscal arrangements will have ensured that this is enjoyed by all workers. History demonstrates that as income per head grows, people take out a large part of their increased standards in the form of increased leisure, shorter hours, later entry into and earlier retirement from the labour market, longer holidays, and so on. There will be fewer seeking work, and the wage rate will have to be kept down only to the level needed to satisfy this reduced demand for work opportunities.

I must stop this crystal-gazing. The future effects of technological change are still quite unclear. All that I am asserting in this chapter is that it may intensify what I believe to be already a basic problem in our society, namely the need to shift the emphasis from wage-setting to other instruments of policy for the purpose of achieving an acceptable distribution of income and wealth.

So much for the nature of our problem. For now, I must confine myself to a very brief catalogue of the sort of changes in policies and institutions that might set our society on a new course in this direction.

## Proposals for reform

First, the whole armoury of Keynesian instruments for the management of demand – budgetary policies, monetary policies and foreign exchange policies – should be brought into play. But the object would be no longer to control expenditures so as to maintain full employment, but rather to keep the total money expenditures on the products of labour on a steady growth path of, say, 5 per cent per annum.

Secondly, this financial background would mean that producers were safeguarded against any wholesale financial collapse in the markets for their products. But on the other hand they would realize that they could not with impunity raise their selling prices, since the total money demand for their products as a whole would be constrained. This atmosphere should be reinforced by other measures to promote competition and to restrain the setting of monopolistic prices by producers. The free import of foreign competitors' products, the development of the arrangements to control business restrictive practices, monopolistic arrangements and mergers, and where appropriate the control of selling prices, all fall into this category of measures.

Thirdly, these restraints on the power and the willingness of employers to raise the selling prices of their products would increase their resistance to excessive money wage claims. They should be accompanied by measures designed to restrain the formation of over-ambitious wage claims. As in the case of the employers so also in the case of the employed, the knowledge that financial policies are designed to limit the total amount of money income available for re-distribution may help to restrain wage claims. But more positive action may be needed. However, it is not suitable to apply to a trade union precisely the same measures against restrictive practices as are applied to the sellers of other services and products. Existing legislation against restrictive practices in business prohibits agreements among independent sellers to set minimum prices below which they will not sell. To apply this to the sale of a man's labour would be to outlaw all effective trade unionism, since it would prohibit individual workers from getting together to agree on a wage below which they would not sell their labour. But there are in my opinion a number of ways in which existing monopolistic powers of a trade union can be judged excessive. For example, objection may be taken to certain arrangements expressly designed to keep outsiders out of the market, such as pre-entry closed shop arrangements that directly limit entry to the occupation, and unnecessary apprenticeship requirements.

Fourthly, arrangements of this kind to reduce the powers and the incentives of both employers and employed to raise the prices of their products and their services need to be supplemented by a more direct control over the process of Uncontrolled Monopoly Bargaining. The civilized way of setting about this is to develop a nationwide pay board system to which, in the case of an unsettled dispute about pay, either side, employer or employees, could appeal. The pay board in making its award would be under a statutory obligation to put much emphasis on the likely effect of the award in promoting output and employment in the sector of the economy under review. There would be sanctions against those, employer or employees, who took industrial action against the terms of the award. Such a system might be combined with a tax on increases in pay that exceeded some specified upper limit.

Fifthly, there are many ways in which the ability of outsiders to challenge the insiders might be encouraged. Of great importance are adequate arrangements for training unemployed outsiders in the skills needed for the expanding occupations. Another is the need for the encouragement of geographic mobility from a depressed to an expanding locality. In this connection I make special reference to the present state of the housing market because it strikingly illustrates the same principles as those that I am preaching for the labour market itself. I cannot go into all the details, but present tax arrangements, rent controls, tenants' rights of occupation, and methods of allocating and setting rents for council housing have resulted in a situation in which those insiders in the housing market who own their houses or are privileged to occupy protected accommodation are unwilling or unable to move. A great freeing of the housing market would greatly help geographical mobility. The arguments against it rest on possible adverse distributional effects. Some landlords might make large takings in rents; some occupiers might be impoverished by having to pay higher rents. As in the labour market, so in the housing market it is essential to combine the freeing of the market with fiscal and other arrangements for the redistribution of incomes, arrangements that impose high levies on the rich, whatever the source of their riches, and grant generous support to the poor and needy, whatever the cause of their poverty and needs.

Sixthly, for the effective and generous relief of poverty and of needs in a society with otherwise free markets, a reform and integration of social benefits and of personal allowances under the income tax is most desirable. All family units would receive a generous social dividend or general social benefit – call it what you will – that would replace both the personal allowances under the income tax and also the broad range of social benefits for sickness, unemployment, basic state pension, children and other dependants, single-parent families, housing costs, and so on. The amount of the social dividend allotted in any particular case would thus depend upon the beneficiary's age, marital status, housing costs, number and age of dependants, and any other relevant factors. But as each beneficiary received additional income from earnings or other sources, these additional receipts would be taxed at an exceptionally high rate until the whole of the social dividend had been recouped. Suppose that the exceptionally high rate of recoupment tax were 80 per cent. Then, in the case of taxpayers whose social dividends were set at £72, the first £90 of their earnings or other receipt of income would be subject to this 80 per cent rate of tax, which would raise the revenue of £72 (i.e. 80 per cent of £90) needed to recoup the whole of the social dividend, any income over and above this £90 being taxable at a lower basic rate of tax.

With the present system there is a wholly irrational and incomprehensible muddle of complicated rules for the payment of national insurance contributions, of income tax with its various tax allowances, and of various social benefits, some subject and others not subject to means tests that themselves vary from benefit to benefit, and some subject and some not subject to income tax. This results in many people getting help who do not need it, while many who do need it get inadequate or no help. The proposed reform would not merely constitute a great simplification that would be less costly to administer and more easily understood by the man and woman in the street; but in addition the universal payment of the social benefit would ensure that all those in need received help, while the special recoupment tax would mean that the cost of state aid was confined to those at the bottom end of the income scale. The result would be that more generous help could be given to those in real need without running into the existing poverty trap in its present most extreme form. At present, because of the host of different and independent benefits with their different and independent means tests, it is possible that by earning an additional £1 of income the earner will actually be worse off because the loss of various means-tested benefits together with the payment of tax and national insurance contribution will absorb more than the £1 of extra income. With the proposed system everyone would be sure of keeping at least 20 per cent of any additional earnings. A system of this kind could meet the generality of cases, though there might well remain certain special welfare needs that would be best treated outside this general structure.

Seventhly, beyond the first slice of earnings or other income taxed at an exceptionally high rate, there would extend as at present a progressive direct tax system, starting at some basic rate of tax like the present 30 per cent basic rate of income tax [1984] and then leading to progressively higher rates of tax as the individual's taxable receipts rose. I would, however, suggest that the basis of this progressive tax should be the level, not of the taxpayer's income, but of his or her expenditure.

Eighthly, I would also suggest two major reforms of the taxation of wealth and transfers of wealth. In the first place, there might be a progressive annual tax on the ownership of any wealth over and above a given tax-exempt limit, though such a tax raises formidable problems concerning the valuation of accumulated pension rights that in present conditions represent a very important element of private wealth. But, secondly, there should in any case be an effective tax on transfers of wealth by way of gift *inter vivos* or of bequest on death; the present capital transfer tax is so riddled with allowances, exemptions and special arrangements as to be basically ineffective. But the tax I would propose would be levied not, as in theory at present, on the cumulative amount of the gifts or bequests made by any single benefactor but on the cumulative amount of the gifts or bequests received by any single beneficiary, so that transfers to individuals who had received little property would be tax-free while transfers to those who had already been enriched by gift or inheritance would be heavily taxed.

Once again it is not possible to go into details, but the general logic of such arrangements can be clearly stated. If my general analysis is correct, it is desirable by one means or another to ensure that income from property is directly or indirectly more equally distributed. There are, broadly speaking, two ways in which this result might show itself.

The first and direct method would be by taking steps to achieve a more equal distribution of the private ownership of property. If every citizen were a representative owner of property as well as a representative earner of wages, the fact that an efficient use of the price mechanism required a fall in the wage rate relative to the return on property would not affect the distribution of income as between individuals; everyone's property income would go up as their wage income went down.

The tax arrangements that I have outlined are designed to encourage a more equal distribution of the ownership of property. The replacement of income by expenditure as the base for direct tax, together with a progressive annual tax on the ownership of properties above a certain limit, would enable those with small properties to accumulate larger properties without any tax on the savings from which the property was accumulated, while an annual wealth tax would raise revenue but in a way that made it more difficult for further concentration on large properties. In addition, a progressive tax on the total amount of property received by an individual by way of gift or inheritance would give a tax incentive for donors to hand on their property to those who had not already received much, and would make more difficult the continued concentration of property by inheritance by the wealthy from the wealthy.

The second and indirect method of redistributing income from property is for the state to acquire the ownership of property and to use the income from the property so acquired to finance the payment of social benefits to all citizens and in particular for the payment on more generous terms of the basic social dividend of which I have already spoken. The drastic method of transferring the ownership would be by means of a once-for-all capital levy at a progressive rate on all owners of wealth of all forms. An annual wealth tax and the taxation of gifts and bequests that I have suggested are less dramatic means for raising revenue that would be paid largely out of private holdings of wealth, and which the state could use either to redeem national debt or to invest in various ways in other forms of income-yielding property. In the case of previous nationalization schemes, the purpose was to transfer the management of real assets (such as the railway system) from private to public hands but at the expense of full compensation to the previous owners, so that the state made little or no gain or even some net loss on income account after setting the cost of interest payments to the compensated owners against the profits earned by the nationalized concerns. What I am proposing is something quite different. It is not to transfer management into public hands, but by means of the general taxation of wealth and of capital transfers to redeem national debt or to acquire for the public the unencumbered rights to a share of profits in enterprise whose management could be left entirely in private hands. The budgetary reduction in interest on the national debt and/or the receipt of income from the state ownership of shares in private enterprise would provide for the government a lasting net revenue that could contribute towards the costs of a social dividend.

Ninthly, everything that I have said relies somehow or another upon a change in attitudes, in which the stark confrontation between "them" and "us" in working life is greatly reduced. Participation in economic enterprises between the workers and the owners of capital, employed both in management decisions and in sharing the income produced by the enterprise, is a development that would have this desirable result. But, as I have already argued, I am reluctantly driven to the conclusion that if it is to be a real help in solving our basic problem, it will have to be accompanied by a rejection of the principle of equal pay for equal work – a conclusion that reinforces the case for the other redistributive measures that I have just catalogued.

Such in its barest outline is the sort of institutional set-up in the Mixed Economy that would in my opinion serve to meet our present needs. But I hasten to add that it constitutes a single interrelated whole, and none of it can be successfully achieved except by general consensus that as a whole it presents a better way to run our affairs. It certainly will not be easy to achieve such a consensus. Some sections of society will not like what Fascist Beast Meade has said about wage-setting. Others will not be attracted by what Bolshevik Meade has said about the taxation of wealth. The politicians are certainly in for a difficult time. But I must confess that Utopian Meade would like to live in the sort of free-market, egalitarian, participatory society that I have outlined. I think that Tom Marshall would have been interested in these ideas: indeed, I suspect that he might even have welcomed at least some of them. I pay my tribute to him by expounding these thoughts on what I think will prove to be the basic economic issue for the future of his Mixed Society.

# CHAPTER 9

# Citizenship and employment in an age of high technology

## Ronald Dore

This chapter raises an old but recently neglected question. Are technological changes creating a society in which, however good the educational system, there are too few people capable of doing efficiently all the complex jobs there are to do, and too few jobs of the kind that almost anybody can be trained to do – jobs, that is, the market valuation of the product of which allows the wage to be above the welfare minimum? And if that were to be so, what would happen to our notions of citizenship and democracy?

A good place to start is *Citizenship and social class* (Marshall 1950), those splendid and influential (Alfred) Marshall lectures given by T. H. Marshall well over a quarter of a century ago. They read now, in our less optimistic era, not just as a broad-sweep historical analysis, but also as a celebration. From Cromwell and Restoration England to 1949, he is saying, we have come a long way. The story is a story of progress, the establishment of civil rights in the definition of citizenship in the eighteenth century, of political rights in the nineteenth, of social rights in the twentieth. He quotes Trevelyan with approval, speaking of "the work of the Hanoverian period" to establish the rule of law – as if men and events had their appointed place in the unfolding of a great story: a story – with frequent setbacks, to be sure – of continuing progress.

Now the idea of progress has not been fashionable for 70 years, and the sources of disillusionment are well known. And yet, for all the general depreciation of the idea of progress, some of us remain unregenerate. The basis of my own unregeneracy lies in the following beliefs.

First, that there are some reasonably consistent long-term trends that can be discerned in the history of European societies, roughly since the Renaissance, and that if they are not exactly, in the words of Nisbet (1969: 303) as he sought to heap on them the maximum of ridicule, characterized by "unilinealism, continuity, directionality and uniformitarianism", they are at least unidirectional. Secondly, that they are the consequence, sometimes through long chains of knock-on effects, of the steady cumulation of scientific knowledge and applied technologies allowing machines to do more accurately and rapidly things that used to be done by men with the occasional help of animals. Thirdly, that for thinking about the future, an extrapolation of these trends, while not quite as safe a use of the principle of induction as assuming from past experience that the sun will rise tomorrow, is at least the road to useful working hypotheses. Fourthly, I cannot deny a residual urge to cling to the principle of optimism, the belief that the net effect of these trends is, on balance, a secular improvement in the sum of human happiness.

It is true that clinging to that optimism has in recent years become increasingly difficult. The reasons have to do partly with what is happening in society and the economy as a result precisely of those long-term technological trends just mentioned, and partly with the related developments in dominant ideologies.

## Egalitarianism

The long-term trend whose continuance seems most problematic is the growth of egalitarianism, a recurring theme in *Citizenship and social class* where Marshall referred to the growing strength of equality as a principle of social justice, the growth of a conception of "equal social worth", not merely of equal natural rights. He quotes Alfred Marshall's Whig-optimistic view of the future:

> The question is not whether all men will ultimately be equal – they certainly will not – but whether progress must go on steadily, if slowly, till, by occupation at least, everyone is a gentleman. I hold that it may and that it will.

And as for what he meant by everyone becoming a gentleman, he saw it happening around him, skilled artisans, soon to be called the labour aristocrats,

> . . . steadily developing independence and a manly respect for themselves, and, therefore, a courteous respect for others; they are steadily accepting the private and the public duties of a citizen; steadily grasping the truth that they are men, and not producing machines.

Tom Marshall's "conception of equal social worth", Alfred Marshall's "status of gentlemen", Alexis de Tocqueville's earlier "basic equality of condition" (1955) – they all had in mind the same thing. But the concept turns out on examination to be a somewhat elusive one. It is not just a matter of measurable institutional features, the changes in which Marshall charted: the steadily added-to bundle of rights accorded by public institutions to all citizens irrespective of their personal characteristics, hereditary or acquired. Nor is it that with the addition of other features, also in principle measurable, like the degree of formal respect revealed by the terms of address people use to each other in society. We all know how "citoyen" could, and "comrade" can, be uttered with an infinity of nuances. It is those nuances that prevent one from simply saying that "basic equality of condition" exists when, in addition to equal enjoyment of a large bundle of institutionally guaranteed rights, convention forbids the use of any categorizing labels for members of the society that (a) carry derogatory implications, and (b) refer to ascribed (in the Parsonian jargon) characteristics – i.e. inherited characteristics or characteristics not conceivably the result of their possessor's own volition. By this measure we have certainly moved a long way from the Victorian days when the label "pauper" was not only used in a derogatory sense but was a legally defined status involving deprivation of certain civic rights.

But "convention" in heterogeneous societies is a tenuous concept. Conventions about racial labels and the implications that may be attached to them are rather different, for example, among the staff and readership of the *Guardian* and the *Sun* respectively. There are some people – educational authorities – who were distressed at the contemptuous overtones other people packed into the term "mentally deficient", and they invented the clinical acronym ESN (educationally sub-normal) to replace it; whereupon the other people packed the same derogatory implications into that term too, and a new generation of administrators had to invent a new label: "children with severe learning difficulties". And so it will go on.

But there can be little doubt about the overall direction in which conventions have hitherto been changing – towards the increasing outlawing of discriminatory labels. Since one cannot guarantee that any categorization of people by inherited characteristics will not acquire pejorative connotations, the best thing to do is to avoid any such categorization at all. That, I believe, is why such anathema has been heaped on IQ testing, and the very concept of IQ. In 1951 a sensitive and humane man, author of one of the earliest environmentalist tracts, could write that a major problem of our societies is going to be finding themselves short of intelligent people, and suggest that all economic and institutional proposals ought to be costed in terms of their effect on the deployment of the man hours of Alpha-plus people (Roberts 1951). Who could write of such matters with such insouciance today?

It is all about dignity, and, of course, there is a plausible argument, which Maslow's famous "hierarchy of needs" theory would reinforce, that the more automatically society provides security and the satisfaction of basic physical wants, the more important becomes dignity, respect, prestige, honour, esteem. One might find some confirmation in the splendid Radio 4 programme for handicapped people, *Does he take sugar?* Most of the programme is devoted to questions of social service benefits and their intricacies, but the aspect of the handicapped condition that the programme's title chooses to highlight is precisely the dignity aspect; the claim to be treated as fully a person in one's own right.

## Equality versus other values

The distribution of dignity is likely to be a source of problems for any society in which the egalitarian urge, the sentiment of fraternity, the kindly desire to spare others the hurt of disrespect, is present. For there can be no society – no society can hold together for long – without a certain broad consensus about values, a general agreement that certain kinds of activities, certain kinds of qualities, are more valuable than others. And if "value" means anything it means that the people who are best at those activities, who exhibit those valued qualities to the highest degree, will be accorded more respect than others. Adam Smith, ill and not far from death, inserted a new passage in the last edition of his *Theory of moral sentiments* about the kinds of corruption to which our moral sentiments were prone (Smith 1853: 127). "The great mob of mankind", he said, "are the admirers and worshippers, and, what may seem more extraordinary, most frequently the disinterested admirers and worshippers, of wealth and greatness." How much better, he suggested, if they could be brought to admire wisdom and virtue instead. If they did, though, different people would, to be sure, be honoured, but there would still be a dignity distribution problem for anyone of strong egalitarian sentiment.

## The dignity minimum

Two paragraphs back I reeled off "dignity, respect, prestige, honour, esteem" as if they were synonyms. In my view they are. Others would differentiate in order to attach some absolute and non-relative meaning to the notion of "equality of basic condition" or "equal social worth". Thus, Daniel Bell, following Garry Runciman, insists on drawing a distinction between the basic "respect" that can be accorded to all by virtue of their humanity, and "praise" that is differentially, invidiously, accorded to individuals by virtue of the quality of their performance in valued activities (Bell 1974: 456–8). I find it very hard to intuit the difference. It still seems to me more in accordance with the workings of the psychological mechanisms involved, in so far as I know about them from introspection (and in accordance, for example, with the assumptions of those who construct occupational prestige scales), to think of dignity distribution as strictly analogous to income distribution. The welfare minimum, the income guaranteed by supplementary benefit, is not different in kind from the income received by the Chairman of ICI. There is just a lot less of it. The socially guaranteed level below which income is not allowed to fall certainly varies between societies. It is a good deal higher today than in the 1930s; higher here than in the USA or Japan but lower than in Germany. In just the same way when de Tocqueville took his French perceptions of society to America in the middle of the nineteenth century, he was struck by how much the basic dignity minimum was higher there than at home. He just happened, a bit misleadingly, to phrase it in terms of America having established "a basic equality of condition".

But even if one accepts my contention that it is only a matter of a guaranteed minimum in a highly skewed distribution of dignity, there are important distinctions to be drawn that Bell's use of the term "praise" draws attention to. There are some activities for which one receives praise if one does them supremely well, but no great reproach if one does them badly; there are others where excellence is hard to define, but a minimum competence is achieved by a large majority of the population. Athletics, music, politics are examples of the former; learning to read and write, getting a driving licence, attracting a spouse in a society that values the married state, finding a job, are examples of the latter. On the one hand are dimensions where invidious dividing lines are drawn through the top tail of the performance or ability distribution, on the other those where they are drawn through the bottom tail.

That is one important distinction. The second is concealed in the casual reference just made to "performance or ability distribution". One should not, of course, equate the two. Performance is a function of ability plus effort; and ability is a function of native aptitude plus past effort, plus opportunity luck, particularly the economic and cultural circumstances of early childhood. The perceived importance of the three ingredients – genes, effort and opportunity luck – is popularly seen to vary in different fields. Some kinds of performance are commonly seen as predominantly a function of native aptitude – such as the extremes of mathematical performance of the child prodigy and the Down's syndrome child. Some, like getting into the *Guinness book of records* for balancing an egg on one's forehead for 102 consecutive hours, or dying bravely for one's country, are seen as predominantly the product of effort – using "effort" broadly to cover determination, courage, single-mindedness – that is to say, inputs attributable to acts of will.

But what is generally *believed* to be the determining aptitude/effort/opportunity luck mix may not necessarily correspond with the way objective analysis would apportion the sources of variance. Many people have an interest in emphasizing the effort ingredient over the native aptitude ingredient. The successful, after all, may well prefer to attribute their success to effort that is under their own control – under the control of the innermost centre of our onion – like sense of self – the will, the centre of intentionality. That way they can claim the credit, as they could not if they attributed their success to their gene package or to social opportunity luck. But supposing they are modest and do not wish to claim the credit. Let the genius, then, say in self-deprecation that he cannot really claim the credit for having taken infinite pains; it's just his luck to have been born a superior person. No-one will grant him much modesty. He offends, in the way we saw that IQ tests offend, by making categories of people according to hereditary characteristics and attaching derogatory connotations to other people's categories – by seeming to say something, not about people's contingent performance, but about their intrinsic worth.

We are hopelessly ambivalent in these matters because we are all, particularly those of us who have brought up more than one child, very conscious of the importance of heredity in so many fields of differential performance – even for determining the strength of willpower that constitutes a capacity for effort. And yet we are also very conscious of the good comradely reasons for under-emphasizing the importance of heredity in social arrangements. Nowhere is this ambivalence greater than in the educational field. Teachers who are pre-eminently in the business of motivating effort tend naturally to emphasize its overwhelming importance – at least when they are in the classroom. The same teachers might well be found at conventions of progressive educators explaining all differences in school achieve-ment in terms of the maldistribution of opportunity in our class-ridden society. And again the same teachers in the staffroom, chatting with colleagues, might be heard cheerfully talking about pupils who are "over-achievers" or "under-achievers" – words that carry the implication that achievement levels ought to be pretty conclusively set by ability endowments and not too much distorted by effort inputs.

I have drawn two distinctions between the various dimensions of valued performance that lead to differential respect in our society: one according to where the line of invidious distinction is drawn – whether through the top tail, or the bottom tail of the distribution – and one according to the effort/aptitude/luck mix in the determination of performance. I did this to arrive at two rather simple propositions. The first is that dignity distribution problems are most acute – give rise to most anguish and conflict – with respect to performance dimensions where the dividing lines are drawn through the bottom tail of the distribution rather than the top tail. (Being part of the 75 per cent majority in the 1950s who never went to grammar school and did not take O levels was no great detraction from one's sense of worth. Being, after the introduction of CSE, part of, say, the 5 per cent minority of those who leave school without a single CSE might well be.) The second proposition is that dignity distribution problems are most likely to cause conflict and personal anguish in those situations (unlike manifest physical handicap, for instance) where uncertainty and ambivalence concerning the role of effort, aptitude and luck of circumstance in determining performance is at its greatest: where "You haven't tried hard enough" can be answered by "I never had a chance", but "Give me another try" by "Don't bother; you haven't got it in you."

## The retreat from Beveridge

This has some considerable significance for the main subject of this chapter: the experience and significance of unemployment. But first let me go back to the question of long-term trends. I referred to a steady growth of egalitarianism in recent centuries, one part of which was the institutional changes Marshall described in his 1949 lecture, creating equality of civil and political rights, and then of certain social rights – rights to a certain welfare minimum. Another part was the concomitant changing of the dignity distribution: raising the dignity minimum and compressing differentials. This happened partly as a result of the same institutional changes: abandoning the conventions of "lesser eligibility" that required paupers to be humiliated, for instance.

It was partly also the result of independent changes in social conventions. The Beveridge settlement was a landmark, raising the material welfare minimum and the dignity minimum simultaneously. The abolition of means tests, the insurance principles of universality and benefit as of right, envisaged a society where the dignity minimum *could* be high. This was so because, to start with, under policies of full employment everyone within a certain age span could have a useful function in society, the usefulness of which was guaranteed by the fact that someone was prepared to pay wages at market rates to have it performed. The contingencies that got in the way of income earning: unemployment (temporary, frictional unemployment), injury, old age, widowhood, could happen to us all. They could, therefore, be provided for on the mutual insurance principle, without any of the detraction from dignity implied either by charity, or by the invasion of privacy involved in providing proof of need.

Go to Germany and you can find a social security system that still works something like that – but with contribution rates double our levels. In Britain, the reality has come to deviate a long way from that ideal. About a quarter of all transfer payments are now means-tested supplementary benefits. The assumption that unemployment is a contingency that could happen, frictionally, to any of us grows increasingly thin. Leave pensions and pensioners aside for a moment and look only at the rest of the population. The poorest 30 per cent of non-pensioner adults and children get only 40 per cent of their income from earnings and 60 per cent from welfare benefits (calculated from HMSO 1985: Table 5.6). The jungle of payment systems, the administrative costs of supplementary benefit now amounting to 11 per cent of the benefits administered, the poverty traps in the transition points from benefits to earnings, have created such a sense of crisis that every organization in the country concerned with social policy has produced its own plans for reform. Nearly all of them, not only those of the Institute of Directors or the Unit for Social Affairs, even those of the Institute of Fiscal Studies, start off from assumptions that are closer to those of nineteenth-century charity-transfers than they are to Beveridge mutuality. They declare themselves to be concerned with "the relief of poverty". They speak of "the poor", and the assumption that being a member of the poor is a relatively permanent, not just a temporary status, is often implicit in what they say – an assumption, as we shall see, for which there is some evidence. If Beveridge mutuality always was a bit of a fiction, it was a purposeful fiction, like the fiction that all citizens have an equal understanding of political issues and so are entitled to a single vote each. Its purpose was to uphold the dignity minimum. That concern has become a distinctly minor concern in the debates of the rival scheme builders today.

## The structural sources of egalitarianism

What has happened? Can it be that the tide of egalitarianism is on the turn, that the trend that has seemed for centuries to be moving inexorably in a single direction has reached a final limit?

If de Tocqueville were alive today, would he revise his view that the growth of equality is a "providential fact" that "has all the chief characteristics of such a fact: it is universal, it is lasting, it constantly eludes all interference, and all events as well as all men contribute to its progress"? The task of guessing an answer to that question will be made easier if we have some clear idea as to what caused the trend in the first place. Is it just a matter of the steady refinement of moral sensibilities parallel to the increasing sophistication of scientific understanding of the world? That argument assumes that moral truths have the same epistemological status as scientific truths, and are revealed by similar processes of discovery – an assumption that most of us would find hard to endorse. It does not, anyway, explain the mechanisms. What is the moral equivalent of the curiosity that provides the motive power for scientific advance? What historical succession of dominant moral ideas could plausibly claim the sort of cumulative sequence exhibited by the evolving understanding of, say, combustion?

De Tocqueville, who gave much thought to charting the growth of egalitarianism in Europe, confessed himself at a loss to explain it. He could only say that it must be "an unquestionable sign of [God's] will" (1955: 7). His countrymen, Guizot and Bouglé, did rather better. They argued from two historical instances, not one (Bouglé 1908). The last centuries of the Roman Empire also showed a growth in egalitarianism similar to that in Europe since the Renaissance. (They created, indeed, the Christianity that provided such a potent ideological weapon for Europe's later egalitarians.) Guizot's and Bouglé's explanations were in terms of changes in social structure. Egalitarianism is inextricably linked with individualism, with the breakdown of feudal constraints, the growth of the market nexus in cities, mobility, choice and contract. In a feudal society A can be the superior of B in all walks of life; the master at work, the front pew occupant at church, the judge in civil disputes, the patron of village sports. Inequality can be effectively, because consistently, enforced. In a mobile market society with differentiated institutional spheres, B might start off poorer and end up richer than A. B might be A's employee, but at the same time churchwarden in the church where A is a mere member of the congregation. When they go off to the wars it may be B, not A, who comes back a sergeant.

The underlying postulate, it would seem, is something like the following. There is a human need for dignity, just as there is a need for food and sex. And just as, say, running a society in which half the population is required to remain celibate requires a very heavily sanctioned set of rigid institutions, and strong ideological indoctrination, so, institutionalized dignity deprivation, like sex deprivation, requires a pretty rigid set of institutions to maintain it. That is what feudal societies had. Let those institutions crumble, and the demand for compression of dignity differentials, and for raising the dignity minimum, will grow. So, too, once the inevitability and naturalness of income inequalities cease to be believed, in pressures for reduction of material income differentials and the raising of the material welfare minimum can begin to grow.

The two processes reinforce each other. The demand for the one can sometimes be seen as an expression of the other. The starving man in rags cannot easily appear dignified. The raising of the material welfare minimum, likewise, weakens the material sanctions that once enforced dignity deprivation. The mutual feedback produces what Daniel Bell calls the Tocqueville effect – one manifestation of a broader phenomenon that might be called the Cleopatra effect: the appetite growing by what it feeds on. As equality of material wellbeing increases in society, so expectations of equality increase even faster. As de Tocqueville said: people may suffer less but their sensibility is exacerbated. And for sensibility read envy; or, for the principled, nothing-personal-to-gain egalitarianism of the *bien-pensant* middle classes like the writer and the readers of this chapter, read Schoeck's term, "envy-avoidance" (1966). Some of the dystopias of science fiction take grisly pleasure in extrapolating the trend: Vonnegut's *corps de ballet*, all except one issued with handicap weights so that none shall leap higher than her fellows; the society of L. P. Hartley's *Facial justice* where all girls are operated on to give them a uniform Beta-grade face. And so on.

## The turning of the tide? A new hierarchical order?

*Will* it be like that? Given that explanation of the past, what might one conclude about the future? It would be plausible to take the apparent disappearance of a concern with the dignity minimum in current British debates about social security, not as a kink in a long-term trend but as a real turning of the tide, if one saw some way in which our society was once again going to develop a set of rigid constraining institutions that would serve to keep lower orders firmly in their place in deferential submission to higher orders.

And in fact that seems to me not at all unlikely. Perhaps we can begin already to discern the shape of a New Hierarchical Order. There is one other steady trend stemming from the accumulation of scientific and technological knowledge over recent centuries. We all know about the ever more refined and specialized division of labour that is entailed by the increasing sophistication of the technology we use. Durkheim also thought that somehow or other this brought a matching increase in the differentiation of native abilities in society. He quotes Le Bon's figures for the cranial capacities of adult males found in various skeleton populations. The difference between the largest and smallest was 200 cc for gorillas, 280 cc for Indian pariahs, 350 cc for ancient Egyptians, 470 cc for twelfth century Parisians, 600 cc for nineteenth-century Parisians and 700 cc for nineteenth-century Germans (Durkheim 1964: 133). He does not let on whether he thinks that assortative mating or some Lamarckian process is responsible. Cephalometry is such a tabooed pastime these days that I do not know whether these results are still accepted or what significance is attached to them, but the point is of no great importance for the trend I want to identify. It may be enunciated in a general form as follows: the more sophisticated the technology a society uses, the more social arrangements have to take account of differences in learning ability among men and women, and the more salient the general social awareness of such differences is likely to become. Paradoxically, in other words, the more egalitarianism has grown, the more have inequalities – the ineluctable inequalities of genetic endowment, of the sort that distinguish slow learners from quick learners and are roughly measured by IQ tests – come to count.

I cannot offer correlated time series in proof of this proposition; I can only appeal to common-sense perceptions. In pastoral societies almost anyone could master the arithmetic needed for the simple purposes to which arithmetic was put, like counting sheep. Even calendrical arithmetic was simple enough that few astronomers had sons who were not able to grasp the secrets of the trade over a long childhood training. With only primitive voice-training techniques, most people could manage acceptable standards of yodelling. Today, only tenors whose sophisticated training shows them to be gifted get listened to. And the skills required to run an atomic power plant or a jumbo jet, to design an integrated circuit or an experimental corrective institution, are such that it is not within the capacity of all, or even of a large percentage, of the population to acquire them in a reasonable period of time. And it is very much in the interests of the rest of us (a) that those who do these jobs should have acquired those skills, and (b) that people should not embark on a lengthy and expensive training to acquire them unless there are strong reassuring indications that they will succeed. And among the various dimensions of talent that society is likely for these reasons to be concerned with – and to reward – athletic talent, musical talent, television-personality charm, etc., it is the multi-purpose mental talents measured by the various components of IQ tests that are most generally important.

The economy of this kind of talent, in other words, becomes of increasing importance for social efficiency, and through a variety of institutional initiatives, partly by government, partly by those in charge of work organizations and partly by those looking after the interests of professional groups, the devices for channelling talent – for "sponsored mobility" in one sociologist's phrase (Turner 1960) – begin slowly to accumulate. China started 2,000 years ago. In Britain the first formal ability tests for jobs come with the East India Company in the nineteenth century, then for the home civil service, and in the end even the foreign service adopts them. The forerunner of the British Medical Association started in a modest way selecting recruits by general academic ability in 1851. The ICIs, the Unilevers and the Anglo-Burma Oils – eventually even the Vickers and the English Electrics – start recruiting bright university graduates for special management career tracks in the early decades of the century. And today, if you want a machinist's job in Nippon Electric in Livingston, Scotland, you need three O levels to apply, and probably need to do better than that if you hope to be one of the one-in-ten who are chosen.

Educators would be likely to resist the suggestion that academic achievement records are primarily used as proxy measures of general intelligence, but when one of the most perceptive of them says that even at graduate level employers are more concerned with "trainability" than with specific skills, that is, in effect, his implication (Taylor 1985: 107). Educational selection is, however, only a part of a larger syndrome of characteristics, and it is that whole larger syndrome of characteristics that seems to threaten – or to promise, according to taste – the creation of the New Hierarchical Order I spoke of; new restrictive institutions sufficiently constraining to reverse the egalitarian tide.

The other parts of it are, on the one hand, oligopoly and the substitution of administration for markets, and on the other, the phenomenon usually referred to as the growth of internal labour markets – once described 30 years ago, rather significantly from the point of view of our earlier discussion of the origin of egalitarianism, as the growth of a new feudalism. Let us illustrate with an example. Difficulty of entry, oligopoly and the need for administrative regulation produce, say, a stable hierarchy of four airlines. Number one with the largest market share has the highest prestige, offers the best promotion chances. Few of its pilots want to leave it for any of the others and so, for morale requirements if for nothing else, number one gets set up for lifetime employment: structuring career promotion chains, giving some recognition to seniority, and so on. Likewise, none of the pilots in number two wishes to leave it, except to join number one – that they would probably have preferred to join in the first place, if only they had managed to pass its selection procedure. Number one is, indeed, the pioneer in careful selection procedures, because it has more applicants and because it is more likely to be stuck with the people it chooses for life. And educational records, and what those records suggest about their possessor's position in the IQ distribution, play an essential eliminating role in those procedures. To complete the circle, the fact that number one airline gets the best people helps it to stay top. Occasionally a maverick newcomer will appear, Laker-like, to upset the regularity of the pattern, but the others will know well enough how to fix that.

I have nothing but a few fragments of gossip as grounds for suggesting that employment in our airline industry actually does work like that, but I offer as a hypothesis the suggestion that empirical research would show that to be the pattern towards which it is tending. I do so because one can see the logic of every step in the development so clearly, and because I have spent a good deal of time in a society, Japan, where the process started much earlier and has gone further. The great Japanese contribution to the New Hierarchical Order (henceforth NHO) is to develop standardized systems of person-classification. The reluctance to talk IQ in fact came in Japan earlier than in Britain and America. They stick strictly to achievement tests, academic merit. But they perceive that, of the variables in the famous Michael Young (1961) formula, "merit equals IQ plus effort", the effort variable did not fluctuate very much more over the individual's childhood than the IQ variable, and since both effort and IQ have occupational importance, school performance can be used very satisfactorily as a predictor of future work performance.

Nowadays Japanese children are educated until the age of 15 wholly in mixed-ability classes in mixed-ability schools. At 15, competitive entrance examinations sort them out into five or six grades of high school each of which draws on a very narrow segment of the ability range. At 18, pupils from the top two or three grades of high school are again sorted out, according to their performance in university entrance examinations, among a spectrum of universities ranked in a well charted hierarchy of prestige/difficulty of entry. The charting of that hierarchy – and consequently its efficient functioning in providing market signals both to student applicants and to employers of the products of the universities – is the work of the mock-test providers. These are often, also, the operators of cram-school chains in which would-be university entrants spend one or two years hoping, by further study, to raise the level at which they enter the crucial university hierarchy. The tests are standardized on national population norms and have acquired a high level of predictive power. Pupils learn with some accuracy at which point in the prestige hierarchy they might have a chance of entering. Once Tokyo University, at the peak of the hierarchy, used to get seven or eight applicants for every place; today, with unrealistic applicants deterred, only two or three. Thus, the system becomes highly self-reinforcing.

The system is much criticized in Japan but it works. The last piece of the institutional complex is job recruitment. The top firms recruit from top universities and from the best of the third rank high schools whose pupils do not go on to university. The second rank firms recruit from the second rank universities, and so on. It all works smoothly, it even promotes social efficiency, if social efficiency means putting the biggest lumps of capital resource and decision-making power into the hands guided by the keenest brains.

## Recent British trends

I suspect that in the long run that is the way Britain is tending. I may be wrong. It may be that the dedication of our present government to the destruction of oligopoly, to the reversal of the trend for administration to replace markets, to the ending of labour market rigidities and the restoration of mobile flexibility – it may be that all those things will actually have an effect in reversing trends that have after all been faintly visible for a century. What is currently happening in our educational system provides ambiguous clues. On the one hand, the merging of the 16-plus exams is the inertial continuation of the earlier egalitarian trends that produced the comprehensive school – a class abatement measure, as Marshall called it, to ensure true parity of esteem. At the same time the designers of the new test have made clear that it will not be less useful than the old ones, and will possibly be more useful, to employers who want to use it to situate school leavers in the overall ability distribution.

Meanwhile, at the top end, a new pro-active Higher Education Funding Council (formerly the University Grants Committee) is pushing tertiary education gently towards Japanese-type hierarchization. At the extreme tail of the ability distribution the percentile differences become important. In a society with our levels of technology and decision-making complexity it is not enough to be able to conclude that if someone was in the 8 per cent of the age group who got into a university he or she is probably at least in the top 15 per cent of the ability distribution. The rationalization of Oxbridge entry with formal examinations in the last two decades has provided the means of guessing who is and who is not in the top one or two percentiles. The Oxbridge label now means something specific in ability and not – or not just – in class terms, and getting that label has now become so important as to be a dominant preoccupation of our sixth forms. British organizational styles still put a greater premium on personal magnetism, "bottom", natural authority, etc. – qualities that do not much correlate with school results – than do Japanese, so that we are unlikely to go as far in this direction as they do. But there seems little doubt in which direction we are going – and the faster we go the more the premium which technical and organizational complexity puts on brains.

## Technology and skill structures

It is time to look at the other tail of the distribution and to get back to the question of the dignity minimum. I suggested above that the increasing sophistication of our technology (and I include our systems for gathering and sorting and evaluating information and processing it into decisions) makes native abilities – learning capacities, trainability – more important. If one can imagine a scale of the intellectual demandingness of jobs – to be measured, say, by the number of weeks or years it takes a person of given intelligence to master it – then the intellectual demandingness of the average job is continually rising. And the pace of change is fast. In my boyhood there was almost nothing around the house whose workings I could not understand except the radio, and I had friends who knew all about that. Today the house is full of devices I would not have the hubris to remove the lid from. Is it possible that we shall move, or have already moved, into an era when there will be too few bright people to do competently all the difficult jobs that need doing and too few jobs for the less bright people to do?

This was a fear freely and openly discussed some thirty years ago before the more recent manifestations of egalitarianism made it seem like pushing people below the dignity minimum even to single out "people of low ability" as a category. Norbert Wiener in the late 1940s already spoke of the first industrial revolution destroying the jobs that required physical labour and the second industrial revolution destroying the more routine jobs requiring manual and clerical skills (Weiner 1968). Kurt Vonnegut in 1952 wrote a splendid and disturbing novel depicting the NHO that results. In his *Player piano* world, measured IQs alone determine the individual's allocation in a centrally controlled occupational hierarchy. But only the top two or three deciles of the ability range are needed for genuinely productive jobs. The rest of the population are either in the army where, although they have no weapons, they can "hide their hollowness beneath twinkling buttons and buckles, crisp serge and glossy leather" (Vonnegut 1952: 29), or else, more dispiritingly, they are in the make-work Reconstruction and Reclamation Corps – "the reeks and wrecks" – enjoying, as they used to say about workers in the Housing Department of the London Borough of Camden, "leisure on the rates". The welfare minimum is high and rising. The dignity minimum has plummeted, and what is more, the elite's concern with the dignity minimum has disappeared. The

179

older generation of engineers and managers, he records, had been through the war and they knew that valour and comradeship and decency and good feeling were values for judging people as important as brains and learning. So they were always slightly sheepish about their eliteness. But not so the younger generation. Now, he says, "this elite business, this assurance of superiority, this sense of rightness about the hierarchy topped by managers and engineers – this was instilled in all college graduates, and there were no bones about it". He might be describing the transition from the wet generation of the Earl of Stockton, to the generation of the hard young men of Mrs Thatcher's circle.

## The interpretation of current unemployment

Take Vonnegut's novel, as one is entitled to take it, as a serious prediction. Was he right? Does the unemployment of contemporary Britain have anything to do with the change in the job structure consequent on changes in technology?

Of course demand deficiency accounts for a large part of total unemployment. Most economists would also acknowledge that there is a certain problem of structural unemployment resulting from technical change. Equally most would see this as a transitional, frictional problem. Labour-saving capital goods have, to be sure, destroyed jobs but past experience shows that this is a temporary state of affairs that cures itself in two ways. First, the improvement in productivity creates new wealth, which makes a demand for new goods and services that creates jobs. This takes time. If the wealth it creates takes the form of profits that are then invested in South Africa it may take quite a lot of time – particularly if the wealth holders migrate to the south of France. But in the long run it will happen. Secondly, historically the increase in productivity brought by new technology has been taken, as to about 30 per cent, in the form of increased leisure rather than increased goods and services. Shorter working hours, longer annual holidays, have produced an aggregated job sharing effect. That is also bound to happen again, and that also takes a considerable adjustment time. But there is no reason at all to suppose that we will not eventually get back to full employment.

It would take too long to argue fully the contrary view, that for any given level of demand there is an employability threshold that is a function, on the supply side, of the minimum wage set by the guaranteed welfare minimum; on the demand side, of the pattern of final consumption and of the technical coefficients determining the value added of the "job slots" into which labour demand is conventionally packaged. And, secondly, that this threshold at maximum feasible demand has risen. Once it was drawn through the extreme tail of the mental ability distribution to exclude only special categories of people entitled to sheltered employment. Today it may well have moved up to exclude from the likelihood of employment much larger numbers. Here the relevant arguments can only be sketched in outline.

First, there are the a priori arguments why we cannot expect the experience of previous periods of technological change to be repeated. These are arguments from changes not only in mechanization but also in the guaranteed welfare minimum. To be worth a job today, a person has not only got to be able to perform a function more accurately and cheaply than machines that have become much cleverer than they were; the market value of that performance has got to be greater than a welfare minimum that is higher than it was. A crucial area of uncertainty is the development of employment in the service industries in some of which the requirements for job efficiency are less those associated with intelligence and school performance, and have more to do, instead, with personality qualities like kindliness and conscientiousness. What will be the value we place on such services, given tax-allergies and cut-backs in public expenditure, the growth of voluntary community services, and the mechanization even of domestic tasks? How does the empirical evidence look? To begin with, there has been a steady rise in the numbers unemployed at the peak of each business cycle since the mid-1960s, long before our present monetarist era, which argues some kind of structural change. Extrapolation of that trend, it has been suggested, would give us now between one and a quarter and one and a half million unemployed, even without the exacerbation of current deflationary policies.

The changing ratio of vacancies to unemployment also suggests a new structural element in unemployment. In the 1960s there was a fairly clear inverse relation; the number of vacancies went up when unemployment went down and vice versa. But not so since the second quarter of 1981, when vacancies and unemployment began to rise, and employment to fall, simultaneously. The mismatch is partly regional, but mostly occupational. Available skills do not match vacancies, which tells one directly only about developed competencies, not about employability thresholds – the capacity to *acquire* saleable competencies – but may also have indirect implications for the latter.

There are signs, too, of an increasing concentration of unemployment experience within the group of the long-term unemployed. In 1984, as the length of uncompleted terms of unemployment increased (together with the increase in the number of long-term unemployed), the length of completed terms of unemployment decreased; those getting jobs got them quicker (HMSO 1985: 69). There may also be some significance in the fact that unemployment is increasingly concentrated in families. Only 31 per cent of unemployed men had a wife or child working in 1983, compared with 61 per cent of employed men – a gap that has widened by 11 percentage points since 1976 (HMSO 1985: 74). One explanation, and probably the crucial one, is the pound for pound reduction of welfare benefits beyond the first £4 of a wife's earnings. But it may also be evidence of the emergence of an underclass culture of discouraged non-job-seekers, familiar already from the American ghetto.

As for increased concentration of unemployment among the unskilled, the evidence from studies of the flows into and out of unemployment is ambiguous (Daniel 1981, DE 1983, White 1983). A priori one would expect a "bumping down" process to occur, thereby producing a concentration of unemployment among the least employable. The model goes as follows. At the first onset of large-scale unemployment all occupational groups suffer equally. But suppose there are five "grades" of job and five skill "grades" of people to fill them. Top-grade people – grade-five people – not finding a top-grade job in current depressed conditions, settle for a grade-four job, and employers are pleased to get "a better class of worker". But with some grade-four jobs going to grade-fivers, grade-fourers have an even harder time, and a larger proportion of them find themselves queuing for grade-three jobs. And so on down the line until nearly all the grade-one jobs are taken by bumped-down grade-twoers, and the grade-oners bear a disproportionate burden of unemployment.

There are two things to be said about that model. The first is that it assumes a single dimension of employability – or rather "desirability in the eyes of employers" – that is clearly false in ignoring the high degree of specificity of some skills. Yet it is not *so* false as to have no relevance to reality. Consider, for instance, the growingly institution-alized stratification in the youth employment market, a hierarchy that shows a marked correlation with school performance. At the top are those in further and higher education with little fear of unemploy-ment if they are not too selective about the jobs that they will take. One step down are those in apprenticeships and traineeships and jobs with a promotion future. Then come those who have some other regular job, even dead-end. Then come those on employer-based Youth Training Scheme (YTS) schemes or enrolled in YTS ITech Centres. And finally come those who are on other Mode B, non-employer-based, YTS schemes – community projects and the like. It is a "recognized hierarchy", an unidimensional one, in the sense that there is general agreement that anyone in a lower niche would prob-ably acknowledge his preference for being in a higher one – if only he could have succeeded in the competition to enter it. That perception colours both self-perceptions and employers' perceptions of employee desirability.

The second thing implicit in the "bumping down" model is the way reversal takes place when demand picks up. The grade-oners get back their jobs only slowly as they are vacated by the grade-twoers going back to their "proper" level, which depends on the grade three-ers having done likewise, etc. But reversal is not an automatic process since the experience of unemployment itself affects employability. It can be so destructive of self-confidence and of the self-disciplined capacity to take responsibility, that re-entry into employment be-comes difficult.

One particular factor of relevance to the possibility of the emer-gence of an underclass of the permanently unemployed, is the concen-tration of unemployment, not just among the unskilled, but among the unskilled young. Under-25s made up 6 per cent of the long-term (6 months plus) unemployed in 1962, 31 per cent in 1981 (OECD 1982: 141). It is reasonable to assume that this is a consequence of the growth of internal labour markets, the increased emphasis on job security, the decline of hire-and-fire labour practices. In 1983, 88 per cent of British employees had been in their job for more than 12 months (OECD 1984). Increasingly, over a wide range of jobs, those who once get into employment stay in employment. More unem-ployment takes the form of a queue of would-be starters waiting for the chance to get in. (The trend towards "tenured jobs" over a large part of the market also means that employers are more careful in choosing whom they take in from the waiting queue. And if it is new labour market entrants who are in question, school records may be seen as important evidence. Hence the increasing clarity of the "recognized hierarchy" of youth jobs mentioned earlier.)

Whatever the cause, the concentration of unemployment in the younger age groups exacerbates the possibly long-term effects of the experience of unemployment on employability. Nothing is better calculated to reduce a person's mastery of tenuously acquired skills than a prolonged period without the occasion to practise them, nothing more destructive of self-confidence and a sense of responsibility that are also such important ingredients of work capacity.

What all this implies is the possibility that, even if it were irrational to fear continuation of deflationary policies for a generation, even if one could look forward to a future when bumping up will replace bumping down so that everybody, Peter's Principle-wise, moves upward to his or her level of barely tolerable competence, there could still be structural unemployment (i.e. shortage of people of even barely tolerable competence for the jobs on offer), as well as a lot of inefficiency caused by those of merely border-line competence. And this could *include* structural unemployment at the very bottom.

One way of coping with such structural mismatch – or at least of the efficiency side of it – is for the able and qualified to work harder. And arguably there is evidence of that. The distribution of work and leisure is getting more and more skewed. On the one hand, the growing aggregate volume of leisure is increasingly concentrated in the form of the involuntary leisure of the unemployed. On the other, work, too, is getting increasingly concentrated among a minority of the gainfully employed – the workaholic, moonlighters and the 80-hour-a-week executives and civil servants and barristers who are either able and ambitious, or who have so many opportunities in their work for choice and what Maslow called self-actualization that the whole distinction between work and play is blurred. And a neoclassical economist who actually believed in market forces might say that the striking recent increases in relative pay of top business executives was evidence of a real scarcity of talent that really does inhibit overloaded jobs from being shared.

The more obvious and preferable way of curing structural unemployment rooted in the structure of competence levels – including bottom-end unemployment – is, of course, to improve the education and training system. And it is particularly relevant to the present discussion that in, for example, comparisons between Britain and Germany, such as those of Prais and Postlethwaite, it is among those of below-average scores that school attainments are markedly inferior in Britain, not among those of above-average performance. It is the slower learners who are cheated in our school system (Postlethwaite 1958, Prais 1958).

What we are talking about here, however, is the possibility that even if we were to improve our schools' performance to the level of Germany's, or better, the native-ability constraints to learning are such that, given the cheapening of the ways of replacing human labour by machines, given the intellectual and responsibility demands of the remaining jobs where such substitution is impossible or too costly, we would still have competence mismatch, labour shortages and labour surplus. Put the proposition, alternatively, in a form more acceptable to our neoclassical economist: given the structure of demand for different types of labour in a technically advanced society, and the supply of those types of labour in an educationally efficient society, there may well still be types of labour the market-clearing price for which is below the welfare minimum.

## The crux of the problem

It is the context of the NHO in which this is happening that is at the root of the problem. The point about "recognized hierarchies", such as the structure of youth employment destinations mentioned earlier, is that they label people. Schools and their performance rankings label people too. At one time children who found school an experience of failure and frustration and dignity-denial could be liberated by leaving it. Finding a job put them above the dignity minimum, gave them a rightful, citizen's place in a Beveridge society. Now even the labour market is structured in such a way as to confirm their disadvantaged status, to write the label in bigger and clearer letters.

And if, as I suggest we have good reason to fear, a number of them – a growing number of them – find themselves relegated to permanent membership in a clearly socially recognizable unemployed/unemploy-able status, and if, in future, substantial numbers of children are born into that underclass with little chance of getting out of it, what happens to our concept of citizenship? What happens to the dignity minimum? What happens to the basic fictions that sustain our democracy?

## False hopes

First let us deal, briefly, with two quite spurious solutions. First, there are those who say airily that the solution is simple and lies in an adjust-ment of our mistaken values. It is only, the argument goes, in societies that falsely identify work with social worth or "jobs" with work (Handy 1984, Robertson 1984) that there is any problem of dignity deprivation for the unemployed. Technology has made such a value system outmoded. It is time we realized it. Time that we put our schools to educating people for leisure. Do that, our value systems will change, and we shall have no problem of dignity deprivation for those without work.

The fallacies of this argument are, alas, all too obvious. There is still going to be a lot of complex, challenging and interesting work to be done in our society, and the chance of doing it is still going to be highly prized, not just for the money, but also for the power that goes with the decision-making jobs, and the work satisfaction that goes with all the problem-solving jobs. (See the earlier discussion of the workaholic executives.) In the schools, the pupils with prospects of such jobs will be the bright ones, the teachers' favourites, the ones it is most rewarding to teach. It is their prospects and ambitions and prefer-ences that will dominate the ethos of the school. The new leisure ethic – self-cultivation and all that is a superior alternative to getting and spending – is not going to have much of a chance.

There are signs, indeed, that the work ethic might get stronger rather than weaker in industrial countries, at least in laggard countries like Britain, as a result of the dilemma we face in trying to run an international free-trade system on the one hand, while maintaining national sovereignty in economic policy on the other. The stridency with which we are increasingly urged in Britain to restore our ailing economy to competitiveness is evidence thereof. It is another conse-quence of technological change. The cheapening of transport and communications has so intensified international competition that we are forced to pull our socks up. We can no longer afford the hangover effect of our old aristocratic versions of the leisure ethic, let alone cultivate a new one.

The second spurious argument is the political one sometimes heard on the Left. There should be no problem about the dignity of the unemployed, it runs. All we have to do is to give them political education, to make them see that it's not their fault they are unemployed; it's all because of the rottenness of society, the mistaken monetarist, etc. policies of the government. It would be an insensitive argument, even if it were never used by the activists of the intellectual proletariat to mobilize baton fodder among the easily-led (Watts 1983: 86). Supposing you do convince an unemployed man or woman that 15 per cent unemployment is the government's fault. That does not solve his or her dignity problem that is: why should it be me who is the one in ten rejected and not the other nine – especially if, in the New Hierarchical Order the answer "it's just pure luck", and in the welfare state the answer "I never had a chance", both become less plausible.

Among one group, however, the dignity problem can be solved by such arguments – and that is among black people who have, of course, the greatest incidence of unemployment and prospects of long-term unemployment. In so far as they can see themselves – with good evidential support – as the victims of unfair discrimination not of personal deficiencies, their despair can be turned into anger against the discriminators rather than paralysing dissatisfaction with themselves. This therapeutic effect of increasing black militancy and hostility towards the majority society is not greatly consoling, however, to those who are prejudiced in favour of social harmony and fraternity.

It is probably also true – to revert to earlier remarks about the bottom tails of distribution – that the growth in unemployment paradoxically eases the self-image problem. If you are the one in ten who is rejected, that is dispiriting. But it is not so dispiriting as being the one in fifty, when the other forty-nine all get jobs. But it is more dispiriting than if you are part of, say, a 50 per cent unsuccessful minority – if only one in two are getting jobs. *The Economist* was puzzled by a survey that found the unemployed to be feeling "less ashamed, less depressed, less useless and less bored" in December 1982 when their numbers were reaching 3 million than two years earlier when they were half that number – perhaps already a sign of that principle at work (*The Economist*, 4 December 1982).

But nobody who has read Vonnegut's *Player piano* and remembers his comfortable, philistine, welfare-benefit underclass, would look in that direction for a solution to the problem of maintaining the dignity minimum in a society with large numbers of people who cannot claim a share of the jobs that are going. And I, personally, must declare my attachment to the Protestant work ethic. Abolish acquisitiveness if you like, but I would not like to live in a society that did not honour those who perform socially useful functions.

## A new basis for the dignity minimum

So one looks for ways in which the dignity minimum can be maintained because everyone has the chance to perform socially useful functions; everyone has a job. James Meade in his brilliant first Marshall lecture (Ch. 8) pointed the way. We need, he said, some means of lowering the real wage, while raising real incomes, by increasingly managing the distribution of the gains of technical progress in ways independent of the price and wage mechanisms. One possible device that he considers – and which has been around a long time – is the idea of a social dividend paid to everyone. This takes care of the dignity minimum problem, first by making the payment universal, and given as of citizen right, and no longer a means-tested contingency fall-back when what is seen as a "normal" wage income fails. It does so, secondly, by making all wage income an extra supplement to the basic citizen wage, by drastically lowering the feasible minimum wage, the minimum value added that performance of a job function must yield, thereby lowering the employability threshold, and enabling almost everyone to have a job.

Further, Meade suggests, if machines are going to do more and more of the work and men less and less, then allocative efficiency probably requires that the wage share in national income should fall in relation to the capital share. If the state acquired a sizeable share of this increasingly significant capital stock though a capital levy or wealth tax, the social dividend could then be financed from the growing proceeds of this collectively owned capital; more and more of our income would be property income and less and less labour income, while maintaining not too unequal shares.

The difficulty is: how to get from here to there. How to make feasible the financing of the social dividend on a scale big enough to count; how to make a capital levy of the necessary size politically as well as administratively feasible; how to bring about the wage reduction that is a necessary part of it.

## Reordering the basis of income

One possible way of trying to deal with these problems, and in particular of dealing with the transition problem in a way that takes account of the concentration of unemployment among the younger age groups, is as follows.

First, to begin with the least important part, one way to build up the capital fund from which the social dividend is to be paid – the State Patrimony, shall we call it – and of doing it gradually, and in kind, is by the process of equity dilution. For companies, the wealth tax takes the form of giving the fund a free rights issue equal to $x$ per cent of their existing equity every year. The fund could likewise acquire an $x/(100 + x)$ share in the ownership title to real estate and art objects valued over a certain sum, that share to be realized whenever the item changes hands. In this way, the fund could slowly build up. If the dilution were 2 per cent, the fund would acquire half the national wealth (all that not in family houses and modest personal possessions, that is) in 36 years, three-quarters in 72 years.

The most obvious counterpart of the slow build-up of the fund is a slow increase in the level of benefit paid out of it. But there is an alternative. One could start with a large benefit for a few beneficiaries and only gradually increase their number. One could, for example, expand the beneficiary population age group by age group. It could be used first to supplement or replace the pension, and then pensionable age could be brought steadily lower and lower. In the context of the present discussion of youth unemployment and the erosion of dignity, a more attractive alternative might be to start at the other end. Let all those who reach the age of 16 next year receive a social dividend, a variable sum depending on the profitability of the fund's equity holdings, but also age-related, perhaps by some compulsory savings device, so that it builds up over three, or if possible, five years from a teenager dividend to a full adult dividend. And set the capital dilution rate at a level that would provide something like 35 per cent of the average wage – somewhat more for a couple with two children than the 62 per cent of average wage provided by supplementary benefit in 1983. The following year, the 17- and 16-year-olds would be covered, and so on until, in about 80 years time, we have special TV programmes to mark the death of the last unendowed man, or more likely woman, with pictures of her drawing the last old-regime pension.

With the endowment, the teenager might receive the right to study, the right to work, but also duties of unpaid community service, duties that should be compulsory and universal, though widely flexible in form. Only in this way can one achieve, what all the schemes for voluntary youth community service (Tawney Society 1984) cannot achieve – namely a genuine sharing in community work, on equal terms both of motivation and performance, between the bright ones for whom community work is an interruption of their preparation for a rewarding work career, and those for whom the alternative would be unemployment.

## Some implications

The variability of the dividend depending on the performance of the national economy would provide everyone with an additional incentive to take part in the producing economy, over and above the wages they might receive. Clearly, thanks to the "free-rider problem" it would be an extremely tenuous incentive. Only the few who enjoy an enormous sense of self-importance will be able to believe that their own contributions make a measurable impact on their dividend. This is true, but it is also true that everyone *would* have a strong interest in stopping everybody else from being a free-rider. Hence we should see the schools suddenly revitalizing the ethic of duty and responsibility, which would not be at all a bad thing.

The overall reduction of wages which could increase work opportunities would take place gradually as new age groups come on to the market. What the existing Young Workers' Scheme tries to do, selectively, to bring down youth wages, would happen as a result of the manner of the Scheme's introduction. Within a few years the concentration of unemployment among the young should end. The low-wage cure for youth unemployment would inevitably lead to displacement of some older workers at first, and it is admittedly difficult to foresee the counter-measures necessary to deal with the problem of having dividend receivers and non-dividend receivers competing in the same labour markets with different reserve prices. It seems certain that they would involve abandonment of the strict principle of equal pay for equal work in favour of some kind of seniority differential. This is the more easy to envisage in so far as a larger proportion of the jobs that will remain will be the kind of jobs for which incremental scales are already common – middle-class jobs in which accumulated experience counts. The fact that it is existing older workers who dominate the trade unions should also ensure that the lowered labour supply price of younger workers does not simply result in unemployment for older workers.

The other nub of the matter is that factor shares in national income would have to shift over time from something like 70 per cent labour 25 per cent capital (1983 figures: 5 per cent imputed income from personal property excluded) to something closer to a 40:50 ratio. In the early 1980s about 35 per cent of GNP would have been needed to give everyone over 18 35 per cent of the mean of the male and female median wage. This is clearly problematic, though given the large element of conventional determination in factor shares and the nature of the new political forces that a Capital Fund/Social Dividend scheme would set up, not beyond the bounds of possibility.

But could we get by with only 40 per cent of national income distributed according to effort? Can we afford, yet, to have an economy in which choosing to do one's own thing in modest poverty is wholly compatible with citizen dignity, a society in which the material incentive to work is much reduced? That was a major concern for Marshall when he wrote *Citizenship and social class* in 1949. At a time when full employment had been established, by means which we thought would work forever, he did not foresee that beyond the minimum income problem there might be a minimum dignity problem. He did wonder, though, whether people would put their backs into their jobs if income guarantees became too strong – whether, in Mandeville's terms, there was anything but their wants that could "stir workers up to be serviceable" (Marshall 1963: 124). He sought hope in the thought that increasingly the search for status and for the intrinsic satisfactions of work would replace Mandeville's wants as means of stirring us up. A far higher proportion of the jobs that remain today permits the mobilization of those motives than ever before. If the wages for the remaining unpleasant and unskilled jobs have relatively to rise because of the universal minimum, this would be a useful countervailing force to the tendency for market forces working on talent scarcities to exacerbate income inequalities. And the vast array of fascinating gadgetry and travel and holiday possibilities that our new technologies have brought should provide plenty of genuine new wants of a material kind, and if those fail, we always have our advertising industry to provide spurious ones. There should be no serious lack of work incentives; it seems unlikely that the social dividend would turn us into a nation of layabouts, or harm the drive to make Britain competitive.

What it *would* do, would be to redefine the social significance of jobs and the concept of a right to a job. It would destroy the idea that it is through their jobs, and only through their jobs, that men and women have an unquestioned, unscrutinized right even to a basic livelihood, and that consequently the community has an obligation to ensure that anyone who *has* a job should be able to keep it forever, irrespective of all economic considerations, whatever the subsidy costs to the community. And in the light of the mid-1980s miners' strike this would seem a not inconsiderable gain.

The implications of a scheme of this order are clearly very great. The sketch given here is, indeed, less than half-baked. But *prima facie* there is a good chance that the benefits would outweigh the costs, at least for anyone who attaches much importance to maintaining the dignity minimum. It is, at any rate, just as much as State Earnings-Related Pension Scheme (SERPS), a matter on which we need thinking and action now if we are to have a decent society in the first quarter of the next century – even if it is not a matter attended by the actuarial certainties that have forced SERPS to the centre of political attention.

# CHAPTER 10

# Family responsibilities and rights

## Janet Finch

## Introduction

My topic in this chapter is families, and relationships within families in the Britain in which we live today. Selecting from this very broad subject, I shall focus specifically on certain specific aspects of family life. But at the same time it is important to keep a sense of the larger picture, of the significance of families as the place in which all of us live out relationships with people close to us.

I use the term "family" in its broadest possible definition. One problem with studying "the family", as a social scientist, is that the meaning of the term shifts around in different settings. Often we take it to mean the household – people who share a roof over their heads and hold possessions in common. But it can also refer to relationships that are either narrower or broader than the household. When politicians speak of "supporting the family" or "strengthening the family" (as many do, from various political persuasions), they can mean at least three different things, according to the context:

1.  They *may* mean arrangements for looking after children when they are too young to take responsibility for themselves.
2.  They may really mean marriage, trying to encourage young people to marry, to see marriage as a life-long arrangement, to discourage divorce.
3.  They may mean encouraging adult children to take direct responsibility for their elderly parents in old age.

In popular usage, the phrase "the family" can mean any of these things – household, parents and young children, marriage, the wider kin group. We can all decode its meaning according to the context, in our normal daily lives. This chapter focuses on the family in its last meaning – relationships within the wider kin group in adult life, between people who probably do not share a household.

What significance does the family – in any of its meanings – have for most of our fellow citizens today? Is it the central cornerstone of all our lives, as perhaps Margaret Thatcher implied in her much-quoted remark that there is "no such thing as society, only individuals and their families"? Or is it rather, as Edmund Leach said in his Reith Lecture in 1967, the "source of all our discontents"? Indeed, is "discontents" too mild a word for some of the things that go on in families – in large numbers of families we now know – the physical and sexual damage done to children, to women and (we are just beginning to acknowledge) to elderly people? These are all unfortunately characteristics of family life, its dark side, and have long been so. The family can be a dangerous place for precisely those people who are least able to escape from it, and for whom it is supposed to be the main protection – the young, the very old, women whose economic circumstances make escape an impossibility on practical grounds.

In reality our images of "the family" are very mixed and contradictory. This has a long history, well expressed in literature, where the contradictory nature of family relationships is a major theme that has preoccupied novelists and playwrights. To quote a single, popular example, John Galsworthy's series of novels about the Forsyte family supply highly contrasting images. When he introduces us to the family in the opening chapter of *The man of property* (1951), he emphasizes the positives: the solidarity of the large kin group, the memorable impression that they make when all gathered in a single place. Anyone "privileged to be present at a festival of the Forsytes", he writes, can witness "that charming and instructive sight, an upper middle class family in full plumage". At such a gathering, an observer cannot help but be impressed. Our observer will glean evidence, says Galsworthy, of that "mysterious, concrete tenacity which renders a family so formidable a unit of society". As the novels progress, these images are filled out into a much more complex picture, and in many ways a sinister one. Anyone who knows *The Forsyte saga* will know that, contained within those stories, are the very contradictions that I spoke about earlier –

the family as the central organizing focus of people's lives, the group from which each derives some measure of security, material support, social identity; yet at the same time, people bound together in relationships that cause great pain, and from which escape is difficult.

Relationships within families therefore provide a rich area for social scientific research and also a major challenge: how to make sense of the real meaning of relationships that are so inherently contradictory? The particular issues that I explore in this chapter highlight one potential source of these contradictions, namely the nature of responsibilities and rights within family relationships and between family members.

Social science offers various ways in which this topic can be tackled. Necessarily I shall be selective. There are important debates, for example, about individual rights, social rights, the moral claims of individuals, to be found in the writing of moral and political philosophers. T. H. Marshall, whose work has provided the stimulus for the production of this book, was a distinguished contributor to debates about social rights and citizenship. I am not going to engage directly with those debates, though my argument has implications for them. My focus is upon what we might call "lay understandings" of family responsibilities and rights – how people in British society conceive of the claims upon them, of the nature of rights and responsibilities within their own families, of what is reasonable. My focus is upon lived experience, rather than philosophical debates, and upon what an accurate knowledge of lived experience can contribute to those debates.

## Public policies and the family

I shall begin this exploration by making a link between the interior of the family, how family relationships are experienced – which is my main focus – and questions of public policy. To put this another way, it is important to bring the findings of sociological research to bear upon issues in social policy. This follows very much in a tradition that Marshall would have recognized.

My starting point is what I take to be an uncontentious observation. Questions about the family have become much more explicit in the agenda of public policy over the last 15 years. This marks something of a departure – though not a total one – from the way in which British social policy has treated the family. Unlike some of our European neighbours, the emphasis in the UK has been that the family is a private domain in which government should not interfere except unusually. The idea that the family is a private domain that can and should be treated as quite separate from the public world has a long history (Land 1978). Our firm belief that we treat the family as a private matter stems essentially from the early period of our industrial development. The new middle classes of the early nineteenth century, the people whose energy and whose money established manufacturing industry and other business enterprises, also strove to create a particular form of family life, one that would suit their vision of the social world. It was a vision in which home and workplace are quite separate places, each with their own sets of relationships and their own priorities. The home was to be a secure and comfortable haven, the proper sphere of women and children where they could live safely and decently, and to which men could return to recover from their toil in the world of work. Both physically and ideologically, home and family were conceived of as a private place where – among other things – members of the family could be free from external pressures and interference (Hall 1978, Davidoff & Hall 1987).

The distinction between the public and private domains has an important hold on the way in which we think about family life in this country. Traditionally, we have been part of a public culture that shrinks from the idea of family life being the business of anyone other than the people involved in it. Yet one consequence of this is to allow the family to be the dangerous place that, for children and for women in particular, it certainly can be. In intellectual terms, the public/private distinction cannot be sustained if it is examined too closely, but it still has an important effect on the way in which we formulate policies about aspects of family life in this country. The effect is that social policy tends to hold back from interfering. Yet, at the same time, public policy cannot, in reality, treat the family as a black box over which it has no control and in which it has no interest. Policy-makers necessarily make assumptions about how relationships in families do work, and ought to work (Land 1989, Ungerson 1989, Parker 1990).

It is relevant therefore to ask the question: what kinds of expectations about rights and responsibilities in the family are embodied in UK public policy? Full exploration of this subject lies beyond the scope of this chapter. But I need to make some brief remarks about this issue that are relevant to my main theme. In this country, essentially we have tended to take a minimalist approach in terms of formal definitions, consistent with the idea that the family should be treated as a private domain. Certainly the law is little used to embody formal rights and responsibilities that regulate relationships between family members, save in the case of young children. Even laws concerned with inheritance embody minimal rights for family members in this country, by comparison with most European jurisdictions (Mellows 1983).

However, looking at how the law regulates family relationships does not exhaust the importance of public policies in this field. Indeed, it really only scratches the surface. Many of the public expectations that we have of family life are embodied not in the law, but in the ways we make other policies. The assumptions built into those policies speak volumes about what governments expect families to do, how they expect them to behave, and what rights and responsibilities are presumed to reside in family relationships. This has become much more apparent with the recent, more explicit, emphasis on the family in public policy. An example that has been written about very fully has been in relation to community care policies, especially the care of elderly people (Finch 1989, Qureshi & Walker 1989, Parker 1990). The idea that family care is *preferable* to state care has obvious financial attractions for any government. But also it is underscored by an apparently widespread belief that this is something that families do naturally. The important body of feminist writing in this area has, of course, decoded that particular belief and pointed out that assumptions about what women should do for members of their family can be very different indeed from assumptions about what men should do (Land & Rose 1985, Dalley 1988, Ungerson 1990).

These brief examples are intended to illustrate my basic point that in reality "the family" is not a wholly private domain as far as public policy is concerned. What underscores much public policy is the basic, and largely unquestioned, assumption that there *are* certain rights and responsibilities associated with family life that are natural, obvious, acknowledged by all normal decent people. There is – it is assumed – a set of basic rules. The rules may change a bit over time, but they do exist and most people acknowledge them as guiding principles in their own family relationships. That being so, then public policies can incorporate those rules and build upon them.

The key question is: are these assumptions accurate? In reality do people recognize clear rules about the rights and responsibilities between family members? If they do, are they the same rules as those upon which public policy is founded?

## Family rights and responsibilities in practice

This is where my focus on "lay understandings" enters the picture. We need to know what people do and think in reality, in contemporary Britain. At this point, I shall draw upon some research in which I have been involved, along with Jennifer Mason. Data from this study can help answer the questions that I have just posed, in respect of adult kin relationships.

The research was a study of obligations and responsibilities within kin groups, and between adults. We excluded responsibilities for young children, and we were not attempting specifically to study responsibilities in marriage, though we cannot ignore relationships between spouses as part of the total pattern. But our principal focus was on those relationships outside the immediate nuclear family and where there is no significant formal or legal regulation. We were interested to find out whether these relationships are meaningful within British society in the late twentieth century and, in particular, whether they can be characterized by feelings of obligation or responsibility. Other scholars have argued that the responsibility to give help when it is needed is one important element that marks the boundary between family or kinship and other types of social relationship. We were trying to find out whether people think in terms of obligation or responsibility in their family relationships and, if they do, what they mean by this.

Our data are quite varied. We conducted a survey of nearly one thousand individuals of all ages, drawn randomly from electoral registers in the Greater Manchester region. We then interviewed in depth 88 people, trying to build up sets of interviews with members of the same family, so that embedded in those 88 interviews we have 11 "kin groups" where we have interviewed between three and eight members of the same family. Seven of the 88 individuals were of Caribbean or Asian descent, the rest were white British. Most of them also lived in the northwest of England, though where we needed to interview members of families living in other parts of the country, we did so.

In both the survey and the in-depth interviews we were asking about all kinds of help that passes between members of families – giving and lending money, practical help both small and large, personal care of people who are sick or incapacitated. We asked about channels of help passing in all direction in families – passing between children, parents and grandparents, both up and down the generations, between brothers and sisters, cousins – indeed anyone who is considered "family". We let our respondents define for themselves whom they included within their family circle.

Using data from this research, I want to make three main points about "lay understandings" of responsibilities and rights in families, in Britain in the late twentieth century.

First, *family relationships* – defined in this broad way – *continue to be of significance* to the great majority of the population. In the course of our detailed interviews almost all our interviewees emphasized that they did have a family that meant something to them, and which "worked" when it needed to. This included young and older interviewees, people who could name large numbers of kin and people who had very few, people who had very regular contact with kin and people who saw them only occasionally. It was emphasized by both women and men, though it must be said that proportionately more women than men placed strong emphasis on the importance of kin relationships in their own lives. In discussing this elsewhere, we have argued that this is explained – at least in part – by the fact that women still tend to take prime responsibility for certain areas of life (child care, domestic organization) where it is most likely that the help of kin will need to be elicited. Consequently, women are more likely than men to get locked into patterns of exchange relationships with members of their kin group (Finch & Mason 1993: 175–7).

The actual shape of families and the pattern of contacts among our interviewees was highly variable. Yet all wanted to be able to demonstrate to us that their family worked when it needed to. Data from our interviewees enabled us to document a range of different ways in which people report that they themselves, and other members of their kin group, can turn to relatives for help: financial assistance, looking after young children, care for someone who is ill (both long-term and short-term examples), practical help (usually with domestic matters), providing a temporary home for a relative, giving emotional and "moral" support. Interestingly the most common type of experience of exchange in families was financial help – usually small sums, but sometimes major gifts or loans to help, for example, in buying a house or establishing a business (see Finch & Mason 1993: 207–19, for a detailed presentation). Adding together all these examples, we found that 93 per cent of our respondents reported that they themselves had been involved in giving and receiving financial help in families, with women and men equally represented.

Moreover, beyond this range of examples of kin groups operating in practice, an image emerged of what we might call the archetypal case that demonstrates that a family really does "work". This is rallying round in a crisis. People quoted us all manner of examples as proof that this happens – sudden illness most commonly, but there were plenty of other instances. For example, one of our male respondents told us how his mother-in-law had stepped in and paid the fine imposed on him by a court after he had been found guilty of petty thieving. As far as he was concerned this was definitely a crisis – he had no money with which to pay it, and he had lost his job because of the criminal prosecution – and it was a member of his kin group who stepped in to bale him out.

My general point is this. People seem to treat "rallying round in a crisis" as the bottom line, as it were. If your family does *not* do this, then it cannot really be said to have any meaningful existence. This is the implicit message. And it appears that the great majority of people do want to be able to say that they are a member of a family that "works" at this level. Really we have only one exception to this among our 88 interviewees, a woman who lived with her adult son and told us that she had no real contact with other kin and did not wish to have any. However, even she had not taken this stance for her whole adult life, having made a major commitment to the personal care of her elderly mother in her terminal illness.

My second point concerns the question of *responsibility* or *obligation*. How far does this characterize family relationships in practice? Our evidence suggests that people do think in terms of "responsibilities" in families, but the actual meaning attributed to this needs to be specified very carefully. It is easiest to say what it does *not* mean. It does not mean that there is a clear set of rules, or social norms, which governs responsibilities in families, and which tells you what is "the proper thing to do" in different circumstances. Should I loan money to my sister if she needs it for a deposit on a house? Should I offer to look after my brother's children when he has to go abroad on a business trip? Should I make a commitment to go regularly to look after my parent's garden? There are no clear, agreed answers to these questions. They are all examples of the kinds of help that does get given within families. But there does not appear to be anything approaching social norms that would indicate that certain types of help would be widely expected, or that you could expect any decent person to make a particular type of offer.

The lack of agreement about norms of family responsibility is very clear in the data from our large-scale survey. We were specifically using the survey to try to tap any norms that did exist, and we asked questions about a whole range of situations in which they might operate. But we found very little clear agreement on anything except, at the most general level, the idea that families should help and assist each other (Finch & Mason 1991). The clearest kind of agreement came in relationships between parents and children where, as certainly would be expected from earlier research, we come closest to finding something resembling fixed obligations. But even here, the agreement that parents should put themselves out to help their children, and vice versa, breaks down when one comes to specific examples. So much appears to depend upon people's *judgement of relevant circumstances*.

I can illustrate this point by contrasting two questions from the survey, both of which ask whether family members should be prepared to offer a temporary home to relatives. In the first case, we postulated a situation of a young couple with a baby who had recently returned from abroad and needed a home for about six months. Eighty-six percent of our sample thought that relatives should offer to accommodate them, and most of them thought that parents should make that offer. However, in a different question we asked about a family with two children who had been evicted from their council flat because they could not pay the rent. Again we specified that a home might be needed for about six months, but in this case only 65 per cent of our sample thought that relatives should make the offer. Twenty-one per cent of them had made a different judgement about family responsibilities in these two questions. It seems that a judgement was being made here about the relative "deservingness" of the two cases. Deservingness is one factor that does seem to be built into people's judgements about family responsibilities, but only one. In giving answers to these two questions, it was a factor that swayed about one fifth of our sample. For the rest, it apparently did not.

My main point is that, across our whole survey data set, the message comes through that, whilst people are generally supportive of the idea that families have a responsibility to help each other, what that means in practice both can and should depend on the specific circumstances of the case. The way that different individuals judge what is relevant is also highly variable. For example, we cannot predict that building in a particular factor like deservingness (or undeservingness) will sway the majority of the sample. It will sway some, but not others. And whether it does sway people is not split on any obvious lines: neither social class, nor age, nor gender makes a clear and consistent difference to the way in which people answer these questions that tap ideas and norms about family responsibilities.

Giving attention to specific circumstances also apparently is how people behave in practice within their own families. Our interview data provide many examples of this point but I shall select just one illustration, on the topic of children's responsibilities to get involved in the care of elderly and infirm parents. Most of our interviewees had past or present experience of this issue in their own families, or could anticipate that they would need to confront it in the future. Yet there were considerable variations not only in what level of involvement different individuals actually accepted but also – and more important for my present argument – how people approached the issue of what they and others "ought" to be doing (Finch & Mason 1990). In approaching this definition of responsibility at the practical level no very clear "rules" emerged, not even that daughters ought to get more involved than sons, nor that eldest children have a special type of responsibility. Our interview data suggest that it is much more complex than that, and highly dependent on the circumstances both of the elderly person and on each of their children. Ideas such as the gendered nature of responsibilities may get woven into such considerations, but they do not drive them unambiguously.

As an illustration of this type of complexity, I shall use a quotation from one of our interviewees, Jean Crabtree, a women in her twenties, who talked at length about her mother's significant involvement in the care of her own parents, in the period before each of them died. Her mother also had a brother, whose involvement had been much less. Alert to the possibility that gendered rules were in operation here, we asked her specifically whether she thought that her uncle had "tried to get out of" responsibilities which he should have acknowledged. She responded thus,

> I think partly, because with his first wife he had an awful lot of trouble for years and years. They didn't get on at all and she was a bit um, mentally disturbed in a lot of ways, so he did have a lot on his plate in that respect, you know sort of trying to cope with his wife and such a large family, and the home. So he did have a lot of other things to consider as well as my grandma and granddad. And I don't, in a way, I don't really think he thought he was capable of helping for some reason. He, I mean, he used to go and visit them that type of thing, but he never seemed to take it much further. He didn't seem to feel that he was *able* to for some reason. He'd not really had a lot of close contact with them, for a long time, mainly while he was with his first wife. He used to visit them, I don't even think it was once a week, occasionally he'd visit them and take one or other of the grandchildren to see them, but so up until he left his wife, you know, he had little contact with them. (emphasis original)

Jean's account places little emphasis on the idea that, as a man, her uncle had a lesser level of responsibility to look after his parents. She does not really explain the situation in terms of norms and beliefs at all. Rather it is a historical account of how her uncle's relationship with his parents had been shaped over time by other factors in his own life – the fact that he was coping with a "mentally disturbed" wife, that he had a large family, that as a consequence he had relatively limited contact with his parents. Jean adds to this that he "didn't seem to feel that he was *able*" to become more involved with the care of his parents – a possible reference to gendered expectations though Jean does not present it that way, adding with slight puzzlement, "for some reason". Meanwhile Jean's mother's relationship with her parents had a very different history, as was apparent in our interview with the mother as well as with Jean herself. It had been a much closer relationship over her whole adult lifetime, characterized by mutual aid flowing in both directions until her parents' infirmity eventually meant that the flow became one-way.

The pattern that this specific example takes is repeated again and again in our interview data, though the details of course are different. But the idea that different personal histories produce not only different outcomes but also different understandings of "responsibility" is the common theme. We have concluded therefore that there are very few clearly identifiable rules about how responsibilities should operate in families, and that we have to see family responsibilities as understandings that are worked out within specific families, and between specific individuals, over time.

Responsibilities build up over time through a process of which reciprocity is an important component – a gift is given, which then creates a responsibility to repay, and so on (Sahlins 1965, Bulmer 1987, Finch 1989). Over time, different individuals become committed to each other in different ways through this process, so that one daughter, for example, may get locked into a set of mutually reinforcing commitments with her mother, whereas another – perhaps living in a situation where she needs to rely less on her mother's help – does not build up a parallel set of commitments. The two end up with different effective responsibilities within their own family, though they are both in the same genealogical position (daughters). This reinforces my point about there being no fixed rules of obligation in families. If there were, just being a daughter would carry certain specific responsibilities (Finch & Mason 1990).

My third point concerns the *concept of rights within families*. In one sense, rights are inextricably bound up with responsibilities. If I have a responsibility to help my children, then surely they have the right to expect this from me. However, this does *not* appear to be the way in which people approach family relationships in adult life. Indeed, our data suggest a strong aversion to the idea that anyone has a "right to expect" anything from another member of their family, even between parents and children. More than that, if someone "acts as if" they are expecting a loan of money, or some practical help, this will be strongly disapproved of. I include here dropping hints as well as asking directly. If you are going to drop hints, it seems, you have to be very subtle about it. You have to do it in a way that is not at all obvious, and where you can always claim that you had no intention of expecting help.

I think that the key to understanding people's feelings – often quite strongly expressed feelings – about this issue is that we are talking about gift-giving (Cheal 1988). Giving and receiving gifts in the broadest sense, not just material objects but time, effort and emotional energy. In this process of gift-giving the initiative must always lie with the donor. It is for the donor to decide to put themselves out for someone else, to make a sacrifice. If I behave as if I have the right to demand money, time or effort this takes away that initiative from the donor, and in the process it reflects badly on me. I have gone beyond what is seen as reasonable within families.

This seems to be the logic on which people operate within their own families. It applies even in situations where an outsider might think that someone had a perfectly legitimate right to expect something from a relative. A rather extreme case of this kind in our data set concerns an elderly woman who had lent money to one of her sons several years previously, with the promise of repayment. Nothing had been repaid and her son had not mentioned the topic to her – a situation that she deeply resented, although that was not entirely unexpected since she described this particular son as "a bit dodgy", not like her other son who was a paragon of virtue. Other relatives had urged her to demand repayment but she refused, saying, "It's never been mentioned and I won't mention it." When pressed to explain why, she said "I wouldn't lower myself." I think that this situation makes clear that our elderly respondent could not contemplate behaving in a way that makes demands on a relative or asserts rights over them. To do so would reflect badly on her own identity ("I wouldn't lower myself").

To summarize: what does our research tell us about lay understandings of responsibilities and rights in families? It shows us that people generally treat families (in their broad sense) as important to them, and expect that family life will entail certain responsibilities. But what the precise nature of those responsibilities is going to be are not prescribed by social norms, certainly not in any straightforward way. They are worked out within particular families, and as a consequence they are highly variable.

This means that it is impossible to predict what kinds of help will flow between family members just by knowing the composition of a family. One person can treat it as a normal part of *their* family relationships to buy each of their children a car when he or she reaches the age of 21. Another parent, equally able to afford this and equally caring for their children, will see that as completely inappropriate. Any suggestions on the part of their children that they expect their parents to buy them a car because friends' parents do so will get short shrift.

This perhaps is a trivial example because it concerns a luxury item, but the same point applies across the whole gamut of help that is given and received in families. Because there are no *fixed* responsibilities between relatives, the idea that anyone has a right to expect something is inappropriate. The right to give must always remain with the donor, and this must include the right to withhold a gift. Any sense of being forced into giving is resisted strongly.

## The right not to have to rely on your family

This brings me to my conclusion, where I shall return to the link with social policy and to suggest that we can identify a principle that people acknowledge in reality, but which hitherto has been quite foreign to social policy thinking. This is that people should have *the right not to have to rely on their families* for help – practical, financial or any other sort. This is a particular kind of social right that in principle could be incorporated as an aim of social policy. No doubt this line of argument is somewhat provocative, but I will develop it a little further.

The right not to have to rely on your family accords readily with the way in which family life is lived in contemporary society – as I have shown. Many of us are very happy with a situation where we help members of our family in various ways. We like to do it. What we do not like is any suggestion that we *have to* do it. Pressure from within the family is seen as inappropriate. But pressure from outside the family can also be relevant. This can come through the kind of social polices that, for example, deny housing benefit to large categories of young people under the age of 25, because it is presumed that they should be living with parents, and partially subsidized by them; or, to use a different example, by rules that ration access to home help services for an elderly person who has a daughter living nearby, on the assumption that this daughter has a responsibility to provide domestic help for her mother. Some parents may well be happy to have their 25-year-old children living in their home on a subsidized basis. Some daughters may be happy to do their mother's housework for them. For some this will seem a natural part of their family relationships, but for others it will not. The kinds of variability that our research shows, and the reasons for it, should make us very cautious about any social policies that assume that particular types of responsibility are normal in families.

Let us now look at this situation from the other side, from the perspective of the potential recipient of help. Where does that leave her or him? The answer is, in a very uncomfortable position, knowing that a son or sister or a parent feels obliged to give them help that is beyond what they regard as reasonable. It puts the recipient in the position of making demands, or claiming rights, either directly or indirectly. Most people find this extremely uncomfortable. Elderly people feel it particularly keenly. We know not only from our research but from many other studies (Wenger 1984, Sixsmith 1986, Waerness 1989) that elderly people strive very hard to remain independent of the assistance of others, including assistance from members of their family, where they see a real danger of becoming "too dependent".

So I would argue for the principle that a basic social right of all citizens should be not to have to rely on members of their family for help, certainly that they should not "have to rely" for want of alternatives. To put the point another way, the family should not be seen as the option of first resort for giving assistance to its adult members, either financial or practical. In expressing it that way, I am not trying to deprecate impulses to generosity, support, mutual care within families. My point is that people expect these to be optional, voluntary, freely given. So "having to" rely on relatives puts someone in an exceptionally invidious position.

I realize that building this principle into public policy might imply a reassertion of the rights of individual citizens to make claims upon collective resources, on the state, on public services, as an option of first resort. Though very much in line with ideas current at the time the welfare state was created – and so ably analyzed by Marshall – I realize that it sounds quite different half a century later. Indeed, it probably sounds like a Utopian programme and impossibly expensive for any government to contemplate.

I acknowledge that this may be true, and that there are political imperatives that are likely to militate against the incorporation of this principle into social policies. But at least we might honestly acknowledge that financial pressures may require us to have public policies that – at least in the short term – place more burdens on the family than many people find reasonable. As a minimum, I would like to see this principle acknowledged – the principle that we all should have the right not to have to rely on our families – as a desirable aim for public policy, something that we should work towards over a period of time. I find that preferable to the present situation where we run the risk of making a virtue out of necessity, relying on the family because it is expedient on financial grounds but justifying it as morally desirable.

My principle of "the right not to have to rely" on your family is a principle that I believe to be in tune with people's experience of contemporary family life. It is much more characteristic than the idea that there are responsibilities associated with the family that people will automatically acknowledge. I have no doubt that some people will see it as a view that undermines the importance of the family but I would argue that it is precisely the opposite. In seeking to remove external pressures on what is given and received within families, I would argue that our fellow-citizens would thereby be given greater freedom to develop, in ways that they themselves have chosen, those relationships that are personally satisfying.

## Notes

The study referred to in this chapter was funded by the Economic and Social Research Council (Grant number G00232197), whose support I acknowledge gratefully.

# CHAPTER 11

# Citizenship in a green world: global commons and human stewardship

## Howard Newby

## Introduction

At the time that Marshall wrote his seminal work *Citizenship and social class*, the term "environment" scarcely existed in common parlance, and the set of issues concerning global environmental change was not recognized. Global climate change, ozone depletion, the decline of biodiversity – each of these depended upon a string of scientific observations and discoveries during the 1980s. Yet the themes laid out in Marshall's work on citizenship were extraordinarily prescient, dealing as he does with the rights and obligations of members of society seeking to sustain themselves with scarce resources. It is therefore illuminating to re-examine Marshall's ideas with regard to recent debates on global environmental change and to investigate how far Marshall's concept of citizenship can be re-worked to apply on a global, not merely national, basis.

In the early 1990s the environment re-emerged as an issue that captured the public imagination. The growing suspicion that we may, in ways that remain not yet fully understood, be irreversibly tampering with the habitability of our planet has given environmentalism an apocalyptic urgency. This is a concern, moreover, which is not going to go away. The Inter-Governmental Panel on Climate Change (IPCC) in 1990 published the report of its working groups. This confirmed that the greenhouse effect is real: that by 2020 mean global temperatures will have risen by around 2°C, with higher levels over large land masses; that sea levels will rise by about 20 cm by 2030; and that within the next century there will be a major outflow of ice from the West Antarctic ice-sheet due directly to greenhouse warming. The belief, yet to be confirmed, is that much of this change is due to *human* intervention in natural systems.

Alongside this recognition of climate change there has also emerged a new awareness of scarcity: that the earth's resources are finite and that current patterns of economic development are simply not sustainable in the long run. We are all now touched by a deep, atavistic fear that the world will end, if not in the bang of nuclear holocaust, then in the whimper of global entropy (Newby 1990). We should not, therefore, be too surprised that environmental issues are once more in the forefront of political debate, for in the broadest sense they are deeply political, raising concerns about the expansion of individual choice and the satisfaction of social needs; about individual freedom versus a planned allocation of resources; about distributional justice and the defence of private property rights; and about the impact of science and technology on society. Beneath the concern for "the environment" there is therefore a much deeper conflict involving fundamental political principles and the kind of society we wish to create for the future.

Debates about "the environment" do not therefore transcend politics, but they do, arguably, transcend the conventional division within the social sciences between the "economy" and "civil society". The notion of "sustainability" as employed, for example, by the Brundtland commission (Brundtland 1987) points both towards the global system of production, distribution and exchange, and to the nature of the global citizen's status and role: our rights, duties and powers within an ultimately irrevocable global community of citizens. Environmentalism has provoked a much sharper recognition of the fact that economic wellbeing in itself does not promote civility, social cohesion or even a sense of enlightened self-interest.

This perspective on current environmental concerns also highlights an issue that is as old as social science itself, namely, the Hobbesian problem of order. This is given added contemporary relevance after a decade that has stressed economic individualism, acquisitive consumerism and the protection of private and sectional interests as guarantors of the public good. How, in other words, can the amoral "anarchy of the market" be reconciled with the promotion of a moral order

210

(whether or not this is encapsulated with the values of contemporary environmentalism) that will regulate the social, political and cultural lives of our threatened planet? What new forms of institutions need to be established that will knit together a social and economic order that is globally sustainable?

Such questions are not, of course, immediately answerable, but they do indicate why the current debate about environmental change is so emblematic of the modern age. Such questions also demonstrate that environmental change can never be simply a scientific and technological issue. Advances in the natural sciences will alter the parameters of environmental change, but they will describe the symptoms rather than explain the causes. The causes – and therefore the necessary corrective measures designed to deal with the impacts – lie in human societies and their systems of economic development.

## Citizenship in a green world

These introductory remarks have deliberately been couched in terms that Tom Marshall would have recognized, even though the world in which he originally framed his views on citizenship now scarcely exists. This is not the place, however, to assess the contribution of Marshall's work to the development of post-war social theory. Others, such as David Lockwood (1974) and Bryan Turner (1986), have done this far more eloquently and more thoroughly than I could attempt here. My purpose, rather, is to demonstrate the continuing relevance of Marshall's analysis of citizenship to an issue he could not have foreseen, and thereby to illuminate part of a social science agenda for research into global environmental change, an agenda on which work has, as yet, scarcely begun.

In setting out on this task I take as my starting point Maurice Roche's comment that "Marshall may have put citizenship 'on the map' in post-war social theory and social policy studies, but his map stopped at a number of limits we need to push beyond" (Roche 1987: 394). This is entirely consistent with Marshall's own pragmatic approach to the analysis of citizenship. In his seminal essay of 1949 on *Citizenship and social class* he described his analysis as "dictated by history even more clearly than by logic" (Marshall 1963: 11). Marshall identified three elements of citizenship – civil, political and social that had their formative period in, respectively, the eighteenth, nineteenth and twentieth centuries. For Marshall, civil citizenship was associated with the attainment of equality before the law; political citizenship with the attainment of the franchise; and social citizenship with the growth of the welfare state. To these he subsequently added the notion of industrial citizenship that emerges through the demands and struggles of trade unionism and which shields the worker from the full rigour of the labour market. It is at least arguable that we are now witnessing the growth of what might be termed "environmental citizenship" that will add to the stock of citizenship rights – and duties – to which Marshall devoted his attention. To some degree this chapter explores the scope and development of such environmental citizenship and the institutional issues that it raises.

Here I am concurring with Turner's approach to citizenship whereby it "can be conceived as a series of expanding circles that are pushed forward by the momentum of conflict and struggle" (Turner 1986: xii). And, like Turner, I recognize that some of the assumptions on which Marshall based his analysis of citizenship need to be modified in the light of subsequent experience. As far as the relationship to environmentalism is concerned, there are three that are particularly relevant:

1. First, there is Marshall's assumption that social classes are the principal actors in modern, industrial societies. This is not the place to explore the validity of such a claim (see, in any case, Marshall et al. 1988); nor is it necessary for the purposes of this analysis. We simply need to acknowledge that the historic fate of the working class was the starting point of Marshall's analysis and that he regarded the growth of citizenship as the outcome of working-class struggles. Indeed, Marshall's major contribution to sociological theory has been his analysis of how citizenship has come to constitute the basis of an abatement of class conflict and to diminish the scope of market-based power. But Marshall's analysis applies equally to the attempts by non-class-based groupings to obtain full citizenship rights – for example, social movements based upon race, gender, age, etc. Marshall's theory is merely modified and extended, but not undermined, by leaving open the question of the continuing centrality of social class.

2. Secondly, Marshall, writing in the more optimistic period of the late 1940s and early 1950s, presumes a more or less evolutionary

212

progress towards the attainment of citizenship rights. We may merely note that such reformist optimism might now look distinctly jaded and that such rights can, under appropriate conditions, be reduced as well as expanded.

3. Thirdly, Marshall assumes that the relevant actor in the granting of citizenship rights is the nation-state and it is this that is capable on the one hand of empowering citizens, recognizing their rights and developing their skills, and, on the other, of exacting the performance of duties and subjecting them to legitimate power. However, the growth of an international economic order during the post-war period and the subsequent emergence of transnational states (such as the EU) have added a new dimension. In the case of environmentalism, for example, while local and national concerns have lain at the origins of the environmental movement, what characterizes the most recent debate is the global character of environmental change and, therefore, the international character of the appropriate remedies and obligations. Moreover, it is this characteristic that is going to provide the most difficult obstacle to agreement on how to limit environmental degradation.

## Citizenship, sovereignty and the global system

In Marshall's writing, citizenship and democracy are closely intertwined. Just as the growth of citizenship implies a strengthening of democracy, so a threat to democracy implies a diminution of citizenship rights. In the modern world more and more political causes are being fought in the name of democracy and increasing numbers of states are being recast in a democratic mould. Yet, as Held (1991) has pointed out, not far beneath the surface of democracy's triumph there is an apparent paradox. "Nations", he writes, "are heralding democracy at the very moment at which changes in the international order are compromising the possibility of an independent democratic nation-state. As vast areas of human endeavour are progressively organised on a global level, the fate of democracy is fraught with uncertainty." (Held 1991: 197)

Held specifically identifies ecological change as one example of how the global interconnectedness of modern economic and social activity may leave today's "citizens" institutionally disenfranchised. The processes of globalization break down the symmetrical and congruent relationship between decision-makers and the recipients of their decisions in ways that go to the heart of liberal democratic theory. As Held puts it: "The modern theory of the sovereign state presupposes the idea of a 'national community of fate' – a community that rightly governs itself and determines its own future. This idea is challenged fundamentally by the nature of the pattern of global interconnections and the issues that have to be confronted by the modern state. National communities by no means exclusively 'programme' the actions, decisions and policies of their governments, and the latter by no means simply determine what is right or appropriate for their own citizens alone."(Held 1991: 200)

The operation of an increasingly complex, and powerful, international system both limits the autonomy and infringes the sovereignty of individual nation-states. Citizenship rights, of the kind referred to by Marshall, are, in this context, at best inadequate and at worst an irrelevancy. An international order has emerged, structured by agencies and forces over which citizens have minimal, if any, control and little or no opportunity to signal their dissent. The institutions of accountability are simply not in place in many, if not most, cases. Consequently, the international agencies that comprise this global system not only lack legitimacy but respond only slowly and imperfectly to the changing demands of a disenfranchised and fragmented citizenry.

These observations provide a timely elaboration of the widely quoted and well meaning conclusion of the Brundtland Commission Report on sustainable development that "The integrated and interdependent nature of the new challenges and issues contrasts sharply with the nature of the institutions that exist today. These institutions tend to be independent, fragmented and working to relatively narrow mandates with closed decision processes ... The real world of interlocked economic and ecological systems will not change; the policies and institutions concerned must." (Brundtland 1987: 310, see also Keohane & Nye 1977) Global governance of global resources will require new institutions of democratic accountability if the rights of all global citizens are not to be infringed.

# The road to environmental citizenship

Thus far I have developed three separate, though related, themes:

1. that environmental change is a socio-economic, and not merely a scientific and technological, issue;
2. that Marshall's concept of citizenship is extendable to the consideration of environmentalism;
3. that recent tendencies towards the globalization of economic and political activity present a problem for liberal democratic theory upon which the concept of citizenship conventionally rests.

I now want to bring these three themes together via a somewhat schematic discussion of the contemporary environmental movement.

In Britain, environmentalism, in a form that we would now recognize, emerged only in the latter half of the nineteenth century. As Lowe & Goyder (1983) have pointed out, a striking feature of the subsequent history of the environmental movement has been its uneven development, marked by distinct periods of organizational expansion and innovation, followed by intervals that saw few new departures. Each phase has not simply replicated the previous one, however. At each stage new issues have been added and the breadth of concern widened. Thus, what began as a specific and separate set of issues involving such matters as landscape change, pesticide use, urban and industrial development, resource depletion, recreation demand and the preservation of wildlife habitats and ancient monuments have been linked together in an amorphous environmental movement. The environmental "lobby" now encompasses a very broad range of pressure groups indeed.

Nevertheless, it is possible, with some oversimplification, to identify four distinct phases in the growth of environmentalism (see also Newby 1990):

1. The first phase was from the mid-1880s to the turn of the century. It is epitomized by the founding of the National Trust, although this is only one of a wide range of organizations established at this time. The dominant theme here was *preservation* – of both natural and human artefacts. It reflected the late Victorian intellectual reaction to many of the tenets of economic liberalism and a growing disenchantment with the consequences of urban industrialization. Environmentalism thus gave expression to doubts about modern industrial society. For its influential proponents

215

like Ruskin and Morris ,what had to be preserved were the tangible elements of an idealized past, not only an indictment of contemporary society but also suggestive of how it might be redeemed.

The appeal was to both a natural and a national heritage, over which organizations like the National Trust (itself an evocative title) were to exercise a stewardship on behalf of all members of society − past, present and future. Also embodied was an appeal to a certain kind of cultural excellence possessed by only a few discerning individuals: hence the emphasis that was (and, to some extent, still is) placed on certain value judgements about what, precisely, constitutes this heritage and in whose interest stewardship is being exercised.

2. The second phase can be located in the interwar years and saw a widening of the social base of environmental concern to include the suburban middle classes, especially in the southeast of England. The focus of attack shifted away from the depredations of economic *laissez-faire* to government itself. Groups formed between the wars were not therefore simply preservationist, but *regulatory*, particularly in relation to land use planning, pollution control and the loss of natural or historic features. A good example of this shifting style of campaigning would be the Council for the Preservation of Rural England and the myriad local watchdog groups engendered by the first tentative steps towards planning control.

The concern with aesthetic judgements remained, articulated by this stage not so much through the notion of "heritage" as that of "amenity" − an equally intangible summation of the quality of life that could be protected by regulation and control. Hence the environmental movement during this period proved to be a strange amalgam of patrician sentiment and socially concerned Fabianism, which believed in the pursuit of social justice through national planning. It proved, however, to be a powerful coalition from which emerged immediately after 1945 the framework of current planning controls − including development control, national parks, green belts and limited public access to open countryside.

3. The third phase began in the early 1960s, but reached its height in the 1970s. Perhaps the term *post-materialism* best summarizes

the predominant concerns, which included (for example in organizations like Friends of the Earth and the Ecology Party, now the Greens) an opposition to crass materialism, a critique of inhuman technology and a broader-based attention to social wellbeing. In certain respects this represented a return to some of the issues that had preoccupied their Victorian predecessors – and for similar reasons. Here, too, there was a rejection of the values that predominated in a market economy and a lack of confidence in the beneficial effects of science and technology, which were seen as part of the problem, rather than as offering a solution. There was a growing anxiety about the future, a loss of confidence in "progress" and a pervasive uncertainty about where current developments were leading. It was provoked by a renewed realization of scarcity, fostered by a rapid increase in knowledge about the terrestrial environment and by new techniques of economic and demographic forecasting. The finite nature of the Earth's resources was repeatedly emphasized, along with the imminent scarcity of food, energy and other raw materials.

It was noticeable, however, that in Britain the environmental movement remained dominated by essentially "amenity" issues, by the recognition that scarcity extended to intangible factors such as natural beauty, open space and pleasing landscapes. Compared with other advanced industrial societies – especially the United States – ecological concerns (narrowly defined) were much less prominent. While there was certainly an awareness of *global* scarcity, the British debate remained comparatively parochial, with wildlife and countryside issues predominating. True to its post-materialist character, this phase of environmental concern was vulnerable to the public re-ordering of priorities attendant upon the economic recession of the early 1980s.

4. The fourth phase has been embarked upon in the last three or four years. It is not so much "post-materialist" as offering the reassertion of an almost neoMalthusian materialism. The emphasis is on *sustainability* and the quest for sustainable economic development (as set out in the Brundtland Report and elsewhere – see Pearce et al. 1989). Although, clearly, it is too early to make any confident generalizations about this phase, a number of trends are discernible. First, there is an emphasis on *global*

environmental change, underscored once more by advances in scientific observation (ozone depletion, climate change, acid deposition, etc.). Questions relating to resource depletion and the material constraints on rising living standards are also to the fore. In other words "ecology" has replaced "amenity" as the focus of public debate. This, at least for policy-makers, has some beguiling attractions, for "ecological" issues are assumed to be amenable to rational, objective enquiry, whereas "amenity" issues are inevitably subjective, value-laden and ultimately a matter of personal preference. This is, of course, a dangerous oversimplification, but for the time being we may merely note that environmental change has been redefined as essentially an ecological problem amenable to scientific solutions.

So much for history, even such a brief and inevitably distorted history as this one. Preservation, regulation, post-materialism, sustainable development: these four themes present a heady brew for a public trying to come to terms with the changes in lifestyles that will inevitably follow if current prescriptions on global environmental change turn out to be scientifically well founded. There is an increasing awareness that the environmental challenges we face today are, increasingly, international, global and potentially more life-threatening than in the past. In this sense, each individual's future is tied, in the title of the Brundtland Report, to "our common future" and we are all, therefore, environmental citizens now. And yet, because of the institutional disenfranchisement that I described earlier, there are no institutions in place capable of articulating the demands for such citizenship rights or for recognizing such rights, assigning appropriate duties and subjecting them to accepted and legitimate forms of control.

## Global commons and citizenship rights

At this point I am quite deliberately employing the vocabulary of constitutional law, reminiscent of the early development of liberal democracy. For there are, indeed, analogies to be drawn between the contemporary political, legal and economic problems of regulating global environmental change and those that existed in the late medieval period concerning the exploitation of common rights over land and their rapid deterioration and overuse associated with increased technological capability and economic growth. Hence the increasing use of the phrase "global commons" to describe those natural resources that do not, or cannot, by their very nature fall under national jurisdiction or individual property rights – ozone layers, oceans, polar ice-sheets, the earth's biosphere, and so on. Global commons do not form a coherent analytical category, but they share a necessity for international regulation and management. No-one "owns" them and to allocate individual property rights over them is, for physical or political reasons, impossible. The problem of the global commons is, therefore, inseparable from that of handling effective international co-operation.

Global environmental change therefore presents a special challenge for several reasons (see Pearce et al. 1989: 12). If the worst effects of, say, global pollution are realized, then some countries will experience catastrophic damage. No one country acting alone can prevent or contain these impacts. Not only are the costs high in relation to consumption patterns, technological change and trading competitiveness, but there are obvious free-rider incentives to avoid such costs yet share in the benefits of the actions of others. Conversely, attempts to conserve resources or to cope with negative externalities will almost inevitably confront the problem of gross inequality in levels of exploitation and demands for redistribution – whether between North and South, or, in the short term, East and West.

We return, then, to one of the classic issues of social theory that I raised at the beginning of this chapter: the problem of co-operation under conditions of anarchy. A political system that at the global level is fragmented and decentralized is confronted with transnational phenomena and high levels of interdependence. Can the tragedy of the global commons be avoided only by the advent of a modern-day Green Leviathan? Or can human stewardship over the global commons be exercised by more democratically accountable means?

Questions like these indicate the ways in which the study of global environmental change can never be regarded *simply* as an issue for the natural sciences alone. Concepts like scarcity, equity, management and development lie at the heart of the social science enterprise. To use the categories of the IPCC report, the processes, impacts and responses relating to global environmental change are social and economic, and not merely ecological, in character. If we are to adapt our lifestyles from unsustainable to sustainable patterns of resource utilization, then the tools of social science analysis are indispensable. The sad fact is, however, that the social science research community has barely scratched the surface of these problems. What is required is a concerted, extensive, multidisciplinary and international research effort in the social sciences that is at least as significant, in its own terms, as, say, the International Geosphere Biosphere Programme in the natural sciences.

To construct such an agenda here would require more time and space than I have available. In any case, I offered some further observations elsewhere (Newby 1990) and the ESRC launched a programme in this area in 1991. However, I do want to conclude by focusing on one particular aspect of the problem to which Tom Marshall's work was relevant: the development of appropriate institutions of environmental citizenship.

As Bryan Turner has remarked:

> The existence of citizenship presupposes a number of political institutions such as the centralised state, a system of political participation, institutions of political education and a variety of institutions associated with the state that protect the individual from the loss of liberties. (Turner 1986: 107, see also 1990)

From the perspective of contemporary environmentalism it is clear that, in this context, we are all what might be called pre-citizens. Systems of political participation are in place that permit the growth of environmental pressure groups and even, as in the case of the various green parties in Europe, political parties. Yet the remaining conditions are largely absent. Moreover, the global nature of existing environmental concerns present particular difficulties over the receding locus of power: how can any one of us claim, let alone exert, our citizenship rights over the preservation of the global commons? Must we witness the rise of transnational bureaucracies that will demand surveillance and control over all the world's citizens in order to render effective the policies necessary to achieve economic sustainability? This version of Weber's pessimistic vision of an "iron cage" of rational bureaucracy and diminishing citizenship will become one of the central issues as international agencies become more effective. Already there are intense discussions about where the dividing line might most appropriately be drawn between market-based solutions and systems of international regulation, but it is a sobering thought that in 1989 the leaders of many of the world's governments sat down to decide upon an international protocol aimed at limiting the emission of greenhouse gases almost without *any* body of social scientific analysis of the theory and practice of international agreements to set beside the natural scientific evidence on global warming. Nor did they have any idea of the effectiveness and the consequences of the range of economic instruments at their disposal in achieving their desired ends.

This could be regarded as a pessimistic comment on the current state of the social sciences, but it is intended, rather, as a statement of the opportunity that is there for the social sciences to seize. During Tom Marshall's heyday, public policy, including social policy, was often research-led. In an era of "conviction politics", the connection between research and policy has seemed tenuous at best. Yet, as I suggested earlier, the public concern about sustainability has been very much influenced by research findings. Politicians, too, have been anxious to found their policies on sound science. But at the end of the day, the natural sciences can only measure, model and describe the symptoms of global change; it is to the social sciences that politicians and policy-makers must turn if they want to understand both the causes and the remedies. Social science techniques and insights are an integral part of finding solutions to our pressing environmental problems. The social science research community will need to offer not only technical expertise, however, but a vision. Like Tom Marshall, they will need to be Utopian in the best sense of the word, combining rational, disinterested analysis with a passion for achieving a better world. In this field, at least, the opportunity is there for policy to be research-led. It is vital for all our futures that the social science community seizes it.

# CHAPTER 12

# The poorest of the urban poor: race, class and social isolation in America's inner-city ghettos

## William Julius Wilson

Inner-city neighbourhoods in large cities in the United States have experienced rapid social deterioration during the 1970s and 1980s. Even the most pessimistic observers of urban life in America during the ghetto riots of the 1960s hardly anticipated the dramatic increases in rates of social dislocation and the massive breakdown of social institutions in the ensuing years. The term "ghetto underclass", rarely invoked during the past two decades, is now frequently used by both social scientists and journalists in descriptions of the growing social problems – joblessness, family disruption, teenage pregnancy, failing schools, crime and drugs – that involve many of those who live in the inner city (Wilson et al. 1988).

For example, in the city of Chicago, the poverty rates in the inner-city neighbourhoods increased by an average of 12 per cent points from 1970 to 1980. In eight of the ten neighbourhoods that represent the historic core of Chicago's "Black Belt", upwards of four families in ten were living in poverty by 1980. In 1970 only one of these neighbourhoods had a family poverty rate that exceeded 40 per cent. Accompanying this increase of poverty has been a sharp growth of single-parent households. In the ghetto neighbourhoods on Chicago's South Side, the percentage of all families headed by women climbed from an average of 40 per cent in 1970 to about 70 per cent in 1980. The growth and spread of public aid receipt was even more spectacular. In 1980 seven of the ten "Black Belt" community areas had rates of receipt of Aid to Families with Dependent Children (AFDC) and

General Assistance that exceeded the 50 per cent mark of its total population, reaching such highs as 61 per cent in the neighbourhood of Grand Boulevard, 71 per cent in Oakland and 84 per cent on the Near South Side.

I hope to provide some new insights into the dimensions of these problems by drawing upon the perceptions and observations of the inner-city residents themselves. This presentation is based on a survey of 2,495 households in Chicago's inner-city neighbourhoods conducted in 1987 and 1988; a second survey of a sub-sample of 175 respondents from the larger survey who were re-interviewed solely with open-ended questions on their perceptions of the opportunity structure and life chances; a survey of a stratified random sample of 185 employers, designed to reflect the distribution of employment across industry and firm size in the Chicago metropolitan area, conducted in 1988; and comprehensive ethnographic research, including participant observation research and life-history interviews conducted in 1987 and 1988 in a sample of the inner-city neighbourhoods.

One of the major problems facing inner-city ghetto residents is weak attachment to the labour force. Weak labour-force attachment used in this context neither refers to nor implies a lack of willingness or desire to work. Indeed, nearly all of the jobless individuals in our random sample of residents from the inner-city neighbourhoods of Chicago expressed a desire to work. Rather "weak labour-force attachment" is a structural concept embedded in a theoretical framework that explains why some groups are more vulnerable to joblessness than others (cf. McLanahan & Garfinkel 1989). In other words, weak labour force attachment refers to the marginal economic position of some people in the labour force because of structural constraints or limited opportunities, including those in their immediate environment, for example, lack of access to the informal job network systems.

For residents of the ghetto, the full dimensions of this problem requires one to do more than simply examine the way that the organization of the economy and racial discrimination affect their job prospects in the larger society and in their immediate environment. For residents of the ghetto, it is also important to investigate the way in which the social organization of their neighbourhoods and the relationship of their neighbourhoods to the larger society further exacerbate their position in the labour market.

The complex dimensions of the problems of joblessness in the inner city are poignantly captured, as we shall soon see, by the statements of the residents themselves. But first let me attempt to put these problems in proper focus.

## The economy and weak labour-force attachment

An important factor in the growing misery of the inner-city ghetto in the cities of the North Central and mid-Atlantic regions of the United States since 1970 has been the major economic transformations that have undermined the manufacturing base of the central-city economies in these regions. The shift from goods-producing to service-producing industries, the increasing polarization of the labour market into low-wage and high-wage sectors, innovations in technology, the relocation of manufacturing industries out of central cities, and periodic recessions have forced up the rate of black joblessness (unemployment and nonparticipation in the labour market), despite the passage of anti-discrimination legislation and the creation of affirmative-action programmes. This has resulted in a sharp reduction in blue-collar jobs that have provided the major source of social mobility for poor blacks (Kasarda 1989, 1990a,b).

In Chicago, where the number of industrial plants had been cut by half from 1954 to 1982, the total number of blue-collar or production workers declined by 63 per cent from nearly a half a million in 1954 to less than 162,000 in 1982. This crumbling of the city's industrial base was accompanied by substantial cuts in trade employment, with over 120,000 jobs lost in retail and wholesale from 1963 to 1982. The mild growth of services – that created an additional 57,000 jobs during the same period, excluding health, financial and social services – came nowhere near to compensating for this collapse of Chicago's low-skilled employment pool (Wacquant & Wilson 1989b).

In recent years, manufacturing industries, historically a major source of urban black employment, have had to absorb the combined shock of periodic recessions, stagflation and increased foreign competition. This has led, with the aid of technological upgrading, to substantial employment cutbacks, periodic layoffs and wage cuts, especially in the older plants in the central cities. The groups most adversely affected by these changes have been the low-wage workers,

newly hired workers and non-union employees – groups disproportionately represented by minorities (Wacquant & Wilson 1989b).

Finally, the economic problems of low-income blacks have been
reinforced by recent demographic factors resulting in a "labour surplus
environment". As the economist Frank Levy has put it:

> During the decade [1970–80], women of all ages sharply
> increased their labour force participation and the large baby-
> boom cohorts of the 1950s came of age. Between 1960 and
> 1970, the labour force (nationwide) had grown by 13 million
> persons. But between 1970 and 1980, the labour force grew
> by 24 million persons. Because of this growth, we can assume
> that employers could be particularly choosy about whom they
> hired. In 1983, more than half of all black household heads in
> central-city poverty areas had not finished high school, a par-
> ticular disadvantage in this kind of job market. (Levy 1986)

In addition to the adverse impact that these changes have had on
poor urban minorities, they have also had a devastating effect on the
social organization of inner-city ghetto neighbourhoods. Consider,
for example, changes that have occurred in the black neighbourhood
of North Lawndale located on Chicago's West Side:

> After a quarter-century of uninterrupted deterioration,
> North Lawndale resembles a war zone. Nearly half of its
> housing stock that remains is, in most cases, rundown or
> dilapidated . . . In its good days, the economy of this West
> Side neighbourhood was anchored by two huge factories, the
> famous Hawthorne plant of Western Electric with over
> 43,000 jobs, and a Harvester plant employing some 14,000
> workers; the world headquarters of Sears, Roebuck and
> Company was located in its midst, bringing another 10,000
> jobs . . . There were, among others, a Zenith and a Sunbeam
> factory, a Copenhagen snuff plant, an Alden's Catalogue store,
> a Dell Farm food market and a post office bulk station. But
> things changed quickly: Harvester closed its gates at the end
> of the sixties and is now a vacant lot. Zenith, Sunbeam, and
> Alden also shut down their facilities. Sears moved most of its
> offices to the downtown Loop in 1973, leaving behind only

its catalogue distribution centre, with a workforce of 3,000 until last year, when it was moved out of the state of Illinois. The Hawthorne factory gradually phased out its operations and finally closed down in 1984. As the big plants went, so did the smaller stores, the banks, and countless other businesses dependent for their sales on the wages paid by large employers. (Wacquant & Wilson 1989a: 91–2)

The problems of job losses in the inner-city black neighbourhoods are clearly perceived by the residents themselves. In our large survey we asked the following question: "Over the past 5 or 10 years, how many friends of yours have lost their jobs because the place where they worked shut down – would you say none, a few, some or most?" Only 26 per cent of the black residents in our sample reported that none of their friends had lost jobs because their workplace shut down.

Some of the inner-city neighbourhoods have experienced more visible job losses than others. The devastation of the North Lawndale community was described above. The residents of that neighbourhood are keenly aware of the rapid depletion of job opportunities.

A 33-year-old unmarried black male of North Lawndale who is employed as a clerical worker stated:

> Because of the way the economy is structured, we're losing more jobs. Chicago is losing jobs by the thousands. There just aren't any starting companies here and it's harder to find a job compared to what it was years ago.

A similar view was expressed by a 41-year-old black female, also from North Lawndale, who works as a nurse's aid. She states:

> Chicago is really full of peoples. Everybody can't get a good job. They don't have enough good jobs to provide for everybody. I don't think they have enough jobs period. And all the factories and the places, they closed up and moved out of the city and stuff like that, you know. I guess it's one of the reasons they haven't got too many jobs now, cause a lot of the jobs now, factories and business, they're done, moved out. So that way it's less jobs for lot of peoples.

Similar views were expressed by respondents from other neighbourhoods. A 33-year-old South Side janitor states:

> The machines are putting a lot of people out of jobs. I worked for *Time* magazine for seven years on a videograph printer and they come along with [a more powerful] printer, it cost them half a million dollars: they did what we did in half the time, eliminated two shifts.

"Jobs were plentiful in the past", states a 29-year-old unemployed black male who lives in one of the poorest neighbourhoods on the South Side. "You could walk out of the house and get a job. Maybe not what you want but you could get a job. Now, you can't find anything."

A similar point was expressed by a 41-year-old hospital worker from another impoverished South Side neighbourhood:

> Well, most of the jobs have moved out of Chicago. Factory jobs have moved out. There are no jobs here. Not like it was 20–30 years ago. And people aren't skilled enough for the jobs that are here. You don't have enough skilled and educated people to fill them.

The problems of joblessness and access to jobs for inner-city residents are exacerbated by the increasing suburbanization of jobs to which they would otherwise have access. Getting to suburban jobs is especially problematic for the jobless individuals in our sample because only 28 per cent overall and a mere 18 per cent who live in ghetto areas, that is areas with poverty rates of at least 40 per cent, have access to an automobile. A 32-year-old unemployed South Side welfare mother describes the problem in this way:

> There's not enough jobs. I thinks Chicago's the only city that does not have a lot of opportunities opening in it. There's not enough factories, there's not enough work. Most all the good jobs are in the suburbs. Sometimes it's hard for the people in the city to get to the suburbs, because everybody don't own a car. Everybody don't drive.

As one 29-year-old unemployed South Side black male put it, after commenting on the lack of jobs in his area:

> You gotta go out in the suburbs, but I can't get out there. The bus go out there but you don't want to catch the bus out there, going two hours each ways. If you have to be at work at eight that mean you have to leave for work at six, that mean you have to get up at five to be at work at eight. Then when wintertime come you be in trouble.

Another unemployed South Side black male had this to say:

> Most of the time . . . the places be too far and you need transportation and I don't have none right now. If I had some I'd probably be able to get one [job]. If I had a car and went way into the suburbs, 'cause there ain't none in the city.

This problem is echoed by an 18-year-old unemployed West Side black male:

> They are most likely hiring in the suburbs. Recently, I think about two years ago, I had a job but they say that I need some transportation and they say that the bus out in the suburbs run at a certain time. So I had to pass that job up because I did not have no transport.

An unemployed single welfare mother of two from the West Side states:

> Well, I'm goin' to tell you: most jobs, more jobs are in the suburbs. It's where the good jobs and stuff is but you gotta have transportation to get there and it's hard to be gettin' out there in the suburbs. Some people don't know where the suburbs is, some people get lost out there. It is really hard, but some make a way.

One employed factory worker from the West Side who works a night shift describes the situation this way:

> From what I, I see, you know, it's hard to find a good job in
> the inner city cause so many people moving, you know, west
> to the suburbs and out of state . . . some people turn jobs
> down because they don't have no way of getting out there . . .
> I just see some people just going to work – and they seem like
> they the type who just used to – they coming all the way from
> the city and go on all the way to the suburbs and, you know,
> you can see 'em all bundled and – catching one bus and the
> next bus. They just used to doing that.

But the problem is not simply one of transportation and the length of
commuting time when one lacks an automobile. There is also the
problem of the travel expense and of whether the long trek to the
suburbs is actually worth it in terms of the income earned. "If you
work in the suburbs you gotta have a car", states an unmarried welfare
mother of three children who lives on Chicago's West Side, "then you
gotta buy gas. You spending more getting to the suburbs to work, then
you is getting paid, so you still ain't getting nowhere."

Indeed, one unemployed 36-year-old black man from the west side
of Chicago actually quit his suburban job because of the transportation
problem:

> It was more expensive going to work in Naperville, transpor-
> tation and all and it wasn't worth it . . . I was spending more
> money getting to work than I earned working.

If transportation poses a problem for those who have to commute
to work from the inner city to the suburbs, it is also a problem for poor
ghetto residents when they travel to the suburbs to look for work. For
example, one unemployed man who lives on the South Side had just
gone out to O'Hare Airport looking for work with no luck. He states:
"The money I spent yesterday, I coulda kept that in my pocket – I
coulda kept that. 'Cause you know I musta spent about $7 or
somethin'. I coulda kept that."

In addition to the problem of getting to where there are jobs, especially higher paying jobs, and the problem of lack of education and
training for a good number of available jobs, inner-city workers also
face the problem of employer attitudes and perception of black workers. Indeed, our interviews of Chicago-area businessmen indicate that

many employers consider inner-city workers – especially young black males – to be uneducated, uncooperative, unstable and dishonest. Accordingly, employers may practise what economists call statistical discrimination – making judgements about an applicant's productivity, which are often too difficult or too expensive to measure, on the basis of his or her race, ethnic or class background.

In interviews of employers in the greater Chicago area conducted by my research assistants (Neckerman & Kirschenman 1990, Kirschenman & Neckerman 1991), employers were asked to give their views on the quality of the workforce in general, black workers in particular, and black workers in comparison with white and Hispanic workers. When asked whether they perceive a difference in the work ethic of black, white and Hispanic workers, 37.7 per cent placed blacks at the lowest level, 7.6 per cent placed both Hispanics and blacks at the bottom, 1.4 per cent ranked Hispanics alone at the bottom, and no-one felt that the work ethic of whites was below that of the other two groups; 51.4 per cent either perceived no differences or refused to categorize workers in terms of the work ethic. In this latter group many qualified their response by saying there was no difference in the work ethic among these three groups when you take into consideration education, family background or environment.

Many of those who viewed blacks in a negative light thought that they possessed few of the qualities of a "good" worker, that "they don't want to work", don't stay on the job", have an "attitude problem", or are "lazy and unreliable". As one employer put it:

> Most of them are not as educated as you might think. I've never seen any of these [black] guys read anything outside a comic book. These Mexicans are sitting here reading novels constantly, even though they are in Spanish. These [black] guys will sit and watch cartoons while the other guys are busy reading. To me that shows laziness. No desire to upgrade yourself.

A manufacturer says:

> The black work ethic. There's no work ethic. At least at the unskilled. I'm sure with the skilled . . . as you go up, its a lot different.

A similar argument along economic class lines was made by another employer. "I find that the less skilled, the less educational background of – and now I'll say black – the more belligerent they are." Black men, in particular, were described in a very unfavourable light. A suburban drugstore manager states, for example, that:

> It's unfortunate but, in my business I think overall [black men] tend to be known to be dishonest. I think that's too bad but that's the image they have. (Interviewer: So you think it's an image problem?) Yeah, a dishonest, an image problem of being dishonest men and lazy. They're known to be lazy. They are (laughs). I hate to tell you, but. It's all an image though. Whether they are or not, I don't know, but, it's an image that is perceived. (Interviewer: I see. How do you think that image was developed?) Go look in the jails (laughs).

However, many of the employers focused on what they perceived to be a lack of basic skills among inner-city workers. A vice-president of a television station in Chicago argued that:

> They are frequently unable to write. They go through the Chicago public schools or they dropped out when they were in the eight grade. They can't read. They can't write. They can hardly talk. I have another opinion which is strictly my own and that is that people who insist on beating themselves to the point where they axe out of the mainstream of the world, suffer the consequences. And I'm talking about languages that are spoken in the ghetto. They are not English.

The employers in our sample expressed concern not only about the quality and level of academic training that inner-city students receive but also about the failure of the public school system to prepare youngsters for the labour market. A Hispanic vice-president of personnel for a large Chicago manufacturing firm relates this problem to the difficulties that black males experience in the workforce:

> If you're handicapped by not having some of the basic skills you need, if you're hired and you can't make it on the job because you don't even have the basic skills, that's part of the

232

problem. Part of the problem may be role models in the families. The business of the discipline of having to be at work every day. If it's not in the school, and they didn't experience it in schools, when you put them in this work environment and all of a sudden try to change habits when there are no role models anywhere, it's not going to work.

A number of employers mentioned that education in the Chicago public school system, which is overwhelmingly black, has become a negative signal, and therefore many applicants from this system are passed over for those from parochial or suburban schools. As one employer explained ". . . the educational skills that they come to the job with are minimal because of the schools in the areas where they generally live".

Many of the employers of clerical workers felt that black applicants tend to lack essential job characteristics. As a black personnel officer put it:

> Unfortunately, there *is* a perception that most of [Chicago public high school] kids are black and they don't have the proper skills. They don't know how to write. They don't know how to speak. They don't act in a business fashion or dress in a business manner, in a way that the business community would like.

Another employer defended his method of screening out most job applicants on the telephone on the basis of their "grammar and English" skills.

> I have every right to say that that's a requirement for this job. I don't care if you're pink, black, green, yellow or orange, I demand someone who speaks well. You want to tell me that I'm a bigot, fine, call me a bigot. I know blacks, you don't even know they're black. So do you.

Clerical employers in particular tended to be sensitive to class distinctions among blacks, and they associate these differences with patterns of speech.

We have a couple of black workers – a friend of mine, one of the black secretaries who's been here several years, said, "Well, they're black but their soul is white" and, because culturally, they're white. They do not have black accents. They do not – I think the accent is a big part of it. If someone – it doesn't matter, if someone is black but they speak with the same accent as a Midwestern white person, it completely changes the perception of them. And then dress is part of it. So, you're dealing with what are almost more socio-economic prejudice than purely racial prejudice.

He goes on to state:

In many businesses the ability to meet the public is paramount and you do not talk street talk to the buying public. Almost all your black welfare people talk street talk. A lot of times I will interview applicants who are black, who are sort of lower class. They'll come to me and I cannot hire them because their language skills are poor. Their speaking voice for one thing is poor, they have no verbal facility with the language, and these, you know, they just don't know how to speak and they'll say "salesmens" instead of "salesmen" and that's a problem.

Another respondent indicated how an inner-city job applicant can signal that these stereotypes are not applicable:

You take somebody from the inner city. They may be right out of the ghetto, they may be right out of the projects. If we feel confident they're not going to steal, I mean, they're sincere, they may be going to school nights or something. They have a little background. They interview well. They're neat and clean . . . We don't have any problems.

Our interviews indicate that it is reasonable to assume that most inner-city applicants are screened out by the skill and educational requirements of clerical jobs. An inner-city manufacturer stated that "when we hear other employers talk, they'll go after primarily the Hispanic and Oriental first, those two, and, I'll qualify that even further, the

Mexican Hispanic, and any Oriental, and after that, that's pretty much it, that's pretty much where they like to draw the line, right there".

Finally, personal references may also be more important for black job applicants than for others.

> All of a sudden, they take a look at a guy, and unless he's got an in, the reason why I hired this black kid the last time is cause my neighbour said to me, yeah I used him for a few [days], he's good. And I said, you know what, I'm going to take a chance. But it was a recommendation. But other than that, I've got a walk-in, and, who knows? And I think that for the most part, a guy sees a black man, he's a bit hesitant, because I don't know.

These responses clearly indicate the problems that inner-city workers, especially black males, face in their job market search. In addition to the structural barriers such as access to informal job information networks and requirements of education and training, there is also the problem of employer perceptions of inner-city workers. Although an overwhelming majority of the respondents did not express overt racist attitudes or a categorical dislike of blacks when explaining their hiring practices, it is clear that many did, in fact, practise statistical discrimination by screening out black applicants very early in the hiring process because of their inner-city residence, their class background and their public-school education. These factors were frequently used as proxies for judgements about worker productivity.

The practice of statistical discrimination reinforces the economic marginality of ghetto residents by further weakening their attachment to the legitimate labour force. But, weak labour-force attachment is also severely exacerbated by the neighbourhoods in which poor urban blacks tend to reside, a subject to which I now turn.

## Weak attachment to the labour and the neighbourhood context

Inner-city ghetto neighbourhoods in America have undergone a profound social transformation over the past several decades. This is reflected not only in their increasing rates of social dislocation but also

235

in their changing class structure. There has been a sharp decline in the number of stable working-class families in these neighbourhoods either because of outmigration of higher income families to other city neighbourhoods or because of downward mobility into the ranks of the persistent jobless due to the devastating effects of deindustrialization and, as suggested by our employer interviews, the problems of statistical discrimination.

The problems of joblessness have aggravated the pattern of social life in the ghetto. As I have suggested, many of these problems are fairly recent. In earlier decades, not only was a substantial majority of the adult population in ghetto neighbourhoods employed, but the black working and middle classes brought stability to these neighbourhoods: they invested their economic and social resources there; they patronized their churches, stores, banks and community organizations; they sent their children to their schools; they reinforced societal norms and values; and they made it meaningful for lower-class blacks in these segregated enclaves to envision the possibility of limited upward mobility.

However, today, inner-city ghetto residents represent almost exclusively the most disadvantaged segments of the urban black population – including those families that have experienced long-term spells of poverty and/or welfare receipt, individuals who lack minimal training and skills and have suffered periods of recurrent and persistent unemployment, adults who have dropped out of the labour force altogether, and those who respond to restricted or limited opportunities by resorting to street crime or involvement in the underground economy. In short, the residents of the inner-city ghetto are collectively different from and much more socially isolated than those that lived in these neighbourhoods in earlier periods. They find themselves in a qualitatively different social and institutional environment, where the structure of economic and social relations makes it increasingly unlikely that they will have access to those minimal channels and resources necessary for escaping poverty, including access to informal job network systems and stable attachment to the labour market (Wilson 1987).

This assessment of the situation in inner-city ghetto neighbourhoods is echoed by the statements of many of the residents themselves. When the black respondents in our large survey were asked how they would rate their neighbourhood as a place to live, only a third rated their area as a good or very good place to live and only 18 per cent of those in extreme poverty or ghetto areas felt that their neighbourhood was a desirable place to live.

As one 33-year-old married father of three from a South Side neighbourhood in which a quarter of the population was destitute in 1980 (incomes 75 per cent below the official poverty line) put it:

> There's no place as depressing, as uninspiring as this neighbourhood right here. This neighbourhood is uninspiring, depressing. At the end of this block, the police just raided these two dope houses, you know. You have that sort of people hanging around, they watch you come and go. We got our house broken into.

A 31-year-old man who works as a labourer and a janitor and lives in a Near West Side public housing project in a census tract in which 72 per cent of the population lived below the poverty line and 61 per cent of the population was destitute in 1980, described his neighbourhood in these emphatic terms:

> See, this is a violent neighbourhood. You always hear somebody gettin' shot, just about everyday or something like every night. Because you know, like I said, I see people are crowded up together, especially in the high rises. I would say it drags you down, because, you know, when people get crazy and everything, it'll drag you down. They gonna robbin' you, you know, tryin' to beat you. They don't wanta work, you know, they'd rather for you to work and then wait for you, you know, to get your paycheck so they can rob you or something.

A 39-year-old divorced schoolteacher and mother of four from a high poverty neighbourhood on the South Side talked about a boy who had been recently shot in her neighbourhood:

> I think he was just gettin', buyin' somethin' or whatever – at the restaurant or somethin' and some kid walked up to him on the street and shot him five times. I – I don't know was it gang related or if kids – you know, just a matter of bein' in the

wrong place at the wrong time, you know. Those are the kinds of things that you have to be careful about when you live in an environment like this.

Many of the respondents describe the negative effects of their neighbourhood on their own personal outlook. An unmarried employed black male who works as a clerical worker and lives in an extreme poverty tract in a West Side neighbourhood said that:

> There is a more positive outlook if you come from an upwardly mobile neighbourhood than you would here. In this type of neighbourhood, all you hear is negative [things] and that can kind of bring you down when you're trying to make it. So your neighbourhood definitely has something to do with it.

A similar point was made by a young 17-year-old black male who works part time and attends college and resides in an extreme poverty neighbourhood on the West Side. Describing the situation of the many alcoholics in his neighbourhood, he states:

> [They say] "Oh, we gonna get high today." "Oh, whoopee!" "What you gonna do tomorrow, man?" "I don't know, man, I don't know." You can ask any of 'em: "What you gonna do tomorrow?" "I don't know, man. I know when [it gets] here." You know, stuff like that. And that's true. Most of them don't know what they going to do the next day. And I can really understand, you know, being in that state. If you around totally negative people, people who are not doing anything, that's the way you gonna be regardless.

A 32-year-old unmarried unemployed black father of one child who resides in an area where three-quarters of the population was destitute in 1980 described his neighbourhood this way:

> No, I don't like this neighbourhood. A lot of friends, they got killed and what not, you know, I saw a lot of killing in this neighbourhood. It's messed up. My mother is going on 66, she ain't got a chance of a young man running up on her and

saying: "Hey give me your money." She ain't got a chance.
The dudes they do a lot of ripping off around here, they do a
lot of stealing, put it that way. They rip off people. Then they
got the drug traffic running through in these buildings. It's all
messed up, man.

Finally, a 40-year-old welfare mother of four children who lives in a
West Side census tract in which nearly half the population was destitute in 1980 describes how the problems in her neighbourhood could
be improved:

> Even this neighbourhood, if they would fix it up, and keep it
> up, keep the drugs out, it would be much better. Take the
> drugs out. Give, uh, let the peoples have more jobs, you
> know, working. They're sitting out on the corner, they're
> doin' nothin'. So I think if a person was workin' – and then,
> even, then even again – I believe if it was more money, like
> even if you're on aid [the inner-city euphemism for welfare],
> if they would give you more money, I don't think there,
> maybe it would be as bad as, you know, stickin' up people and
> killin' people. 'Cause I think they kill, stick up people 'cause
> they don't have, so they figure they can go take it from some-
> one else.

Given the overall negative descriptions the respondents gave of their
neighbourhoods, it is not surprising that a substantial majority desire
to live elsewhere. When the interviewers in our large survey asked the
respondents if they would prefer to live in their neighbourhood,
another neighbourhood in Chicago, in the suburbs or somewhere
else, only 35 per cent of the respondents stated that they would prefer
to live in their own neighbourhood and as few as 23 per cent of the
respondents in the extreme poverty tracts stated a preference for their
own neighbourhood.

A 27-year-old unmarried welfare mother of three who lives in an
extreme poverty tract in North Lawndale in which nearly half the
population was destitute in 1980 describes her situation this way:

> It's the only place I could afford to live at the time when I
> moved in. At the time when I moved I had two children and

I've been here eleven years. No, I don't like it. At the present time I can't afford to move out.

Another welfare mother of three children who is divorced and from the same area complains that: "Taxis don't want to come over here to get you and bring you back either. You know, friends from other places don't want really to come here. And you yourself, you wouldn't want to invite intelligent people here: there's markings and there's writing on the wall, nasty – whatever."

One unmarried 37-year-old women who works part time as a telemarketer and has lived in an extreme poverty tract in a South Side neighbourhood for 23 years, put it this way:

> I really don't like the neighbourhood, but I can't afford right now to go to another neighbourhood, you know to a better apartment 'cause I don't have the money, the rent would be more. Everybody here – I have talked to peoples in the neighbourhood – they feel the same way. You know, they say the building is bad and it's poor. You know, you try to do things about it, you know, and you do. For instance, we had the lock put on the door one day and the next day the lock was off, and the hall was really messed up. So you be really trying to do things, but then there's the next person that come along and just tear it down. So it's basically, everyone is here because the rent is in ranges of their salary and so forth but I think eventually everything will, you know, work itself out.

A 33-year-old married mother of three, who lives in a West Side neighbourhood where nearly half of the population is destitute, sums up the feelings of many of the respondents in our study.

> If you live in an area in your neighbourhood where you have people that don't work, don't have no means of support, you know, don't have no jobs, who're gonna break into your house to steal what you have, to sell to get them some money, then you can't live in a neighbourhood and try to concentrate on tryin' to get ahead, then you get to work and you have to worry if somebody's breakin' into your house or not. So, you

know, it's best to try to move in a decent area, to live in a community with people that works.

In addition to the overall negative perception that people in our sample have of their neighbourhoods, there was a general feeling that conditions have deteriorated and are likely to get worse. In answer to the question as to whether the neighbourhood has changed as a place to live over the years, 71 per cent of the overall sample felt that their neighbourhood had either stayed the same or had gotten worse.

A divorced mother of two children who lives in a poverty tract in which half the population is poor also compares her situation with that of her parents. She states that:

> It wasn't as bad in their [her parents] days. People wasn't there on drugs and stuff like that, as often as they are now. And then you could sleep with your door open, you know, I was told, and now you have to have bars, you know. You're scared to walk the street.

A divorced schoolteacher and mother of four children, who resides in a South Side area in which 38 per cent of the population was poor in 1980, says:

> I've lived in this community for, let's see, since about 1958, so what I've seen is that the community has gone down. 'Cause the businesses are leavin' and nobody is, um, putting back money into the community, so I see it go down, I don't see it, you know, prospering at all.

"Well, OK, I realize there was drugs when I was growing up but they weren't as open as they are now", states a divorced Illinois Bell telephone despatcher and mother of five children from a neighbourhood that recently changed from a non-poverty to a poverty area. "It's nothing to see a 10-year-old kid strung out or a 10-year-old kid selling drugs. I mean, when they were doing it back then they were sneaking around doing it. It's like a open thing now."

A divorced mother of one child and employed as a schoolteacher in a South Side neighbourhood that has also recently become poor, states:

I've been in this neighbourhood close to 20 years. I havn't seen changes for the better. There's a lot more crime in this area now than there was when I first moved over here. In this area the opportunities have gone down.

"Only thing that changed is that the neighbourhood going down instead of going back up", states an unemployed black male from a West Side housing project in one of the most destitute census tracts in the city. "It ain't like it used to be. They laid off a lot of people. There used to be a time when you got a broken window, you call up housing and they send someone over to fix it, but it ain't like that no more."

The 17-year-old black college student from the West Side that I quoted earlier described how drugs have created a problem for his neighbourhood:

When I first moved over here this neighbourhood was quite OK . . . But, when drugs start flowing in, people start having drugs fights and you couldn't sleep because there were cars coming up and down the street all night long. And, you know, that's bad 'cause that makes your community look bad.

Finally, a 41-year-old married but separated mother of two who is employed as a nurse's aide and lives in an extreme poverty tract on the West Side describes how the situation in her neighbourhood has changed for the children.

Before, you know, the young peoples they had this Youth Corps and all this you know, but they done cut out this all. They don't have anything for the young peoples now. All they do when they get out of school in summertime is rap up and down the street, and get into trouble 'cause they don't have anything to do. And I felt like the Youth Corps, when I was in school, I was in Youth Corps and it really helped out a lot. It taught me a lot, taught me – I learned to hold on a job when I am working it 'cause they train you. But now they don't have anything for the young kids, really you know.

In recent media descriptions of the problems of the ghetto underclass one gets the distinct impression that the values of people in the inner-city ghetto, to quote a *Time* article, "are often at radical odds with those of the majority – even the majority of the poor". However, our research reveals that the beliefs of inner-city residents bear little resemblance to such blanket views.

What is so striking is that, despite the overwhelming poverty, black residents in inner-city ghetto neighbourhoods actually reinforce, not undermine the basic American values on individual initiative. For example, in our large random survey, we found that nearly all the respondents felt that plain hard work is either very important or somewhat important for getting ahead. Indeed only 2.5 per cent of the black residents who live in extreme poverty neighbourhoods denied the importance of plain hard work for getting ahead in society. And 66 per cent expressed the view that it is very important (Tienda & Stier 1989).

Nonetheless, given the constraints and limited opportunities confronting people in inner-city neighbourhoods, it is altogether reasonable to assume that many of those who subscribe to these values will, in the final analysis, fail to or be unable to live up to them. Take for example the special problems created by joblessness in these neighbourhoods. As Pierre Bourdieu (1965) has pointed out, work is not simply a means of making a living and supporting one's family. It also constitutes the framework for daily behaviour and patterns of interaction because of the disciplines and regularities it imposes.

Thus in the absence of regular employment, what is lacking is not only a place in which to work and the receipt of regular income, but also a coherent organization of the present, that is, a system of concrete expectations and goals. Regular employment provides the anchor for the temporal and spatial aspects of daily life. In the absence of regular employment, life, including family life, becomes more incoherent. Unemployment and irregular employment preclude the elaboration of a rational plan of life, the necessary condition of adaptation to an industrial economy. This problem is most severe for jobless individuals and families in neighbourhoods with low rates of employment. The relative absence of rational planning in a jobless family is reinforced by the similar condition of other families in the neighbourhood.

One of the most severe problems created by the decline of inner-city neighbourhoods has been the effects of these changes on the children of the neighbourhood and their future attachment to the labour market. For example, youngsters who grow up in a family with a steady breadwinner and in a neighbourhood in which most of the adults are employed will tend to develop some of the disciplined habits that automatically emerge with stable or steady employment, habits that are reflected in the behaviour of his or her parents and in the conduct of other neighbourhood adults. Accordingly, when this youngster enters the labour market, he or she has a distinct advantage over the youngsters who grow up in a household where there has not been a steady breadwinner and in a neighbourhood that is not organized around work – in other words, a milieu in which one is more exposed to the less disciplined habits associated with casual or infrequent work.

Unlike many of the inner-city ghetto neighbourhoods in our study, in a neighbourhood that includes a good number of working and professional families (neighbourhoods in which poor urban whites overwhelmingly reside), perceptive youngsters may observe idleness but they will also witness many individuals regularly going to and from work; they may see many school drop-outs but they can also see a clear connection between education and meaningful employment; they may observe family breakups, but they will also be aware of the presence of many intact families; they may notice welfare dependency, but they can also see a significant number of non-welfare families; they may be cognizant of neighbourhood crime, but they can recognize that many individuals in their neighbourhoods are not involved in criminal activity.

But in neighbourhoods with a small proportion of regularly employed families and with a substantial majority of families experiencing spells of long-term joblessness, people become isolated and are excluded from the job network system that permeates other neighbourhoods and that is so important in learning about or being recommended for jobs that become available in various parts of the city. As the prospects for employment diminish, other alternatives such as the underground economy and welfare are not only increasingly relied on, but also, in some cases, they come to be seen as a way of life. Moreover, unlike the situation in earlier years, girls who become pregnant out of wedlock are far more likely to give birth out of wedlock because of a shrinking pool of marriageable, that is, employed, black males.

Thus, in such neighbourhoods the chances are that children seldom experience sustained interaction with people who are employed or

with families that have a steady breadwinner. The result is that joblessness becomes a way of life and takes on a different social meaning; the
relationship between schooling and post-school employment carries a
different meaning. The development of linguistic, cognitive, and other
educational and job-related skills necessary for the work world in the
mainstream economy is thereby impaired. In such neighbourhoods,
teachers become frustrated and do not or are unable to teach and children do not learn. A vicious cycle is perpetuated through the family,
through the neighbourhood and through the schools (Wilson 1987).

The residents of poor inner-city neighbourhoods clearly see this
process themselves and many of them discuss the situations more
graphically and more clearly than some of the social scientists who are
researching these neighbourhoods. Let me once again quote the perceptive college student who lives on the West Side:

> Well, basically, I feel that if you are raised in a neighbourhood
> and all you see is negative things then you are going to be
> negative because you don't see anything positive. Guys and
> black males see drug dealers on the corner and they see fancy
> cars and flashy money and they figure: "Hey, if I get into
> drugs I can be like him."

He goes on to state:

> And I think about how, you know, the kids around there, all
> they see, OK, they see these drug addicts, and then what else
> do they see? Oh, they see thugs, you know, they see the gang-
> bangers. So, who do they, who do they really look, model
> themselves after? Who is their role model? They have none
> but the thugs. So that's what they wind up being, you know.
> They [the children in the neighbourhood] deal with the only
> male role model that they can find and most of the time that
> be pimps, dope dealers so what do they do they model them-
> selves after them. Not intentionally trying to but if, you
> know, that's the only male you're around and that's the only
> one you come in close contact with, you tend to want to be
> like that person. And that's why you have so many young drug
> dealers.

A 25-year-old West Side father of two who works two jobs to make ends meet raised a similar point:

> And they see what's around 'em and they follow that same pattern, you know. The society says: "Well, you can sell dope. You can do this. You can do that." A lot of 'em even got to the point where they can accept a few years in jail, uh, as a result of what they might do . . . They don't see nobody getting up early in the morning, going to work or going to school all the time. The guys they − they be with don't do that . . . 'cause that's the crowd that you choose − well, that's been presented to you by your neighbourhood.

An unemployed black male who lives on the South Side describes how the children in his neighbourhood get into drugs and alcohol.

> They're in an environment where if you don't get high you're square. You know what I'm saying? If you don't get high some kind of way or another . . . and then, you know, kids are gonna emulate what they come up under . . . I've watched a couple of generations − I've been here since '61. I watched kids, I saw their fathers ruined, and I seen 'em grow up and do the very same thing . . . The children, they don't have any means of recreation whatsoever out here, other than their back yards, the streets, nothing . . . The only way it can be intervened if the child has something outside the house to go to, because it is just go by the environment of the house he's destined to be an alcoholic or a drug addict.

A 40-year-old mother of six who lives in an extreme poverty tract on the South Side related the problems of children in her neighbourhood to the limited opportunity structure.

> There's less opportunities over here: it's no jobs. The kids aren't in school, you know, they're not getting any education, there's a lot of drugs on the streets. So, you know, wrong environment, bad associations. So you have to be in some kind of environment where the kids are more, you know, ready to go to school to get an education instead of, you

know, droppin' out to sell drugs because they see their friends, on the corner, makin' money: they got a pocket fulla money, you know. They got kids walkin' around here that's ten years old selling drugs.

A 37-year-old unemployed black male from the South Side describes the different situation for males and females:

Some kids just seem like they don't want to learn, but others, they stick to it. Especially the females, they stick to it. The males either become – they see the street life. They see guys out here making big bucks with fancy cars, jewellery and stuff, and they try to emulate them. That's our problem, you know. The males, they're pretty impressionable. That's why they drop out . . . They see their peers out here, they didn't go to school, they makin' it. But they making it the wrong way.

Finally, an unmarried 19-year-old West Side male who works at a MacDonald's restaurant reflects on his own situation in terms of the negative influences in his environment:

I missed a lot of days out of school just hanging – trying to do what my friends do, that is what messed me up and I regret it. It was, like, for a while I was going to my classes, then when classes started getting boring I was, like, "Man, I'm not going to do this." So me and my friends would go and ride the El together and that is what basically messed me up . . . I regret it because I am cheating myself out of an education. I know some things but I cheated myself out of bettering my education. Now, it ain't too late. It's just that if I would have went to school, I would have accomplished some of the things that I want to accomplish but now it will be harder.

# Conclusion

The legacy of historic racial oppression in the United States is a massive and growing ghetto underclass, highly concentrated in the nation's largest central cities and adversely affected by the ongoing restructuring of the American urban economy. Indeed, despite the Great Society programmes ushered in by the Lyndon Baines Johnson administration and despite the sweeping anti-discrimination legislation and affirmative-action programmes of the 1970s, the vulnerability of the urban minority poor to sectoral economic shifts and cyclical downturns, especially since 1970, and to the insidious practice of statistical discrimination has resulted in sharp increases in inner-city joblessness and related problems such as persistent poverty, poor single-parent households, welfare receipt, educational failure, housing deterioration and crime.

These outcomes are most clearly seen in the most concentrated poverty areas in the inner city. The precipitous rise in joblessness together with the outmigration of working- and middle-class families from these areas have altered the class structure of these neighbourhoods and magnified the deleterious effects of periodic recessions, spatial and industrial changes in the economy, and low-wage employment. The dwindling presence of non-poor families in these neighbourhoods makes it considerably more difficult for the remaining residents to sustain basic formal and informal institutions. And as the basic institutions decline, the social organization of inner-city ghetto neighbourhoods deteriorates, further depleting the social resources and life chances of those who are trapped in these blighted areas.

As we approach the end of the twentieth century, the problems of poverty, joblessness and social isolation in the inner-city ghetto remain among the most serious challenges facing municipal and national policy-makers. As suggested in this chapter, a successful public policy initiative to address these problems requires a close look not only at the declining labour-market opportunities for the truly disadvantaged, but also at the declining social organization of inner-city neighbourhoods that have and continue to reinforce the economic marginality of their residents.

# CHAPTER 13

# Social justice in a global economy?

## Patricia Hewitt

This chapter does not pretend to offer a neatly wrapped solution to the question of whether the global economy makes social justice impossible. But I hope that I can at least take the debate forwards, by considering the more pessimistic and the more optimistic responses to that question and by looking at the conditions that would make it possible for the industrialized nations of Europe to sustain our welfare states against competition from low-cost producers.

These issues lay at the heart of our work on the Social Justice Commission whose report was published in October 1994 (Commission on Social Justice 1994). But I also want to take the opportunity to reflect upon our conclusions and suggest how we might develop what seem to me to be the most important aspects of the Commission's proposals. I must stress, therefore, that I am not writing on behalf of my colleagues on the Commission, nor indeed on behalf of Andersen Consulting; I can only offer a personal view.

I shall frame my argument in the terms of Marshall's classic essay, *Citizenship and social class*, and the three generations of rights whose development he traced. In summary, I want to argue: first, that the proposition that globalization makes social justice unachievable is a latter-day version of the conflict that Marshall perceived between the civil and the social rights of citizenship; secondly, that there are many different reasons for challenging that proposition, most of which I will summarize only briefly; and thirdly, the main point I want to develop, that in order to give an optimistic answer to the question that is my title, we have to reformulate the relationship between civil and social rights. In other words, we have to rethink the purpose and the nature of the welfare state in Britain and other industrialized countries. And in doing so, we can learn from the very countries whose success we now perceive as a threat to our own welfare state way of life.

## Civil and social rights

I can no longer remember when I first read *Citizenship and social class*, the work of an outstandingly original and generous thinker. Certainly, I absorbed a long time ago Marshall's central argument about the development of citizenship through three generations of rights – civil, political and social – and his elegant attribution of them, respectively, to the eighteenth, nineteenth and twentieth centuries. In recollection at least, there seemed a comforting logic, a sense of the onward march of citizenship, of the necessary development of social rights upon a foundation that was itself being strengthened and developed.

I was dismayed to find, however, on rereading Marshall, that I had failed to absorb his much less comforting argument: that civil and social rights are necessarily in conflict. For the civil rights whose development he traced were, as he said: "indispensable to a competitive market economy. They gave to each man, as part of his individual status, the power to engage as an independent unit in the economic struggle and made it possible to deny to him social protection on the ground that he was equipped with the means to protect himself." The right to work, to earn, to save, to buy property, to make contracts – these created a status for individuals that was no longer dependent upon, nor protected by, a feudal position acquired at birth.

These new civil rights, however, could not co-exist with the earlier, pre-capitalist generation of social rights that had derived in medieval times from membership of local communities and functional associations and had given rise to the Elizabethan Poor Law and an extensive system of wage regulation. As Marshall puts it: ". . . at the very end of the eighteenth century there occurred a final struggle between the old and the new, between the planned (or patterned) society and the competitive economy. And in this battle citizenship was divided against itself; social rights sided with the old and civil with the new."

Two hundred years later, we find ourselves engaged in a latter-day version of the same battle. On one side, the neoliberals – the champions, in Marshall's terms, of civil rights – who argue that Europe can only survive in the modern global economy by slashing its social costs, deregulating its labour markets and dismantling its welfare institutions. On the other, social and Christian democrats alike who believe that an extension of social rights must go hand-in-hand with the expansion of the market, if economic efficiency as well as social justice is to be realized.

## The challenge of globalization

My second surprise, on rereading Marshall, was the *Englishness* of his essay. The story of citizenship that Marshall told was a history of England over seven centuries – but a history in which England's economic and political relationships with other countries were never referred to. The silent presence that lies behind Marshall's story is the "global economy" that England had helped to create, in its relations not only with the other nations of Britain and Ireland but with all those parts of the globe that England had colonized, with which it traded, to which it sent its convicts.

You will understand that I do not make this point in any spirit of criticism: the Englishness of Marshall's essay reflected, I imagine, a confidence in English institutions that we no longer feel and, perhaps too, a sense that Britain's post-war welfare state was at the forefront of radical social reform. But today, it is impossible for us to contemplate the present condition or future direction of the welfare state, in the United Kingdom or within the European Union, without confronting the challenge of globalization.

The post-war welfare state depended to a significant extent upon international conditions that no longer exist. In the long post-war boom, American military and economic hegemony in the capitalist world provided the West with a free-trade system, which included access to American consumer and capital markets; a relatively open and stable international financial system, agreed at Bretton Woods; secure and cheap oil supplies from the Middle East; an end to war between the liberal capitalist states with the creation of NATO; and the Marshall Plan that helped to make possible the reconstruction of western Europe and the creation of the European Communities.

Within this extraordinarily stable international order, the countries of the West pursued – of course, with significant variations, depending upon their political and social inheritance – policies of full employment, in most though not all cases primarily for men; established far-reaching social welfare and transfer programmes; secured rising real standards of living and, generally, reduced inequalities of both income and status.

But the world's political geography has changed irrevocably. It is not my purpose here to evaluate the argument about the extent of globalization, or even to rehearse the numbers about the growth of foreign trade and inward investment. We are all familiar with the transformation of the countries of the Pacific Rim, and with the addition of communism to capitalism, with what we might call the forward march – by no means yet complete – of civil rights, of economic individualism, across the globe. I hope you will forgive me therefore if I take for granted this thing we can reasonably call the global economy, together with the intensification of the political, demographic and technological forces that are making for globalization. And the picture we are offered of this new global economy is, from the perspective of social justice, pretty gloomy.

Unstable and apparently uncontrollable world capital markets – trading in a single day more than one trillion dollars – have destroyed the ability of national governments to pursue Keynesian policies of demand management and thereby to maintain full employment. The ceaseless pursuit by transnational companies of the lowest-cost location – together with the ability of modern technology to eliminate routine work, and to export even highly sophisticated work through a computer modem to the other side of the world – is destroying demand in the industrialized countries for unskilled labour, and challenging the security even of those involved in more highly skilled employment. Emblematic of this new world order are the code-cutters of Bombay, just some of the 60 million Indians with the equivalent of an undergraduate degree, but earning just one-eighth of a comparable American graduate.

Alongside this globalization of markets for capital, labour and goods, most – although not all – industrialized countries have experienced a marked growth in inequality over the last decade and a half, inequality driven by changes at both ends of the labour market. And, however much the weight of different contributory factors is contested, clearly globalization and technological changes are playing a part. For the bottom third or so, the result is higher unemployment, as in Germany, or lower wages, as in the USA, or – as in this country – both. For those at the top, however, we can see substantial increases in real incomes and opportunities – in part explained by the extraordinary returns to human capital that can be generated in constantly enlarging world markets. And that fortunate minority – whom Robert Reich calls "symbolic analysts" and Marx called more simply "workers by brain" – for reasons Marshall alluded to and which are familiar to sociologists, appears to be increasingly unwilling to throw its lot in with their fellow citizens, whether "throwing their lot in" involves paying higher taxes or simply living in the same street.

Now, if globalization implies, in Marshall's terms, a geographical extension of civil rights in the economic sphere, then it is not the only extension of civil rights that is taking place. The civil rights that Marshall described belonged, as he rightly said, to each individual *man* and it is only in the last 40 years – to an extent that varies, of course, between different countries and classes – that women have claimed for themselves the promise of civil rights, and above all the right to participate in education and employment. As a result, the transformation in production that is driven in large part by the combination of forces we call globalization, produces quite uneven effects within the industrialized countries, uneven not only between the well- and ill-educated but between men and women as well. In general, across the industrialized economies, we can see a reduction in the opportunities traditionally available to working-class men, and an expansion in the opportunities generally thought of as being available to women, in particular to women with intermediate or higher levels of education. Thus, inequalities have not simply grown between individuals and classes: they are deepening between the "work-rich" families, of men and women who can thrive or at least survive in this rapidly changing economy, and "work-poor" families where no adult has more than a very precarious position in the workforce.

The fragility of the welfare state in the face of these changes, both global and domestic, is compounded by demographics. In the mature industrialized countries – in this case including Japan – the ageing of the population, we are constantly told, appears to make it impossible to sustain our traditional health and welfare services, or anything resembling a generous, state-organized pension scheme.

The result in the West is, simultaneously, a growing class of the socially excluded and a declining willingness to meet the costs of supporting them.

Now this is only the briefest summary of a complex argument. But this story, or something like it, is used by the neoliberal Right – including the former Secretary of State for Employment, Michael Portillo – to conclude that we can only survive in the global market by dismantling our social rights, and by the protectionist right – including the French Member of the European Parliament, James Goldsmith – to argue (1993) that we can only protect our social systems by disengaging from world trade.

There are several reasons for rejecting both conclusions.

First, social justice is not the preserve of one country or one region of the world. Any of us who are interested in social justice must surely regard the growth of the newly industrialized economies as a very substantial good. And, whatever other models of development might theoretically have been available, that growth has in reality been driven by the development of manufactured exports and access to world markets. Of course, it is true that there are appalling conditions for workers in many of the factories and mines of the new economies. Of course, there are environmental threats – and probably worse to come, as India and China start to meet their exploding energy needs. And we need urgently to find ways of reforming the world's trading system, not only to slow down environmental degradation, but also to reverse the deterioration in the terms of trade that have so penalized the poorest countries. But the idea that we can achieve some greater measure of social justice across the world by seeking to cut off the developing countries from a substantial source of trade is surely both wrong in principle and doomed to failure in practice.

Secondly, from a stance of self-interest rather than principle, market challengers are themselves new markets. The unification of Germany has already imposed very substantial tax increases upon the citizens of the former West Germany: but even if unification is proving much tougher in practice than most people imagined five years ago, few doubt that the result will be a long-run increase in prosperity in the eastern Länder, with beneficial effects across the entire country. Indeed, the toughest challenge facing the European Union is not how to protect itself against the countries of, respectively, the CEE and Sub-Saharan Africa, but how to engage them in sustainable economic development. That, in the case of the CEE, means how to reform our most costly protectionist institution, the Common Agricultural Policy; and in the case of Sub-Saharan Africa must involve a radical transformation of financial and trading relationships.

The third point to make – qualifying the sketch I drew earlier of globalization – is that in reality, most trade continues to be within, rather than between global regions. There are very good reasons, even from the most hard-headed business perspective, to locate production close to the consumer. Just-in-time production techniques require components, as well as final assembly, plants near the markets they serve – one reason for the extent of Japanese inward investment to this country over the last decade. Furthermore, as a recent Andersen Consulting international benchmarking study showed, it is process control and close management of the supply chain – rather than simply costs – that make for competitiveness. That study warned: "Global investors beware: betting on taking advantage of only one positive aspect of a location – labour rates, for example – is a false hope."

Fourthly, we should challenge the simplicity of the neoliberals, who believe that most of the countries with which Europe competes are characterized by low social costs. There is, for instance, the view that, thanks to its miserly unemployment benefits system, low minimum wage and weak employment laws, the USA has achieved far lower unemployment. But, if we look at the various forms of non-employment that characterize the American economy, we find virtually the same rate of employment amongst prime working age males as that achieved in high social cost Germany. Indeed, as a recent OECD study (1994) concluded: "labour standards do not have much influence on external competitiveness and trade performance . . . Cross-country differences in regulations and arrangement on labour standards do not alter supply and demand forces in a fundamental way."

It is also instructive to consider the social institutions – the welfare states, as it were – of the Pacific Rim and other developing economies. There is, for instance, the education system, with public investment in Japan absorbing nearly the same proportion of GDP as in Germany and the UK, and that in Hungary substantially more. In Japan and the South East Asian economies, furthermore, a substantial share of private income is also invested in education. Above all, education investment in the Asian economies is spent in a way that maximizes participation and achievement amongst the great majority of the population, instead of, as in this country, deepening the divide between those who achieve and those who do not.

We are also becoming more aware of the means by which Japan maintains its high employment levels – not, as in the Swedish model, by using tax transfers to finance employment in the public service sector, but by using high consumer prices to finance employment in the private service sector. There is, of course, intense pressure – both internally and externally – to open up Japan's domestic markets to foreign competition, and it seems likely that consumer prices, and with them employment, will fall as a result. But if Japan is to avoid the social dislocation of high unemployment, it will have to find – as we have to find – ways of transferring demand from its tradeable sector to those parts of the economy that can employ the people who cannot be absorbed in the most competitive sectors.

Economists and social policy analysts are, however, much less aware of a third kind of social institution that fulfils in the South East Asian economies many of the functions of the European welfare state. The Central Provident Fund is at its most developed in Singapore, where it has been in operation for the last 40 years – nearly as long as the NHS and the national insurance retirement pension. Originally designed to provide financial security for old age and a safety net for the permanently disabled, the Fund has evolved a fourfold purpose of providing funds for economic development; raising the savings ratio; promoting home-ownership; and meeting a variety of social needs, notably for retirement and medical care but, most recently, for further education. Compulsory contributions from employee and employer reach a total of 40 per cent of income for people below the age of 55. Furthermore, contributions are payable by the employer regardless of whether the employee is full-time or part-time, permanent or temporary: a provision that, no doubt, would appal opponents of Europe's Social Chapter. The result is that, although Singapore is perceived and praised as a low-tax regime, the reality is one of social costs upon employees and employers alike that are directly comparable with those in the EU: the sharp contrast that the neoliberals offer between a Europe crippled by the welfare state and "Asian trading rivals, whose economies are unburdened by social costs" (*Daily Telegraph*, 31 January 1995) begins to dissolve rather rapidly. The question becomes not high against low social costs, but rather how different kinds of institutions can, in different countries, best promote social inclusion.

There are, therefore, several reasons for rejecting the pessimistic proposition that social justice, European-style, is doomed to failure in the global economy. But we need to go further in order to meet the challenge to our welfare state institutions.

## The nature of social rights

I want to turn now to the central point of my argument, which concerns the nature of the welfare state – the nature of the social rights – that those committed to social justice should seek to defend in western Europe.

In Marshall's view, as you will remember, social rights created "a universal right to real income which is not proportionate to the market value of the claimant". Following him, the author of *The three worlds of welfare capitalism*, Gøsta Esping-Andersen (1989) argues that "If social rights are given the legal and practical status of property rights, if they are inviolable, and if they are granted on the basis of citizenship rather than performance, they will entail a decommodification of the status of individuals vis-a-vis the market." Perhaps the most effective, and certainly the most popular, expression of that principle in this country is the National Health Service; and it is quite clear that any move, in line with proposals from the neoliberal right, to substitute individual insurance and savings for a tax-funded health care system would involve quite unacceptable losses in equity.

But the notion of decommodification goes much further than the health service. Esping Andersen (1989) goes on to say that: "A minimal definition [of a decommodifying welfare state] must entail that citizens can freely, and without potential loss of job, income or general welfare, opt out of work when they themselves consider it necessary." He rightly argues that if this indeed is the test of social rights, then the ultimate expression of the welfare state would be the creation of a Citizen's Income – a basic income, independent of past, present or future participation in the labour market.

But that route – to the disappointment of many – we explicitly rejected in the Social Justice Commission, at least for the time being. Although our discussions were not framed in terms of decommodification, implicit in many of our proposals was rejection or, at least, substantial qualification. We found it impossible to reach full agreement on this issue, and many of my colleagues on the Commission take a very different view of Citizen's Income.

Many of those who support a Citizen's Income do so precisely because they fear that the global economy will deprive a growing number of our citizens of the ability to earn a living. My fear is a different one: that Citizen's Income is too weak an instrument to promote social citizenship in the face of the inegalitarian forces at work in the global economy.

Citizen's Income is, above all, conceived of as a means of social inclusion. Having started our discussions rather sympathetic to the whole idea, I found myself increasingly fearful that, in reality, it would become an instrument of social *exclusion*. Belgium introduced Citizen's Income in the form of an unconditional payment to young people, designed as a springboard for participation in education, training, voluntary and paid work. The Belgian scheme produced participation rates that, if anything, were *lower* at the end of the monitoring period than at the beginning. As a result, the Belgian government has introduced new qualification conditions for receipt of the benefit.

It is not difficult to see that, if a Citizen's Income were paid to the long-term unemployed in this country – and I include in that group not only those officially registered as unemployed, but those lone mothers who have been outside employment for several years – then the result might well be far less, rather than more, concern about how to get the long-term unemployed into employment. Indeed, universal receipt of Citizen's Income – precisely because of its universalism – would presumably dissolve the category of long-term unemployed completely.

If Citizen's Income is indeed designed as a means of social inclusion, one is entitled to ask "inclusion in what?" Inclusion in the wider community of which one is a citizen, clearly. But as Marshall himself remarked, in the context of a discussion about reconciling social rights with the individual's responsibility to work, "the national community is too large and remote to command this kind of loyalty and to make of it a continual driving force": and, conversely, it may well prove too large and remote to take much interest in its citizens once it had offered them the supposedly emancipatory entitlement to Citizen's Income. But it is quite clear to anyone who listens that those now excluded from employment want, above all, to be included in the opportunities and communities formed around paid work.

If, as is the case in many variants of the proposal, Citizen's Income requires higher marginal tax rates and a lower tax threshold, we can anticipate another effect that is the opposite of that intended, the deepening of disincentive effects – not for all of those who are now most disadvantaged by the labour market, but for many married women whom, as we know from extensive empirical evidence, are far more likely than married men to take into account the tax and benefit withdrawal rates that they face when deciding whether or not to take a job.

In theory, Citizen's Income appears as a generous move to value and support the unpaid work now done by women within families. In reality, it might turn out to be a poor bargain, deepening rather than relieving the gendered division of labour as it detached women from the labour market without any of the re-entry mechanisms supplied by measures such as paid maternity leave and unpaid career breaks.

The view of social rights as the means by which workers can escape the commodifying clutches of the market economy, has always been paralleled by a different perspective, in which social policy is not only emancipatory, but also a precondition for economic efficiency. The strategic value and, indeed, necessity of welfare policies is precisely that they promote the onward march of the productive forces of capitalism. It is that line of argument upon which we need to call in the reconstruction of European welfare states. Our aim should be to create a welfare state that enables people not only to participate more effectively in the market economy but also to choose more freely the terms upon which they do so.

As I have indicated, this is not a new argument. But it takes on a new meaning, in the light of the transformations taking place within production. The drop in demand for unskilled, and particularly male labour, which is producing such appalling social dislocation in this and other Western economies has as its counterpart the intensification of demand in these same economies for more flexible, better educated and more responsible workers in production as well as in more obviously knowledge-based work. In practice, we can see two quite contradictory forces at work within organizations: one emancipatory, the other oppressive. On the one hand, technology is being used to eliminate routine, low-skill jobs, so that production workers who used to perform the same mechanical task on the assembly line may now be called upon to work as part of teams, to take collective responsibility for the production of the entire output rather than just one part of it, to maintain and even program the robots to whom much of the routine production has now been delegated, and so on. It is a move summed up by the senior executive at the Rover Group, who said that: "We used to treat our workers as the hands. Then we discovered that with every pair of hands, we get a free brain."

On the other hand, technology is also being used by some employers to push Taylorism to its limits, so that clerical workers, for instance, find that their document production system is also counting their keystrokes to make sure they never take a break, and their voicemail system monitors their phonecalls to make sure they never make personal calls. On the one hand, labour as an asset: on the other, labour as a commodity.

Employers in both camps are seeking to control costs as well as to raise productivity. But the labour-as-commodity strategy is overwhelmingly driven by the desire to cut costs, rather than to improve quality: and globalization is peculiarly threatening to the people who work in cost-cutting organizations, for the simple reason that there is always somewhere else in the world who can cut those costs further. The logic of what is happening at the higher value-added end of the industrialized economies is that it is *only* by decommodifying labour that companies can earn Western standards of living for those who work in them. Social rights, then, take on a different guise as the means by which individuals and families are empowered to engage with the market economy and, crucially, to move as far as they can out of commodified labour and into work that is both demanding and rewarding.

## Implications for policy

I want now to consider the implications for policy of thinking about social rights as the partner, rather than necessarily the opponent, of civil rights in the economic sphere. Three principles should guide the reinvention of the welfare state. First, it should be designed to promote participation in social institutions and particularly, the labour market. Secondly, it should be designed to build the capacity of individuals – their capacity to learn, to earn, to take responsibility, and to contribute to relationships with others, within families and the wider community.

Thirdly – and derived from the first two – social programmes should wherever possible be "owned" by individuals, families and local communities, rather than by the more remote institutions of the local or national state.

Let me illustrate these principles by reference, first, to the delivery of services within communities and, secondly, to the future of the national insurance system – both areas where, I believe, we could usefully learn from some of the experience in the newly industrializing countries.

Through the National Health Service (NHS), through education and social services, the welfare state used the proceeds of taxation to finance socially essential work. In the reinvention of the welfare state, community development should be part of a strategy to find new ways of paying for the work that needs to be done – and new ways of providing work for the people who need to do it. There is, after all, no shortage of work that needs doing – and, crucially, in the light of the debate about globalization, no shortage of work that can only be done within the domestic economy, developing and caring for people and places. Much of that, as in the NHS and the schools, has to be done through tax-financed public services. But it cannot all be done that way. From the perspective of the economic modellers, taxation and public service employment may well be the most efficient way of reducing unemployment: but if the aim is to build people's own capacity, to develop potential, increase autonomy and mobilize political support, then we need to supplement traditional services with different forms of community development.

Within the development community, it is well known that the programmes most likely to succeed are those that are built from the bottom up, defined and driven by the people whom they are intended to benefit. There are examples from every region of the world, including Latin America that is beginning to rival South East Asia in its growth rates. In Chile, for example, the revenues from tax rises equivalent to 2 per cent of GDP have been dedicated to structural anti-poverty programmes, including a micro-entrepreneurs' investment fund that enables people on poverty wages to build their own tiny business and move into the broader network of production. In Mexico, local communities can bid for funds from Solidarity, a $2.7 billion a year anti-poverty programme, which supports local people to design and build the facilities they need – roads, a school, a health clinic.

It was partly with models like this in mind that the Social Justice Commission proposed a new approach to community development in the marginalized estates of Britain – the places like Easterhouse, on the outskirts of Glasgow – that were scarcely touched by the boom of the mid-1980s and are equally untouched by the present economic recovery. Even without new government funding, a Community Regeneration Fund could take the funds now used for property-led development and invest them instead in development that builds the capacity of local communities to sustain their own economic and social future.

Self-build and self-rehabilitation projects, for instance, could help to tackle homelessness, poor housing, lack of skills and unemployment. Part of this strategy, too, could be "social franchising" where the aim of policy is to replicate, in different parts of the country, an initiative that has already proved its worth. The *Big Issue*, which gives homeless people access to an income by giving them access to work, has given birth to a Scottish and a French, as well as several local English, copies of the original project. In Glasgow, there is the Wise Group, a charitable company that trains and employs unemployed young men by providing environmental and energy services for local communities. Social franchising would invite communities in other high-unemployment towns and estates to set up their own Wise Group, offering expertise, management advice and support, as well as access to funding. A new focus on building people's capacity would also alert us to the possibility of mobilizing resources in the form of people's time, and not simply their money. Amongst older people who have, willingly or unwillingly, taken early retirement are many who would welcome the opportunity to work in schools, whether helping on after-school clubs or in under-fives centres, or providing specialist support to teachers, inside or outside the classroom.

Clearly, however, services are not enough. We also have to consider one of the central functions of the welfare state – allocating income across the life-cycle. When William Beveridge designed the national insurance system over 50 years ago, he assumed relative stability in the post-war workplace and family, in which the wage-earner's ability to provide a family wage would mainly be threatened by temporary spells of unemployment, by sickness or disability, or – for those who lived long enough – by retirement, and where marriage would remain the norm, divorce the rare exception.

Today, however, income distribution systems have to cope with turbulent change in both workplace and family, where most men and women can expect not just several changes of job but one or more changes of occupation as well, and where cohabitation, separation and divorce make the family unit much less effective as a means of income redistribution. To quote Esping-Andersen again, reaching a conclusion that implies something rather different from the view I quoted earlier of a decommodifying welfare state, we need an active welfare state that enables people to change within constantly changing economic and social circumstances. That implies a transformation of opportunities for education during people's adult lives and, in our view on the Social Justice Commission, a radical change in the way we finance further and higher education. But it also requires a social security system that allows people to engage with the labour market on different terms at different stages in their lives, making possible periods of part-time or full-time family responsibilities, education sabbaticals, voluntary and community work, leisure and retirement.

The modernized social insurance that we proposed in the Commission is one way of achieving that objective. We sought to bring Beveridge's vision of national insurance into the modern world, to exploit to the full the opportunity it offers of individual entitlements in return for individual contributions, and to fit those entitlements to the different needs of individuals and families today. But it may be that the national insurance system cannot bear the weight we wanted to put upon it. There is, first, the question of whether taxes on earnings – such as national insurance contributions – are the most efficient form of revenue-raising, particularly in the European economies where we urgently need to encourage employment and discourage environmental pollution. Despite the distributional problems, we can expect to see a long-term shift away from direct and towards indirect taxation, particularly of an environmental kind.

Secondly, there is the problem of mobilizing political consent for the taxation required to finance lifetime income-smoothing. Transferring income from periods in to periods out of employment was a relatively modest challenge when a working lifetime of, say, 45 years was required to sustain a retirement of perhaps a third of that. It is much harder for a pay-as-you-go system to command the political consent needed when earnings that may last for little more than 30 years have to sustain a similar period in education, family responsibilities and retirement. The National Association of Pension Funds, for instance, estimates that someone aged 30 who wants to retire at 60 with a second pension of 50 per cent of their earnings needs to invest 15 per cent of their annual pay for that purpose alone – about three times the amount of the rebate given on SERPS contributions to people who contract out into a personal or occupational scheme.

In Sweden, an all-party committee recently concluded that its generous, earnings-related, pay-as-you-go pension system is simply not sustainable, and proposed a gradual shift towards funded schemes, with benefits much more closely based on the actuarial value of contributions. Australia, similarly, has introduced a national system of funded, earnings-linked pension schemes. By contrast, Germany has stood by the virtues of its pay-as-you-go system, although some observers, particularly from business, believe that adjustment will eventually be unavoidable. Certainly, we concluded on the Commission that we should not try to undo Britain's present mixed economy of pension provision – with its substantial role for occupational and personal pension schemes.

Indeed, we proposed to develop that mixed economy with a system of truly universal second-tier, earnings-related pensions. As many of you know, we offered two options for achieving that goal: one based around SERPS, the other involving a wider range of funded pension schemes, including one based on National Savings. My personal view is that it is most improbable that any government would propose, or win political support for, the restoration of the original SERPS formula, the value of which has been halved and halved again by the present government.

Instead, I want to suggest a development of the Commission's second option for funded pension schemes, which draws on some of Frank Field's ideas and also borrows some features of the Provident Funds in the South East Asian economies to which I referred earlier and which I have been looking at with colleagues from Andersen Consulting. The goal would be to build, on top of the present national insurance system, a national insurance investment fund for each individual – a fund that could be used, not only in retirement, but to help finance earlier withdrawals, part- or full-time, from the labour market.

Under this system, the national insurance contributions paid in respect of each individual would be divided in two. The first would remain with the National Insurance Fund, to pay for the continuing liabilities of the pay-as-you-go system, in particular the basic retirement pension. The second part of the contribution, however, would be allocated to an investment fund chosen by the individual contributor, and including existing occupational and personal pension schemes. To start with, the total contribution should be no higher than it is at present: in effect, everybody would receive a contracted-out rebate from SERPS. But the aim should be, as in Australia, to increase the level of investment contribution gradually as the economy and people's earnings grow. Furthermore, every contributor should receive regular information about the size of their fund and the income they could expect to receive if they continued to contribute at their present level, the aim being to encourage people to make whatever extra voluntary contributions that they could afford.

Of course, not everyone could afford to contribute sufficiently or at all. In particular, different provision would need to be made for people whose disabilities make any employment impossible. But government could also provide contribution credits – perhaps in the form of government bonds – in return for various forms of social participation: for instance, to people involved in further and higher education; and parents at home caring for small children or those looking after elderly people. A future government that decided to introduce the Citizen's Service we proposed on the Commission could also extend to its volunteers credits into their national insurance fund. The tax relief now available on various forms of savings could, similarly, be extended to those below the tax threshold in the form of national insurance credits.

In Singapore and other South East Asian countries, there is a single Provident Fund, managed by government and largely invested in government bonds. It is hard to see that model being viable in the West, and indeed the Singapore Fund now allows members to accumulate a discretionary fund that can be used for higher education, or for equity investment on the Singapore Stock Exchange. Presumably, they rule out gambling on Japanese futures! Here, the second feature of the national insurance fund would be effective regulation of pension schemes and investment managers from amongst whom individuals could choose their preferred provider. In addition to direct regulation, the mis-selling of personal pensions and other savings products – consider the recent publicity about endowment mortgages, for instance – could be severely inhibited by the creation of low-cost, low-risk competitors. These could come from trade union sponsored industry pension funds, which are being established in Britain on the model of the Australian schemes that were themselves stimulated by the Labour Government pension reforms there. But effective competition could also come from a new National Savings Pension Fund, of the kind we outlined in the Commission's report.

The third change would be to extend the use to which people can put their pension funds at present, or their national insurance funds in future. One small, but sensible change would be to allow pension schemes to offer insurance for long-term care – something currently denied by the Inland Revenue's rules on tax relief. The more complex change needed to make sense of income transfers across people's increasingly varied life-cycles is to allow individual funds to be used to help finance parental leave and education sabbaticals as well as partial or full retirement – within, of course, limits to prevent the retirement fund from being exhausted before retirement is even reached.

Linked to this change is the Commission's proposal for an Education Bank, made up of individual learning accounts from which people could draw to finance both maintenance and a proportion of tuition fees for further and higher education, and which they could pay back during subsequent periods of higher earnings. Employers could be encouraged to contribute – and, indeed, in a variation of proposals for a training levy, required to do so if they were unable to provide education and training themselves. And government would make additional contributions for priority groups, including in particular the long-term unemployed and those who, although in employment, had few or no educational qualifications. Individual learning accounts could simply represent one aspect of the new individual national insurance fund that I am proposing.

If the national insurance fund is to fulfil its potential of giving individuals more control and more choice about how they distribute income over their lives, then it needs, finally, to be accompanied by changes in the labour market, to open up a greater variety of working patterns. This may seem odd, when perhaps the most pressing concern is to create more full-time jobs at a time when most of the jobs available to the unemployed are part-time and, all too often, temporary. But looking at the changes that are taking place in the organization and distribution of working time in industrialized economies, I am struck not so much by the growth in part-time and other forms of non-standard employment, but by the unmet demand for other than full-time work. And this is not simply the case amongst women with young children – including a significant proportion of mothers with high educational qualifications, who are most likely at the moment to be working full-time – and even amongst a minority of fathers too. It is also true among men in their fifties and sixties, including many of those who have been forced to give up employment altogether.

Organizations as different as the Inland Revenue and British Airways who have offered their full-time staff the option of reducing their hours have found no shortage of volunteers and have succeeded in meeting organizational imperatives as well as individual needs. Forty years ago, the good employer was the one who set up an occupational pension scheme. Tomorrow, the good employer may be the one who turns the pension scheme into a time bank that, like the scheme that already operates in British Columbia, allows employees to save up part of their earnings for, say, three years – and then take the fourth year off, with a right to come back at the same level as before.

In a place like Britain, with no general tradition of regulating working hours, there seems to me no prospect of reducing working hours by legislation, in the way that the French have proposed to do, although we should certainly build upon the example of statutory paid maternity leave by creating, for example, a right for every employee to at least five days learning a year. There are many ways of reducing working hours by consent, of enabling individuals to trade off time and money and – in the course of doing so – to increase the number of people employed for at least part of their notionally "working" lifetimes.

I have moved a long way from Marshall's theme of the rights of citizenship. I have suggested that there are opportunities, as well as threats, in the world's rapidly enlarging market economy – opportunities that require on our part a radical transformation of our view of social rights.

I hope, however, that I have not given the impression of an uncontrollable wave of economic individualism surging across the globe. It feels like that sometimes, particularly when we consider the revolution in computing and communications that is just beginning to transform production. But the reality is far more complex than the simple picture of globalization suggests. As many authors have noted, the collapse of the Soviet economies has made it easier to see the different forms of capitalism that operate within the global economy: easier, too, for those on the Left to see the different kinds of social institutions upon which market economies depend.

In Britain, in particular, we should resist any temptation to cede the ground to Anglo-Saxon neoliberalism. Here, in the country where the neoliberal experiment went furthest, we can not only see its limitations and failures most vividly, we can see, too, a political right divided against itself, divided not only between neoliberal deregulators and economic protectionists, but divided too between the deregulators and those who, like John Gray, hark back to an earlier Conservative tradition – a tradition of social institutions and social rights. Tony Blair's appeal to the tradition of ethical socialism, and his language of responsibility rather than rights, may discomfort some on the Left, but it clearly resonates with many citizens of this country whose disenchantment with the Thatcherite experiment is paralleled perhaps only by their disenchantment, at the end of the 1970s, with the limitations of the post-war settlement. In our own history, in the innovative projects that are making a difference in some of the most deprived parts of this and other European countries, and – not least – in the countries that are our economic competitors, we have, I believe, much to learn about how we can create and sustain a modern welfare state in the context of a rapidly changing global economy.

# CHAPTER 14

# Conclusion: citizenship in the twenty-first century

## Martin Bulmer & Anthony M. Rees

T. H. Marshall's original formulation of the concept of citizenship nearly half a century ago remains of continuing significance. It was at once modest and powerful, relevant to the society of his day but with wide theoretical and social philosophical resonance. Social scientists responded to it and developed it as a way of understanding the ramifications of what membership of a "society" entails. "Citizenship" enabled the concept of a "society" to be deconstructed, so that it became possible to examine the extent to which full membership was accorded to all who lived within its boundaries (however these might be delineated). The concept remains at the centre of debates of what is meant by "society", "social welfare", "civil society" and related terms. (For some of the relevant recent literature to set alongside that cited in earlier chapters see Giddens 1982; Turner 1986; Roche 1987; Keane 1988; King & Waldron 1988; Hall & Held 1989; Turner 1990; Crouch 1992; Culpitt 1992; Roche 1992; Tester 1992; Turner 1993a,b; Gellner 1994; Twine 1994; van Steenbergen 1994; Hall 1995; Minogue 1995; Stewart 1995.) Some would argue that "citizenship" is a more illuminating way of casting light upon the nature of social integration than the rather nebulous and ill-specified term "society" that sociologists constantly invoke without making it clear what it refers to.

Marshall's seminal formulation was nevertheless circumscribed by place and by time, as several of the contributors to this volume observe. Mann, for example, draws attention to the Englishness of Marshall's approach, his failure to encompass other parts of the British

Isles, let alone citizenship as an issue in other countries. Also, *Citizenship and social class* was written in the first flush of optimism associated with the creation of the post-1945 "welfare state". In one sense Marshall's conception of "social" citizenship set the imprimatur of academic social science upon the swathe of social legislation that was enacted in that period. In another it sought to interpret changes in a more theoretical frame, and it is to this that we must now turn.

## The theoretical status of Marshall's typology

Marshall's typology of citizenship has been very influential, but there is a good deal of uncertainty about its precise status. Was it put forward as a historical hypothesis, or as an ideal type to serve a heuristic purpose in analysis? The more usual approach is to treat it as a set of hypotheses about historical development. Marshall himself treated the three types century by century: "The formative period for civil citizenship was the eighteenth century . . Political citizenship emerged in the nineteenth century . . . The third stage, social citizenship, developed through the twentieth century." Yet Mann has maintained (1993: 19–20) that citizenship has not been such a singular process as Marshall indicated, and that citizenship developed various forms and rhythms, some of which undercut others. Further distinctions are required, he argued, between individual and collective rights in the case of legal citizenship, and between ideological and economic citizenship with respect to social citizenship.

Such distinctions come close to treating the three concepts each as an ideal type, that heuristic device beloved of the theoretical micro-economist and the comparative sociologist, the one-sided accentuation of reality in order to understand at an abstract level what are the properties of a class of events or processes and their workings. Viewed in this light, Marshall's typology of citizenship may be more comparable to Weber's typologies of action or of authority than to a specifically historical hypothesis about linear social development.

We can fill this out with the aid of Hirschman's famous triad of exit, voice and loyalty (Hirschman 1970). Although there has been considerable variation within each discipline, different kinds of social scientists have typically been more at ease with one of Marshall's categories of citizenship than with the others. Economists, for instance, with their penchant for exchange relationships in a relatively depoliticized market place, have tended not to favour the concept of positive rights. Instead, they stress the importance of the negative liberties of civil citizenship: freedom of association, equality before the law, freedom of contract, and non-discrimination on such grounds as race, gender or prescribed status. Most of these civil liberties are essential if capitalism is to function effectively, and they also provide much of the somewhat exiguous moral backup to which the system can lay claim. Thus the characteristic economic mode of response to perceived deteriorations in the quality of goods and services is "exit": the conditions of production, distribution and exchange should be such that dissatisfied consumer-citizens can take their trade elsewhere, and they also ought not – if they are rational – to have any compunction about doing so.

Political scientists, on the other hand, understandably have a particular interest in political citizenship, which may be understood as active involvement in the affairs of the community and as dialogic relationships both within and between bounded political units. "Voice", therefore, is almost a shorthand term for political modes of expression, or at least for those generally favoured in a democracy, since force is always an alternative political response.

Lastly, sociologists seem to have an especial affinity with social citizenship. This must be, at least in part, because of their concern with social cohesion, the glue that does or should stick societies together. It may, therefore, not be fanciful to claim "loyalty" for the sociologists' corner.

## Social class and social cleavage

We can extend this line of thought to apply it to historical progressions themselves, provided that these are not conceived of as linear. Take the trajectory of welfare state development since Marshall wrote *Citizenship and social class*. Here we may unashamedly concentrate on Britain, although the passage of events in other comparable countries was often similar.

We need to start with one very prominent feature of Marshall's writing, his preoccupation with social class as the principal line of cleavage in society. Such a preoccupation was totally justified at the time that Marshall was writing, and reflected the central feature of

English society. It also had a more general justification. Max Weber regarded the issue of citizenship as peculiar to Western civilization and bound up with the concept of social class. "The citizen [he wrote] in the quality of membership of a class is always the citizen of a particular city, and the city in this sense has only existed in the Western world, or elsewhere, as in the early period in Mesopotamia, only in an incipient stage" (Weber quoted in Käsler 1988: 49).

Marshall's typology traced the progressive incorporation of the working classes into mainstream society through the extension of citizenship rights to them. Perhaps "incorporation" is not quite the right word, with its links to corporatism, the corporate state, and the structures of "Rhine capitalism" (Albert 1990, Saunders 1995) that include the direct representation of workers' interests on the boards of institutions. Doubtless for this reason many commentators have preferred the rather weaker term "inclusion", which has as a bonus a readily available converse, "exclusion". And indeed Marshall's social citizenship is about inclusion and exclusion, even though he does not use these terms in *Citizenship and social class*, preferring instead to talk of "equality" and "inequality".

However, when Marshall wrote about "class-abatement" or "class fusion", precisely what kind of equality did he desire to promote, or inequality to diminish? The crucial passage here is the following:

> What matters is that there is a general enrichment of the concrete substance of civilized life, a general reduction of risk and insecurity, an equalization between the more and the less fortunate at all levels – between the healthy and the sick, the employed and the unemployed, the old and the active, the bachelor and the father of a large family. Equalization is not so much between classes as between individuals in a population that is now treated for this purpose as if it were one class. Equality of status is more important than equality of income. (Marshall 1963: 107)

To the modern reader one of the more surprising things about *Citizenship and social class* is the dismissive tone in which Marshall refers to more direct methods of equalization. In the passage immediately preceding the foregoing he writes:

The extension of the social services is not primarily a means of equalizing incomes. In some cases it may, in others it may not. The question is relatively unimportant: it belongs to a different department of social policy. (Marshall 1963: 107)

Thus the equality to be established through social citizenship was above all equality of access. In Dahrendorf's parlance, it was a matter of entitlements more than it was a matter of provisions. In the main, it was Marshall's prescriptions along with the similar agendas of Tawney, Beveridge, Keynes and others, that were given flesh and blood by the post-war Labour Government. We can see why Mishra maintains, at the end of a long discussion of the views of Marshall and some of his successors, that:

Part of the appeal of citizenship is, no doubt, that it offers a neat and in many ways an apolitical conception of the social services. Its justification for a limited but useful and honourable place for the social services forms a basis for consensus among people of "reason and goodwill" about the role of the welfare state in capitalist society. (Mishra 1981: 36)

However, not so long after Marshall wrote, a sea change occurred. This had the effect of undermining the walls separating the compartments into which Marshall had so carefully placed political and social citizenship. A much wider range of inequalities became seen as appropriate objects for direct redress through the political system. This shift is associated with the rise, first of all to intellectual pre-eminence in the late 1950s, and then (for a time) to political dominance in the 1960s, of a new breed of democratic socialist. Ironically perhaps, the chief progenitors of these views were the revisionists, especially Antony Crosland (1956), one of whose main aims was to wean the Labour Party off its addiction to questions of ownership. The Labour Left rejected these aspects of the new version of socialism, but were happy to go along with a more full-blooded interpretation of inequality.

Thus what Le Grand (1982) calls "the strategy of equality" was born: a new formulation, even if the phrase was borrowed from Tawney (1952). It should be noted that even where this approach appears to resonate with Marshallian themes – for example, Townsend's reconceptualization of poverty as a level of income below which households are unable to participate in customary social practices and styles of life (Townsend 1979) – the resemblances were rather superficial: Marshall was not in the business of setting poverty lines in *Citizenship and social class*, and Townsend was advocating more comprehensive redistribution and a more relativistic view of poverty than Marshall found it easy to endorse (Marshall 1975: 184). Le Grand (1982: 18) lists five kinds of equality: of public expenditure, of final income, of use, of cost and of outcome. It may be argued – as Powell has argued in a recent article (1995) – that none of these was the species of equality that the architects of the welfare state in the 1940s were aiming to bring about.

By the time Le Grand's book appeared (1982) there had been a further paradigmatic shift, with the ascendancy of the neoliberal New Right, which again was both intellectual (although always, of course, disputed) and carried with it access to the levers of political power. Le Grand's strictures therefore became merely another stick that could be used to belabour large-scale state-provided welfare for its failure to achieve its presumed objectives. Under the dispensation of the New Right, political citizenship was downplayed and social citizenship disappeared almost entirely as a distinguishable and acceptable aim. Civil citizenship (in its more individualistic forms, that is) was more and more identified as the only form of citizenship that could be granted full legitimacy. Under John Major, with the introduction of internal or "quasi-" markets into several of the main areas of social policy, relationships between the agents of the welfare state have become increasingly regulated by contract. Patients, clients and claimants are alike renamed "consumers". The "Citizen's Charter" (with the apostrophe in that singular position) has provided new scope for individual complainants, but little for purposeful collective action. All this has been accompanied by a considerable growth in inequality, which would certainly have distressed Marshall. Some critics – Ralf Dahrendorf among them – have detected the emergence of a sizeable, although rather variously characterized, group outside and underneath the occupational class structure, to which the term "underclass" has therefore been attached. William Julius Wilson's discussion in Chapter 12 is concerned with this group, although he has now himself disavowed the use of the term because of its pejorative political connotations.

It is obviously difficult to tell where this merry-go-round, with its stopping-off points at different models of citizenship, will get to next. It is, however, at least possible that it will come to rest at what has usually been termed the mixed economy of welfare (although mixed polity or mixed society would be equally appropriate descriptions). If so, the wheel will in some ways have come full circle, back to Marshall's own vision, especially as summed up in his later formulation of the "hyphenated" society of democratic-welfare-capitalism (Marshall 1981).

## The omissions from Marshall's schema

Many commentators have noted that Marshall's schema contains significant omissions. Rees's earlier contribution om Chapter 1 considered some of these in relation to the long timespan covered in Marshall's account in *Citizenship and social class*. The omissions have, however, come to be if anything more obvious as we move closer to the twenty-first century. The principal gaps are women and the family; persons lacking in self-determination; the very poor; racial and ethnic minorities; and other countries. We will consider these in this order, although the last has such wide ramifications that we reserve our discussion for the next part of the chapter. In this section we want to discuss aspects of the citizenship debate that have come to be of importance in contemporary British politics. Some of these relate to developments that Marshall, not having a crystal ball built into his cranium, could not have been expected to foresee: others, however, were already significant when *Citizenship and social class* was written.

One preliminary point needs to be made at the outset, to stress the importance of partial citizenship. There is a danger of perpetuating a mode of analysis that views society as akin to the Greek *polis*, made up of two or more classes of beings, the first of whom enjoy full citizenship, and the second of which for reasons of status or condition are debarred from it. The employment of the all-or-nothing words "inclusion" and "exclusion " tends to compound this risk. There are several groups that may better be viewed as part in, and part out, of citizenship.

The neglect of women and the family is an obvious lacuna. *Citizenship and social class* refers to a society of men, and its generalizations about the extension of legal, political and social rights relate to men. The account would be different if women were concerned, and less optimistic. The position of women within modern Western welfare systems is by no means as clear-cut as Marshall implies. Marshall also does not consider the position of those whose citizenship is questionable or incomplete – for example, children (who are future citizens, but who in Marshall's discussion are invisible), severely deteriorated elderly people suffering perhaps from Alzheimer's disease (who might be regarded as ex-citizens), or the mentally ill or those with severe learning difficulties. Marshall did not ground his conception of citizenship in such notions as agency, capability, autonomy or responsibility, although it could be argued that these are implicit in his formulation. However, many recent writers (for example, Weale 1983, Plant 1991, Gray 1992) have justified their views about welfare and other entitlements in this way. Such a move creates major problems, especially concerning whether any viable version of citizenship requires to be supplemented by recourse to a quite different principle, such as benevolence or compassion. Some of the duties here may be justified by reference to the obligations of citizenship – for example, the requirement to bring up one's own children, and, more contentiously, to bring them up properly. However, benevolent or compassionate sentiments or behaviour can in general neither be enjoined as an obligation nor expected or experienced as a right.

In many cases, moreover, there is no-one on whom to affix the responsibility, apart from the state. Even where there are extant relatives the relevant obligations are rarely legally enforceable in Britain, although the legal systems of some other comparable countries are less permissive in this respect. It would clearly be morally disreputable to suggest that the protection of the interests of people with limited or no autonomy should assume a lesser priority because of their lack of the necessary entry qualifications for admission to citizenship status. However, this may be what happens quite often in practice, as the melancholy catalogue of scandals in long-stay institutions bears testimony.

A less stark point also needs to be made here. The wishes and the interests of these "incomplete citizens" (and indeed of anyone in a state of dependency, whether *compos mentis* or not) are very often interpreted and communicated by others. The assessments of the situation, for example, made by carers and those for whom they care may very well diverge. This raises the question of who exactly is the client of the social services. Children are largely invisible, yet it is they, not their parents, who are the direct users of the school system, and who may well have strong views of their own about their education. The usual way of treating such questions is to ascribe more rights to children – to be heard, to be consulted, to have the final say the nearer they approach the threshold of adulthood.

It is, however, also worth noting that there are others with a legitimate involvement, apart from children and their parents. The evaluations of teachers may differ from those of both. And there are many other professionals – medical practitioners, social workers, etc. – who are charged with the responsibility of arriving at independent diagnoses and taking, or perhaps only recommending, appropriate action. In real life situations, therefore, where individuals are not cut off and sharply distinguishable from significant others, are sometimes not sure of their desires and often not aware of their interests, are frequently not in possession of the knowledge and capacities to plan and pursue effectively their projects, and most generally are not sole masters or mistresses of their own fates, there is an inevitable zone of indeterminacy surrounding the concept of the "consumer citizen".

Inequalities of condition may lead to the diminution of citizenship rights. This is particularly the case in societies characterized by dual-labour markets (Piore 1979). There is also often a marked degree of residential segregation. Some American evidence is presented by William Julius Wilson in Chapter 12. In Britain this does not only occur in the inner cities, but also in housing developments on the urban fringes, often poorly serviced by public transport and lacking in other amenities. Most British cities and larger towns possess one or more heavily stigmatized council estates, where only a few of the male inhabitants are in full-time work, there are concentrations of single-parent families, and high crime rates prevail especially among juveniles. Some of these are the famed concrete jungles of the 1960s, but others are older areas of low-rise family-style housing, like Ferguslie Park in Paisley or Meadow Well in North Tyneside. It is in such places where an "underclass", distinguished by its detachment from traditional working-class behavioural norms, may most easily be sought and perhaps be found, as Norman Dennis testified when he cycled into Meadow Well in the aftermath of rioting in September 1991 (Dennis & Erdos 1992).

If segments of a society containing a high concentration of those with low incomes are in practice excluded from many citizenship rights, the basis of Marshall's optimism is somewhat dented. And there is increasing evidence that this is the case, particularly perhaps in the United States, a society that also remains a magnet for in-migration, in terms of capitalist opportunity and the attainment of prosperity through competitiveness (cf. Shklar 1991). Where there is a considerable overlap between membership of the "underclass" and of an ethnic minority, the denial of effective citizenship rights is powerful, as Chapter 12 demonstrates. Recent evidence comparing the United States with Europe is available in McFate et al. (1995).

In some countries, most notably Germany, citizenship has been first and foremost a matter of ethnic descent: there is currently a debate going on there about whether children born into the third generation of non-German guestworker families may be granted full citizenship status. In Britain, almost all post-war immigrants from the New Commonwealth have enjoyed full citizenship rights from the moment they reached its shores. However, the Nationality Act of 1981 did a good deal to refashion British immigration law on racially discriminatory lines, even if in recent times "the discourse on patriotism", in Paul Rich's words, has "tended to take more the form of an ideology in search of territorial roots rather than a systematic theory of racial identity" (Rich 1991: 102). Organizations representing ethnic minority interests are very alarmed at the prospect of the introduction of identity cards, fearing that they would be used by zealous authorities to root out illegal immigrants and to revive by the back door the "sus" laws, which were disproportionately applied to black youths. Indices of residential segregation on ethnic lines remain high (Smith 1989), although the areas in question are often quite distinct from the estates where the indigenous "poor whites" have been concentrated. There is little reason for Britons to be complacent in this regard.

There are thus good grounds for challenging the optimism implicit in Marshall's original formulation, and pointing out its analytical limitations. This has a bearing, too, on the relationship between the Marshallian view of citizenship and present politics. Marshall's view was not explicitly evaluative and political, but it was implicitly that of a twentieth-century liberal democrat. The issues that he raised intersect with politics at a number of points. The concept of citizenship has played a not insignificant role in post-war political discourse, first in setting the welfare state historically in theoretical context, and secondly in sharpening in the contemporary world the analysis of social inclusion and exclusion. Questions of citizenship are very pertinent politically, as Patricia Hewitt shows in Chapter 13. Even if A. H. Halsey's attempt to claim Marshall for democratic socialism seems on reflection somewhat implausible, there is no doubt that his legacy has a good deal of substance to contribute to key debates in social democratic politics. Whether he himself stands foursquare in that tradition, despite his standing as a Labour parliamentary candidate in the 1922 General Election, is more open to doubt. Robert Pinker's assessment is surely right:

> we should note the quality of detachment which pervades Marshall's writings. This is not to imply that he either ignores the key value issues in social welfare or fails to make his own values explicit, but he approaches questions of value in a spirit of scholarship rather than partisanship . . . He poses the truly awkward questions about the nature of welfare and relationship between its political, economic and social components, often without having to hand an answer which will be immediately comforting to social administrators. (Pinker 1981: 8)

## The study of citizenship entering the twenty-first century

What do the contributions to this book suggest should be some of the main issues for study concerning citizenship as we move towards the millennium and enter the next century? A primary point, made by several contributors, is that a focus on England is no longer enough. Marshall's "Englishness" had its time and place, but that has passed. A wider perspective is needed, without losing sight of the significant link he made between citizenship and social stratification, which remains a central preoccupation of sociology and social policy. Citizenship and its definition takes different forms in different societies, as the German definition of citizenship as being based on descent suggests. Mann argues in Chapter 7 that the adoption of a comparative perspective requires the reformulation of the concept.

Geographically, a wider focus is required. It enables us to appreciate the very different understandings of citizenship in countries at an apparently similar level of economic, political and social development.

The diverse interpretations in Britain, France and Germany of the nature of the relationship between ethnic descent and political and other rights are a case in point (cf. Brubaker 1989, 1992). Marshall's definition of legal and political rights was perhaps too narrow, and insufficiently attentive to historical context. Consider the following example. In relation to legal rights the American constitution guarantees the citizen's right to bear arms. In the contemporary United States there are approximately 220 million firearms in private ownership, on average roughly one for each adult and child member of the population. This right is staunchly defended by groups such as the National Rifle Association, which lobbies ferociously in favour of preserving the right to own and carry weapons of all kinds and to oppose legislation that would limit this right. Deaths in the United States from firearm-related homicide, suicide and accidental shootings are considerably higher than in most other industrial countries. Yet in Canada and European countries, private gun ownership is severely restricted and banned, and is the rare exception rather than the rule, and then mainly limited to sporting guns like shotguns. There is no significant or effective lobby on behalf of gun owners. The pattern of firearm ownership is almost the obverse of what it is in the United States. In what senses, then, can one postulate a "right" to bear arms as a universal legal right? This example overstates the issue, but demonstrates some of the problems that there are in postulating universal rights enjoyed by all.

For those in the United Kingdom, the last 25 years in Northern Ireland serve as a reminder that aspirations for different forms and symbols of citizenship can clash bloodily in quite a confined geographical space. In a gentler fashion (so far) the assertion has been growing that separate Scottish and Welsh identities need to be embodied in new devolved or even sovereign governmental institutions. Increasingly, too, European citizenship attracts attention. The strengthening and enlargement of the European Union raises a variety of questions, both politically and analytically, which are only just being grappled with (cf. Brubaker 1992, Meehan 1993, Soysal 1994).

Certain rights (e.g. of appeal to the European Court) are conferred by membership of the European Union, other rights (e.g. through participation in the Social Chapter) are currently matters of acute domestic political controversy and would almost certainly be speedily imported into Britain with any change of government, while the basically federal nature of these pan–European arrangements means that the generation of new rights could extend in the future to several other areas. At present each country retains its own definition of citizenship: the European Union is not a nation, and shows few signs of becoming one, but the implication of moves towards common rights is that European citizenship is now far from a meaningless concept, as the standard red EU passport bears witness. The study of European citizenship will be an expanding area for attention in future.

Beyond the confines of the prosperous European Union, citizenship is a topical issue in societies in dissolution and reconstitution such as eastern Europe and South Africa. In such societies currently the nature of the relationship between the state and civil society is acutely observed and widely debated, and raises more questions than can be immediately resolved. In both cases, the replacement of an overwhelming centre by more open and democratic forms has acutely posed the question of whether in the absence of a strongly centralist and controlling state, democratic institutions can develop with space for the rights of citizenship to be extended. In eastern Europe the outcome is partly contingent on relations with more prosperous western neighbours (cf. Gellner 1994, Liebich & Warner 1995). In South Africa, legal and political rights have been extended rapidly and dramatically to all races. Will the extension of social rights follow, or will this prove an insurmountable obstacle given the stark inequalities inherited from apartheid (Adam & Moodley 1993)?

A third field for enquiry concerns the implications of global citizenship and global developments. As both Howard Newby and Patricia Hewitt point out in Chapter 11, we are all now much more aware of our global interdependency and that no nation is an island unto itself. There have always been trading minorities scattered around the world's major urban centres, but the movement of labour is becoming easier and in many parts of the world has grown in response to economic demand, whether this is for Indian professionals in the United States, Filipino and South Asian female domestic servants in other parts of Asia and the Middle East, Central and South American workers in North America, southern Europeans in northern Europe, Japanese executives in other industrial countries where Japanese plants are located, and so on. Political refugees in various countries are not new, but their volume increases with the scale of local wars and the facility of international air travel. Such movements have consequences for the meaning and implementation of citizenship in the modern world. They draw attention to the urgency of the project referred to by Dahrendorf – Kant's project – to create a "general" (i.e. worldwide) "civil society under the rule of law".

Viewed philosophically rather than geographically, citizenship posits new problems for the social analyst. Is citizenship still a matter largely of positive rights, or does it now, as W. G. Runciman in Chapter 3 and Janet Finch in Chapter 10 suggest, also involve the idea of negative rights? The right *not* to do something may be a product of affluence or the meeting adequately of basic needs. Moreover, the satisfaction of claims to rights does not necessarily have universally beneficial consequences. The exercise of your rights may mean my exclusion. Consider the issue of positive discrimination/affirmative action. Policies based upon premises in favour of such policies seek to extend certain social rights to members of minority sub-groups of the population who hitherto were excluded from certain benefits. The implementation of such policies, however, may involve the denial to other members of majority groups access to rights they might have enjoyed. The *Bakke* case in California, over entry to medical school of a white applicant denied a place to make space for black applicants with lower grades, illustrates the dilemma, and the general issue has been a matter of keen political controversy, along partisan lines, in the United States. In South Africa today, similar issues are faced in extending to the majority black population not only legal and political rights but the expectation of economic advancement for the poor and very ill-housed and inadequately provided-for African majority. There is a real sense in which this gain in rights can only be at the expense of the white minority who enjoy privileges created under apartheid.

## Citizenship – the perennial tension

Citizenship as a topic links the social sciences to wider public debate. The importance of scholarly work on citizenship lies in linking the discourse of social scientists directly into discussion of these public issues. A focus on citizenship demonstrates the continuing relevance of sociology, social policy, political science and related fields to the major issues of the day, such as "social exclusion" in the European Union. Such an issue leads back to a consideration of legal, political, and social rights, to T. H. Marshall's original distinctions, which for all their imperfections, still have a robust usefulness. Their deployment, moreover, throws into stark relief, just as it did in Marshall's day, the contrast between inequalities of class, income, race and gender, and the egalitarian aspirations – however they may be constructed – embedded in the concept of citizenship. This tension between the reality of equality and the ideal of equality is a timeless one that gives the topic its continuing appeal and its contemporary relevance.

# Bibliography

Abrams, P. 1980. *Historical sociology*. Bath: Open Books.

Adam, H. & K. Moodley 1993. *The opening of the apartheid mind: options for the new South Africa*. Berkeley: University of California Press.

Addison, P. 1975. *The road to 1945*. London: Cape.

Albert, M. 1990. *Capitalism against capitalism*. London: Whurr Publishers.

Anderson, M. 1971. *Family structure in nineteenth century Lancashire*. Cambridge: Cambridge University Press.

Anderson, P. 1974a. *Lineages of the absolutist state*. London: New Left Books.

Anderson, P. 1974b. *Passages from antiquity to feudalism*. London: New Left Books.

Andreski, S. 1986. Review of Bulmer, M. (ed.) *Essays on the history of British sociological research*. *Sociology* **20**(1), 107–9.

Andrews, G. (ed.) 1991. *Citizenship*. London: Lawrence & Wishart.

Aristotle, 1988. *The politics* (ed. S. Everson). Cambridge: Cambridge University Press.

Aron, R. 1974. Is multinational citizenship possible? *Social Research* **41**(4) (Winter), 638–56.

Bairoch, P. 1968. *The working population and its structure*. Brussels: Université Libre de Bruxelles.

Bairoch, P. 1982. International industrialization levels from 1750 to 1980. *Journal of European Economic History*, **11**, 269–333.

Baker, J. 1986. Comparing national priorities: family and population policy in Britain and France. *Journal of Social Policy* **15**(4), 421–42.

Barbalet, J. M. 1988. *Citizenship*. Milton Keynes, England: Open University Press.

Barnett, S. & A. Barnett 1915. *Practicable socialism*. London: Longman.

Barry, B. 1973. *The liberal theory of justice*. Oxford: Clarendon Press.

Becker, C. 1955. What are historical facts? In *The philosophy of history in our time*, H. Meyerhoff (ed.). New York: Doubleday.

Bell, C. & H. Newby 1981. Narcissism or reflexivity in modern sociology, *Polish Sociological Bulletin.* **1**, 5–19.

Bell, D. 1974. *The coming of post-industrial society.* London: Heinemann.

Bendix, R. 1978. *Kings or people. Power and the mandate to rule.* Berkeley: University of California Press.

Berghahn, V. 1973. *Germany and the approach of war in 1914.* London: St. Martin's Press.

Bierstedt, R. 1959. Toynbee and sociology. *British Journal of Sociology* **10**(2), 95–104.

Blackbourne, D. & G. Eley 1984. *The peculiarities of German history.* Oxford: Oxford University Press.

Bonnell, V. E. 1983. *Roots of rebellion: workers politics and organizations in St. Petersburg and Moscow, 1900–1914.* Berkeley: University of California Press.

Bottomore, T. 1992. Citizenship and social class: forty years on. In *Citizenship and social class*, T. H. Marshall and T. Bottomore (eds), 55–93. London: Pluto.

Bouglé, C. 1908. *Les Idées égalitaires: étude sociologique*, 2nd edn. Paris: Alcan.

Brooke, S. 1991. Problems of socialist planning: Evan Durbin and the Labour Government of 1945. *Historical Journal* **34**, 687–702.

Brubaker, R. (ed.) 1989. *Immigration and the politics of citizenship in Europe and North America.* London: University Press of America.

Brubaker, R. 1992. *Citizenship and nationhood in France and Germany.* Cambridge, Mass.: Harvard University Press.

Brundtland, G. H. 1987. *Our common future.* Oxford: Oxford University Press.

Brunton, D. & D. H. Pennington 1954. *Members of the Long Parliament.* London: Allen & Unwin.

Bryant, J. M. 1994. Evidence and explanation in history and sociology: critical reflections on Goldthorpe's critique of historical sociology. *British Journal of Sociology* **45**(1), 3–19.

Buchanan, J. 1975. *The limits of liberty.* Chicago: University of Chicago Press.

Buck, N. 1992. Labour market inactivity and polarisation: a household perspective on the idea of an underclass. In *Understanding the underclass*, D. J. Smith (ed.), 9–31. London: Policy Studies Institute.

Bulmer, M. (ed.) 1983. *Sociological research methods: an introduction.* London: Macmillan.

Bulmer, M. 1987. *The social basis of community care.* London: Allen & Unwin.

Calleo, D. 1978. *The German problem reconsidered: Germany and the world order, 1870 to the present.* Cambridge: Cambridge University Press.

Campbell, M. 1942. *The English yeoman.* New Haven, Connecticut: Yale University Press.

Carr, E. H. 1961. *What is history?* London: Macmillan.

Carus-Wilson, E. M. 1954. *Essays in economic history.* London: Edward Arnold.

Cheal, D. 1988. *The gift economy.* London: Routledge.

Clark, J. C. D. 1986. *Revolution and rebellion.* Cambridge: Cambridge University Press.

Clarke, P. 1978. *Liberals and Social Democrats*. Cambridge: Cambridge University Press.

Clubb, J. M. 1980. The new quantitative history: social science or old wine in new bottles? In *Historical social research*, J. M. Clubb & K. Scheuch (eds), 13–24. Stuttgart: Klett-Cotta.

Cobbett, W. 1936. *Rural rides*, vols I & II. London: Dent.

Collingwood, R. G. 1946. *The idea of history*. Oxford: Oxford University Press.

Commission on Social Justice 1994. *Social justice: strategies for national renewal*. London: Verso.

Coote, A. (ed.) 1992. *The welfare of citizens: developing new social rights*. London: Institute for Public Policy Research.

Corrigan, P. & D. Sayer 1985. *The great arch: English state formation as cultural revolution*. Oxford: Basil Blackwell.

Crosland, A. 1956. *The future of socialism*. London: Jonathan Cape.

Crouch, C. 1992. Citizenship and community. In *Social research and social reform*, C. Crouch & A. Heath, (eds), 69–95. Oxford: Clarendon Press.

Culpitt, I. 1992. *Welfare and citizenship: beyond the crisis of the welfare state?* London: Sage.

Dahl, R. A. 1985. *A preface to economic democracy*. New Haven, Connecticut: Yale University Press.

Dahrendorf, R. 1959. *Class and class conflict in an industrial society*. London: Routledge & Kegan Paul.

Dahrendorf, R. 1973. A personal vote of thanks. *British Journal of Sociology* **24**(4), 410–11.

Dalley, G. 1988. *Ideologies of caring*. London: Macmillan.

Daniel, W. W. 1981. *The unemployed flow*. London: Policy Studies Institute.

Davidoff, L. & C. Hall 1987. *Family fortunes: men and women of the English middle class 1780–1850*. London: Hutchinson.

DE 1983. *Employment Gazette*. London: Department of Employment.

de Tocqueville, A. 1955 *Democracy in America*. New York: Vintage Books.

Dennis, N. & G. Erdos 1992. *Families without fatherhood*. London: Institute of Economic Affairs.

Dennis, N. & A. H. Halsey 1988. *English ethical socialism: Thomas More to R. H. Tawney*. Oxford: Clarendon Press.

Donnison, D. 1982. *The politics of poverty*. Oxford: Martin Robertson.

Durkheim, E. 1964. *The division of labour in society*. New York: Free Press.

Eckstein, H. 1984. Civic inclusion and its discontents. *Daedalus* **113**(4) (Fall), 107–45.

Eisenstadt, S. N. 1963. *The political systems of empires*. New York: Free Press.

Erikson, K. 1966. *Wayward Puritans*. New York: John Wiley.

Erikson, R. & J. H. Goldthorpe 1987. Commonality and variation in social fluidity in industrial nations. Part I: a model for evaluating the FJH Hypothesis; Part II: the model of core social fluidity applied. *European Sociological Review* **3** (1) (May), 54–77; (2) (September), 145–66.

Esping-Andersen, G. 1985. *Politics against markets: the social democratic road to power*. Princeton, New Jersey: Princeton University Press.

Esping-Andersen, G. 1989. The three political economies of the welfare state. *Canadian Review of Sociology and Anthropology* **26**(1), 10–36.

Finch, J. 1989. *Family obligations and social change*. Cambridge: Polity.

Finch, J. & J. Mason 1990. Filial obligations for elderly people. *Ageing and Society* **10**, 151–75.

Finch, J. & J. Mason 1991. Obligations of kinship in Britain: is there normative agreement? *British Journal of Sociology* **42**(3), 345–67.

Finch, J. & J. Mason 1993. *Negotiating family responsibilities*. London: Routledge.

Fischer, C. 1982. *To dwell among friends*. Chicago: University of Chicago Press.

Flora, P. & J. Alber 1981. Modernization, democratization, and the development of welfare states in Western Europe. In *The development of welfare states in Europe and America*, P. Flora & A. J. Heidenheimer (eds), 37–80. New Brunswick, New Jersey: Transaction Books.

Flora, P. & A. J. Heidenheimer 1981 Introduction in *The development of welfare states in Europe and America*, P. Flora & A. J. Heidenheimer (eds), 5–14. New Brunswick, New Jersey: Transaction Books.

Fogel, R. W. & G. R. Elton 1983. *Which road to the past?* New Haven, Connecticut: Yale University Press.

Foster, J. 1974. *Class struggle and the Industrial Revolution: capitalism in three English towns*. Cambridge: Cambridge University Press.

Friedman, M. 1962. *Capitalism and freedom*. Chicago: University of Chicago Press.

Froude, J. A. 1884. *Short studies on great subjects*. London: Longman.

Gallie, D. & C. Marsh 1994. The experience of unemployment. In *Social change and the experience of unemployment*, D. Gallie et al. (eds), 1–30. Oxford: Oxford University Press.

Galsworthy, J. 1951. *The man of property*. London: Penguin.

Galtung, J. 1979. Om makrohistoriens epistemologi og metodologi: en skisse. In Nordisk Fagkonferanse for Historik Metodelaere, *Makrohistorie*. Oslo: Universitetsforlaget.

Gellner, E. 1994. *Conditions of liberty: civil society and its rivals*. London: Hamish Hamilton.

Gewirth, A. 1982. *Human rights*. Chicago: University of Chicago Press.

Giddens, A. 1979. *Central problems in social theory*. London: Macmillan.

Giddens, A. 1982. Class division, class conflict and citizenship rights. In *Profiles and critiques in social theory*. London: Macmillan.

Giddens, A. 1985. *The nation state and violence*. Cambridge: Polity.

Glass, D. V. 1954 Preface. In *Social mobility in Britain*, D. V. Glass (ed.), v–vi. London: Routledge & Kegan Paul.

Goldsmith, J. 1993. *The trap*. London: Macmillan.

Goldstein, R. J. 1983. *Political repression in 19th century Europe*. London: Croom Helm.

Goldthorpe, J. H. 1962. The relevance of history to sociology. *Cambridge Opinion* **28**, 26–9 [reprinted in Bulmer (1983): 162–74].

Goldthorpe, J. H. 1971. Theories of industrial society. *Archives Européennes de Sociologie*, **12**(2), 263–88.

Goldthorpe, J. H. 1979. Intellectuals and the working class in modern Britain. Fuller Memorial Bequest Lecture, University of Essex.

Goldthorpe, J. H. 1994. The uses of history in sociology: a reply. *British Journal of Sociology* **45**(1), 55–77.

Goldthorpe, J. H. in collaboration with C. Llewellyn & C. Payne 1980. *Social mobility and class structure in modern Britain*. Oxford: Clarendon Press.

Gough, J. W. 1957. *The social contract*, 2nd edn. Oxford: Clarendon Press.

Gray, J. 1992. *The moral foundations of market institutions*. London: Institute of Economic Affairs.

Habermas, J. 1985. *Theorie des kommunikativen Handelns*. Frankfurt: Suhrkamp.

Haimson, L. H. 1964, 1965. The problem of social stability in urban Russia, 1905–1917, parts 1 and 2, *Slavic Review* **23**, **24**.

Hall, C. 1978. The early formation of Victorian domestic ideology. In *Fit work for women*, S. Burman (ed.), 15–32. London: Croom Helm.

Hall, J. 1985. *Powers and liberties*. Oxford: Basil Blackwell.

Hall, J. A. 1995. *Civil society: theory, history, comparison*, 2nd edn. Cambridge: Polity.

Hall, S & D. Held 1989. Citizens and citizenship. In *New times: the changing face of politics in the 1990s*, S. Hall & D. Held (eds). London: Lawrence & Wishart.

Halsey, A. H. 1984. T. H. Marshall: past and present, 1893–1981. *Sociology* **18**(1), 1–18.

Handy, C. B. 1984. *The future of work: a guide to a changing society*. Oxford: Basil Blackwell.

Hannerz, U. 1969. *Soulside: inquiries into ghetto culture and community*. New York: Columbia University Press.

Harris, J. 1986. Political ideas and the debate on state welfare, 1940–45. In *War and Social Change*, H. L. Smith (ed.). Manchester: Manchester University Press.

Hart, N. 1994. John Goldthorpe and the relics of sociology. *British Journal of Sociology* **45**(1), 21–30.

Heilbroner, R. L. 1985. *The nature and logic of capitalism*. New York: W. W. Norton.

Held, D. 1991. Democracy, the nation-state and the global system. In *Political theory today*, D. Held (ed.), 197–235. Cambridge: Polity.

Henderson J. & V. Karn. 1987. *Race, class and state housing: inequality and the allocation of public housing in Britain*. Aldershot, England: Gower.

Hexter, J. H. 1958. Storm over the gentry. *Encounter* **105**(May), 23–34.

Hexter, J. H. 1961. *Reappraisals in history*. London: Longman.

Himmelfarb, G. 1984. *The idea of poverty: England in the early industrial age*. New York: Alfred A. Knopf.

Hirsch, F. 1977. *Social limits to growth*. London: Routledge & Kegan Paul.

Hirschman, A. O. 1970. *Exit, voice and loyalty: responses to decline in firms, organizations and states*. Cambridge, Mass.: Harvard University Press.

Hirschman, A. O. 1991. *The rhetoric of reaction; perversity, futility, jeopardy*. Cambridge, Mass.: Belknap Press of Harvard University.

HMSO 1985. *Social trends*. London: HMSO.

Hobbes, T. 1934. *Leviathan*. London.

Hobhouse, L. T. 1911. *Liberalism*. London: Williams & Norgate.

Hobhouse, L. T. 1924. *Social development: its nature and condition*. London: Allen & Unwin.

Jenkins, P. 1987. *Mrs Thatcher's revolution: the ending of the socialist era*. London: Jonathan Cape.

Jensen, A. 1972. *Genetics and education*. London: Methuen.

Jessop, B. 1978. Capitalism and democracy: the best possible political shell? In *Power and the state*, C. Littlejohn et al. (eds), 10–51. London: Croom Helm.

Jones, G. S. 1983. *Languages of class: studies in English working class history 1832–1982*. Cambridge: Cambridge University Press.

Jordan, B. 1981. *Automatic poverty*. London: Routledge & Kegan Paul.

Kaiser, D. E. 1983. Germany and the origins of the First World War, *Journal of Modern History* 55, 442–74.

Kann, R. E. 1964. *The multinational empire* [2 volumes]. New York: Octagon Books.

Kasarda, J. D. 1989. Urban industrial transition and the underclass. *Annals of the American Academy of Political and Social Science* 501 (January), 26–47.

Kasarda, J. D. 1990a. Structural factors affecting the location and timing of urban underclass growth. *Urban Geography* 11, 234–64.

Kasarda, J. D. 1990b. City jobs and residents on a collision course: the urban underclass dilemma. *Economic Development Quarterly* 4 (November) 313–19.

Käsler, D. 1988. *Max Weber: an introduction to his life and work*. Cambridge: Polity.

Katznelson, I. 1981. *City trenches: urban politics and the patterning of class in the United States*. New York: Pantheon Books.

Keane, J. B. (ed.) 1988. *Civil society and the state: new European perspectives*. London: Verso.

Keohane, R. O. & S. Nye 1977. *Power and interdependence: world politics in transition*. Boston, Mass.: Little Brown.

Ketchum, J. D. 1965. *Ruhleben: a prison camp society*. Toronto: University of Toronto Press.

King, D. S. & J. Waldron 1988. Citizenship, social citizenship and the defence of welfare provision. *British Journal of Political Science* 18, 415–43.

Kirschenman, J. & K. Neckerman 1991. We'd love to hire them, but . . .: the meaning of race for employers. In *The urban underclass*, C. Jencks & P. Peterson (eds), 203–34. Washington District of Columbia: Brookings Institution Press.

Land, H. 1978. Who cares for the family? *Journal of Social Policy* 7(3), 257–84.

Land, H. 1989. The construction of dependency. In *The goals of social policy*, M. Bulmer, J. Lewis, D. Piachaud (eds), 141–59. London: Unwin Hyman.

Land, H. & H. Rose 1985. Compulsory altruism for some or an altruistic society for all? In *In defence of welfare*, P. Bean, J. Ferris, D. Wynes (eds), 74–96. London: Tavistock Publications.

Layton-Henry, Z. 1991. Citizenship and migrant workers in western Europe. In

*The frontiers of citizenship*, U. Vogel & M. Moran (eds), 107–24. London: Macmillan.

Le Grand, J. 1982. *The strategy of equality*. London: Allen & Unwin.

Levy, F. 1986. Poverty and economic growth. Unpublished manuscript, School of Public Affairs, University of Maryland, College Park, Maryland.

Liebich, A. & D. Warner (eds) 1995. *Citizenship East and West*. London: Kegan Paul International.

Lipset, S. M. 1964. Introduction. In *Class, citizenship and social development*, T. H. Marshall (ed.), v–xx. New York: Doubleday.

Lipset, S. M. 1973. Tom Marshall – man of wisdom. *British Journal of Sociology* **24**, 412–17.

Lipset, S. M. 1985. *Consensus and conflict: essays in political sociology*. New Brunswick, New Jersey: Transaction Books.

Lockwood, D. 1974. For T. H. Marshall. *Sociology* **8**(3), 363–7.

Lowe, P. & J. Goyder 1983. *Environmental groups in politics*. London: Allen & Unwin.

Macintyre, A. 1981. *After virtue: a study in moral theory*. London: Duckworth.

MacIver, R. M. 1926. *The modern state*. Oxford: Oxford University Press.

Macrae, D. G. 1974. For his eightieth birthday. *British Journal of Sociology* **24**, 409–10.

Macrae, D. G. 1982. Tom Marshall 1893–1981: a personal memoir. *British Journal of Sociology* **33**(3), iii–vii.

Maier, C. S. 1981. The two postwar eras and the conditions for stability in twentieth century western Europe. *American Historical Review* **86** 327–52.

Maitland, F. W. 1911. The body politic. In *Collected papers*, F. W. Maitland & H. A. L. Fisher (eds). Cambridge: Cambridge University Press.

Mann, M. 1980. State and society, 1130–1815: an analysis of English state finances. In *Political power and social theory*, vol. I, M. Zeitlin (ed.). Westport, Connecticut: JAI Press.

Mann, M. 1984. The autonomous power of the state. *Archives Européennes de Sociologie* **25**, 185–213.

Mann, M. 1986. *The sources of social power: a history of power from the beginning to 1760 AD*, vol. I. Cambridge: Cambridge University Press.

Mann, M. 1987. War and social theory: into battle with classes, nations and states. In *The sociology of war and peace*, C. Creighton & M. Shaw (eds), 54–72. London: Macmillan.

Mann, M. 1993. *The sources of social power: the rise of classes and nation states, 1760–1914*, vol. II. Cambridge: Cambridge University Press.

Mann, M. 1994. In praise of macro-sociology: a reply to Goldthorpe. *British Journal of Sociology* **45**, 37–54.

Marquand, D. 1992. *The progressive dilemma: from Lloyd George to Kinnock*, new edn. London: Heinemann.

Marshall, A. 1925. In *Memorials of Alfred Marshall*, A. C. Pigou (ed.). London: Macmillan.

Marshall, G. 1980. *Presbyteries and profits*. Oxford: Oxford University Press.

Marshall, G. et al. 1987. Distributional struggle and moral order in a market society. *Sociology* **21**, 55–73.

Marshall, G., H. Newby, D. Rose, C. Vogler 1988. *Social class in modern Britain*. London: Routledge.

Marshall, T. H. 1950. *Citizenship and social class and other essays*. Cambridge: Cambridge University Press.

Marshall, T. H. 1963. *Sociology at the crossroads and other essays*. London: Heinemann.

Marshall, T. H. 1964. *Class, citizenship and social development*. Garden City, New York: Doubleday [with an introduction by S. M. Lipset].

Marshall, T. H. 1965. *Social policy*, 1st edn. London: Hutchinson.

Marshall, T. H. 1967a. *Social policy in the twentieth century*, 2nd edn. London: Hutchinson.

Marshall, T. H. 1967b. Review of Ketchum (1965). *Sociology* **1**(1), 90–93.

Marshall, T. H. 1970. *Social policy in the twentieth century*, 3rd rev. edn. London: Hutchinson.

Marshall, T. H. 1973. A British sociological career. *International Social Science Journal* **25**(1/2), 88–100 [partially republished in *British Journal of Sociology* **24**(4): 399–408].

Marshall, T. H. 1975. *Social policy in the twentieth century*, 4th rev. edn. London: Hutchinson [see also Rees 1985].

Marshall, T. H. 1981. *The right to welfare and other essays*. London: Heinemann

Marwick, A. 1964. Middle opinion in the thirties. *English Historical Review* **79**.

Mayer, A. J. 1981. *The persistence of the old regime*. London: Croom Helm.

McCrone, D. 1992. *Understanding Scotland: the sociology of a stateless nation*. London: Routledge.

McFate, K., R. Lawson, W. J. Wilson (eds) 1995. *Poverty, inequality and the future of social policy: Western states in the new world order*. New York: Russell Sage Foundation.

McLanahan, S. & I. Garfinkel 1989. Single mothers, the underclass, and social policy. *Annals of the American Academy of Political and Social Science* **501**(January), 92–104.

Mead, L. M. 1986. *Beyond entitlement: the social obligations of citizenship*. New York: Free Press.

Meade, J. 1982. *Stagflation: wage fixing*, vol. I. London: Allen & Unwin.

Meehan, E. 1993. *Citizenship and the European Community*. London: Sage.

Mellows, A. R. 1983. *The law of succession*. London: Butterworth.

Mill, J. S. 1989. *On liberty*. Cambridge: Cambridge University Press.

Miller, D. 1989. *Market, state and community: theoretical foundations of market socialism* Oxford: Clarendon Press.

Minogue, K. 1995. Two concepts of citizenship. In *Citizenship East and West*, A. Liebich & D. Warner (eds), 9–22. London: Kegan Paul International.

Mishra, R. 1981. *Society and social policy: theories and practice of welfare*, 2nd edn. London: Macmillan.

Moore, B. 1966. *The social origins of dictatorship and democracy*. London: Penguin.

Moran, M. 1991. In *The frontiers of social citizenship: the case of health care entitlements*, U.Vogel & M. Moran (eds), 32–57.

More, T. (G. M. Logan & R. M. Adams eds) 1988. *Utopia*. Cambridge: Cambridge University Press.

Mouzelis, N. 1994. In defence of grand historical sociology. *British Journal of Sociology* **45**(1), March, 31–6.

Mowat, C. L. 1955. *Britain between the wars 1918–1940*. London: Methuen.

Murphey, M. 1973. *Our knowledge of the historical past*. Indianapolis: Bobbs-Merrill.

Neckerman, K. M. & J. Kirschenman 1990. Statistical discrimination and inner-city workers: an investigation of employers hiring decisions. Paper presented at the Annual Meeting of the American Sociological Association, Washington DC, 11–15 August.

Newby, H. J. 1990. Ecology, amenity and society: social sciences and environmental change. *Town Planning Review* **60**(1), 3–13.

Newman, J. H. 1903. *The scope and nature of university education*. London [first published 1859].

Nisbet, R. A. 1969. *Social change and history*. New York: Oxford University Press.

Nozick, R. 1974. *Anarchy, state and Utopia*. New York: Basic Books.

Oakeshott, M. 1975. *On human conduct*. Oxford: Oxford University Press.

OECD 1982. *The challenge of unemployment: a report to Labour ministers*. Paris: OECD.

OECD 1984. *Employment outlook*. Paris: OECD.

OECD 1994. *Employment outlook*. Paris: OECD.

Page, R. 1984. *Stigma*. London: Routledge & Kegan Paul.

Pahl, R. E. 1984. *Divisions of labour*. Oxford: Basil Blackwell.

Parker, G. 1990. *With due care and attention: a review of research on informal care*. London: Family Policy Studies Centre.

Parry, G. 1991. Conclusion: paths to citizenship. In *The frontiers of citizenship*, U. Vogel & M. Moran (eds), 166–201. London: Macmillan.

Partridge, F. 1981. *Memories*. London:Gollanz.

Pearce, D., D. Barbier, A. Markandya 1989. *Blueprint for a green economy*. London: Earthscan.

Pedersen, S. 1993. *Family, dependence and the origins of the welfare state: Britain and France 1914–1945*. Cambridge: Cambridge University Press.

Pelling, H. 1968. The working class and the origins of the welfare state. In *Popular politics and society in late Victorian Britain*, H. Pelling (ed.), 1–18. London: Macmillan.

Phelps, G.(ed.)1947. *Living writers*. London: Sylvan Press.

Pinker, R. 1981. Introduction. In *The right to welfare and other essays*, T. H. Marshall (ed.), 1–28. London: Heinemann.

Piore, M. 1979. *Birds of passage: migrant labour and industrial society*. Cambridge: Cambridge University Press.

Plant, R. 1991. Welfare and the enterprise society. In *The state and social welfare*, T. Wilson & D.Wilson (eds), 73–88. Harlow, England: Longman.

Postlethwaite, N. 1958. The bottom half in lower secondary schooling. See Worswick (1958).

Powell, M. 1995. The strategy of equality revisited. *Journal of Social Policy* 24 (2), 163–85.

Prais, S. 1958. What can we learn from the German system of education and vocational training? See Worswick (1958).

Pressnell, L. 1956. *Country banking in the Industrial Revolution*. Oxford: Clarendon Press.

Przeworski, A. & H. Teune 1970. *The logic of comparative social inquiry*. New York: John Wiley.

Qureshi, H. & A. Walker 1989. *The caring relationship: elderly people and their families*. London: Macmillan.

Rawls, J. 1971. *A theory of justice*. Cambridge, Mass.: Belknap Press of Harvard University.

Rees, A. M. 1985. *T. H. Marshall's social policy in the twentieth century*, 5th edn. London: Hutchinson.

Rees, A. M. 1995. The other T. H. Marshall. *Journal of Social Policy* 24(3), 341–62.

Reisman, D. A. 1984. T. H. Marshall on the middle ground. In *The economics of human betterment*, K. E. Boulding (ed.), 151–73. London: Macmillan.

Renier, G. J. 1950. *History: its purpose and method*. London: Allen & Unwin.

Rich, P. 1991. Patriotism and the idea of citizenship in post-war British politics. In U. Vogel & M. Moran (eds), *The frontiers of citizenship*, 86–106. London: Macmillan.

Roberts, M. 1951. *The estate of man*. London: Faber.

Robertson, J. 1984. The coming transformation of work. In *The future of work: challenge and opportunity*, E. G. Fragnière (ed.). Assen: Van Gorcum, for the European Centre for Work and Society.

Roche, M. 1987. Citizenship, social theory and social change. *Theory and Society* 16(3), 363–99.

Roche, M. 1992. *Rethinking citizenship: welfare, ideology and change in modern society*. Cambridge: Polity.

Rokkan, S. 1970. *Citizens, elections, parties: approaches to the comparative study of the processes of development*. Oslo: Universitetsforlaget.

Rollings, A. 1994. Poor Mr. Butskell: a short life, wrecked by schizophrenia. *Twentieth Century British History* 5(2), 183–205.

Roth, G. 1963. *The social democrats in imperial Germany*. Totowa, New Jersey: Bedminster Press.

Runciman, W. G. 1993. Has British capitalism changed since the First World War? *British Journal of Sociology* 44, 53–67.

Sahlins, M. 1965. On the sociology of primitive exchange. In *The relevance of models in social anthropology*, M. Banton (ed.), 139–236. London, Tavistock Press.

Sandel, M. A. 1982. *Liberalism and the limits of justice*. Cambridge: Cambridge University Press.

Saunders, P. 1995. *Capitalism: a social audit*. Buckingham: Open University Press.

Schiff, M. 1982. *L'Intelligence gaspillée*. Paris.

Schoeck, H. 1966. *Envy: a theory of social behaviour*. New York: Harcourt Brace.

Shaw M. 1987. *The dialectics of total war*. London: Pluto.

Sheehan, J. J. 1976. *Imperial Germany*. New York: Franklin Watts.

Shirley, J. 1646. *Poems*. London.

Shklar, J. 1991. *American citizenship: the quest for inclusion*. Cambridge, Mass.: Harvard University Press.

Sixsmith, A. 1986. Independence and home in later life. In *Dependency and interdependency in old age*, C. Phillipson, M. Barnard, P. Strang (eds). London: Croom Helm.

Skocpol, T. 1979. *States and social revolutions*. Cambridge: Cambridge University Press.

Skocpol, T. 1984. Emerging agendas and recurrent strategies in historical sociology. In *Vision and method in historical sociology*, T. Skocpol (ed.), 356–91. Cambridge: Cambridge University Press.

Smith, A. 1853. *The theory of moral sentiments*. Indianapolis: Liberty Fund [1976 edition].

Smith A. 1961. *The wealth of nations*. London: Allen & Unwin.

Smith, D. (ed.) 1992. *Understanding the underclass*. London: Policy Studies Institute.

Smith, S. 1989. *The politics of "race" and residence: citizenship, segregation and white supremacy in Britain*. Cambridge: Polity.

Sombart, W. (with C. T. Husbands) 1976. *Why is there no socialism in the United States?* London: Macmillan [first published 1906].

Soysal, Y. N. 1994. *Limits of citizenship: migrants and postnational membership in Europe*. Chicago: University of Chicago Press.

Spencer, H. 1861. *Essays on education*. London: Dent [new edition 1911].

Spencer, H. 1904. *An autobiography*. London: Williams & Norgate.

Steenbergen, B. (ed.) 1994. *The condition of citizenship*. London: Sage.

Stewart, A. 1995. Two conceptions of citizenship. *British Journal of Sociology* **46**(1), 63–78.

Stone, L. 1987a. History and the social sciences in the twentieth century. In *The past and present revisited*, L. Stone (ed.), 3–44. London: Routledge.

Stone, L. 1987b. The revival of narrative: reflections on a new old history. In *The past and present revisited*, L. Stone (ed.), 74–96. London: Routledge.

Stone, N. 1975. *The eastern front, 1914–1917*. New York: Charles Scribner's Sons.

Swain, G. 1983. *Russian social democracy and the legal labour movement, 1906–1914*. London: Macmillan.

Tassin, E. 1992. Europe: a political community? In *Dimensions of radical democracy: pluralism, citizenship, community*, D. Mouffe (ed.), 169–92. London: Verso.

Tawney, R. H. 1912. *The agrarian problem in the sixteenth century*. London, Longman.

Tawney, R. H. 1941. The rise of the gentry, 1558–1640. *Economic History Review* **11**(1) [reprinted with a postscript in *Essays in economic history*, E. M. Carus-Wilson (ed.). London: Edward Arnold, 1954].

Tawney, R. H. 1950. Review of Titmuss 1950. *New Statesman and Nation* (1950).

Tawney R. H. 1952. *Equality*, 4th edn. London: Capricorn (first published 1931).

Tawney Society 1984. *Count us in: social action opportunities for young people.* London: Tawney Society Community Service Research Group.

Taylor, A. J. P. 1961. *Bismarck: the man and the statesman.* London: Arrow.

Taylor, W. 1958. Productivity and educational values. See Worswick (1958).

Tester, K. 1992. *Civil society.* London: Routledge.

Thomas, H. & C. Logan 1982. *Mondragon: an economic analysis.* London: Allen & Unwin.

Tienda, M. & H. Stier 1989. Joblessness or shiftlessness: labor force activity in Chicago's inner-city. Paper presented at a conference on the truly disadvantaged, Northwestern University, Evanston, Illinois, 19–21 October.

Tilly, C. 1978. *From mobilization to revolution.* New York: McGraw-Hill.

Titmuss, R. M. 1950. *Problems of social policy.* London: HMSO.

Townsend, P. 1979. *Poverty in the United Kingdom.* London: Allen Lane.

Turner, B. S. 1986. *Citizenship and capitalism: the debate over reformism.* London: Allen & Unwin.

Turner, B. S. 1990. Outline of a theory of citizenship. *Sociology* 24(2), 189–217.

Turner, B. S. (ed.) 1993a. *Citizenship* [2 volumes]. London: Routledge.

Turner, B. S. (ed.) 1993b. *Citizenship and social theory.* London: Routledge.

Turner, R. H. 1960. Sponsored and contest mobility and the school system. *American Sociological Review* 25(6) (December), 855–67.

Twine, F. 1994. *Citizenship and social rights: the interdependence of self and society.* London: Sage.

Ungerson, C. 1989. *Policy is personal: sex, gender and informal care.* London: Tavistock Press.

Ungerson, C. (ed.) 1990. *Gender and caring: work and welfare in Britain and Scandinavia.* Brighton: Harvester Press.

van Gunsteren, H. 1994. Four conceptions of citizenship. In *The condition of citizenship*, B. van Steenbergen (ed.), 36–48. London: Sage.

van Haitsma, M. 1989. A contextual definition of the underclass. *Focus* 12 (Spring and summer), 27–31.

van Steenbergen, B. (ed.) 1994. *The condition of citizenship.* London: Sage.

Vincent, A. & R. Plant 1984. *Philosophy, politics and citizenship.* Oxford: Basil Blackwell.

Vogel, U. & M. Moran (eds) 1991. *The frontiers of citizenship.* London: Macmillan.

von Hayek, F. A. 1960. *The constitution of liberty.* Chicago: University of Chicago Press.

Vonnegut, K. 1952. *Player piano.* London: Granada-Panther [1969 edition].

Wacquant, L. J. D. & W. J. Wilson 1989a. Poverty, joblessness and the social transformation of the inner city. In *Reforming welfare policy*, D. Ellwood & P. Cottingham (eds), 70–102, Cambridge, Mass.: Harvard University Press.

Wacquant, L. J. D. & W. J. Wilson 1989b. The cost of racial and class exclusion in the inner city. *Annals of the American Academy of Political and Social Science* 501 (January), 8–25.

Waerness, K. 1989. Dependency in the welfare state. In *The goals of social policy*, M. Bulmer, J. Lewis, D. Piachaud (eds), 70–75. London: Unwin Hyman.

Wallerstein, I. 1974, 1980, 1989. *The modern world system* [3 volumes]. New York: Academic Press.

Walzer, M. 1983. *Spheres of justice: a defence of pluralism and justice*. Oxford: Martin Robertson.

Watts, A. G. 1983. *Education, unemployment and the future of work*. Milton Keynes, England: Open University Press.

Weale, A. 1983. *Political theory and social policy*. London: Macmillan.

Webb, S. & B. 1932. *Methods of social study*. London: London School of Economics.

Weiner, N. 1968. *The human use of human beings*. London: Sphere.

Weitzman, M. L. 1984. *The share economy: conquering stagflation*. Cambridge: Mass.: Harvard University Press.

Wenger, G. C. 1984. *The supportive network*. London: Allen & Unwin.

White, M. 1983. *Long term unemployment and the labour market*. London: Policy Studies Institute.

Williams, R. 1971. *Orwell*. London: Fontana.

Wilson, W. J. 1987. *The truly disadvantaged: the inner city, the underclass, and public policy*. Chicago: University of Chicago Press.

Wilson, W. J. 1988. The American underclass: inner city ghettos and the norms of citizenship. Godkin Lecture, John F. Kennedy School of Government, Harvard University, Cambridge: Mass., 26 April.

Wilson, W. J., R. Aponte, J. Kirschenman, & L. D. J. Wacquant 1988. The ghetto underclass and the changing structure of American poverty. In *Quiet riots: race and poverty in the United States*, F. R. Harris & R. W. Wilkins (eds), 123–54. New York: Pantheon.

Woodruff, P. 1953. *The men who ruled India*. London: Jonathan Cape.

Woolf, L. 1980. *An autobiography: 1880–1911*, vol. 1. Oxford: Oxford University Press.

Worswick, G. D. N. (ed.) 1958. *Education and economic performance*. Aldershot, England: Gower

Young, M. 1961. *The rise of the meritocracy*. London: Penguin.

Young, M. & P. Wilmott 1973. *The symmetrical family*. London: Routledge & Kegan Paul.

# Index